Is Psychoanalysis a Science or an Art?

**Edited by
Daniel S.
Benveniste**

Is Psychoanalysis a Science or an Art?

Edited by Daniel S. Benveniste

IPBOOKS.net

International Psychoanalytic Books (IPBooks)
New York • www.IPBooks.net

International Psychoanalytic Books (IPBooks), Queens, NY

Online at: www.IPBooks.net

Cover painting: Wassily Kandinsky, Circles in a Circle, 1923

Cover and interior book design by Kathy Kovacic, Blackthorn Studio

ISBN: 978-1-956864-09-0

CONTENTS

Science Needs Criticism: Debating the Clinical Aspects of Diverging Theoretical Schools

Lois Oppenheim Review of Neubauer Twin Study: An Interview about a Controversy or a Controversial Interview?

Nathan Szajnberg Review:
The Emergence of Analytic Oneness:
Into the Heart of Psychoanalysis by Ofra Eshel

Introduction

The book before you is the print edition of the first issue of the IJCD. The IJCD, International Journal of Controversial Discussions, is an online journal that launched in March 2020 and was distributed free by subscription. The IJCD is a forum for discussion and debate about controversial issues within psychoanalysis among colleagues with a variety of different approaches. It offers a meeting place for analysts with diverging theoretical and clinical attitudes whose paths might otherwise not cross.

The theme of the first issue, edited by Daniel Benveniste, addresses the old question "Is Psychoanalysis a Science or an Art?" It includes eleven original contributions accompanied by discussions and some authors' replies to the discussions. The IJCD is a journal of dialogue and we envision that the discussions begun in this issue will be continued in subsequent on-line issues. We feel that this journal fills a need which is not addressed by many of the contemporary journals in the United States and abroad that tend to publish standalone papers with discussions and responses as the exception rather than the rule.

The IJCD is an independent journal not affiliated with any national or international organization. The editorial board of distinguished scholars and clinicians includes former editors of other psychoanalytic journals. This journal is not peer-reviewed in the usual sense. The standard peer review practice is to send each submitted paper to a panel of readers whose names are not shared with the author of the paper. These readers write reviews which may be excerpted for the author and which form the basis for the acceptance or rejection the paper. In the IJCD model of peer review, well written and well-reasoned papers on a selected controversial topic are published. Each published paper is paired with a response by a discussant with a relevant interest. The author is also given the opportunity to respond in the same issue.

The IJCD does not have any theoretical or ideological bias and casts a wide net, including contributors from many disciplines and many geographical locations. It considers a broad array of subjects of interest to mental health professionals. The journal together with its print edition is a work in progress, and we welcome input from the larger mental health community.

–Arnold D. Richards, Editor-In-Chief

Musings on the Question
Is Psychoanalysis a Science or an Art?

Daniel S. Benveniste

The history of psychoanalysis is a history of controversial discussions that have provided a means of resolving problems or clarifying positions regarding theory, technique, and institutional power. Rather than creating yet another journal with a theoretical bias for like-minded theorists and clinicians to develop their ideas, this journal will take on controversial topics and create a forum for discussions between colleagues who specifically do not think alike. The intention here is to create a village square for discussion and debate about controversial issues.

As the first topic to discuss, we have chosen the age-old question, *Is psychoanalysis a science or an art?* If it is a science, what kind of a science is it? If it is an art, what kind of art is it? And if it's not a science or an art, what else could it be? I open this issue of the *International Journal of Controversial Discussions* with a set of musings to orient the reader to some of the matters involved in such questions. The rest of this issue will be dedicated to distinguished psychoanalysts presenting their ideas in concise articles followed by other analysts responding to those articles.

Sigmund Freud was born in 1856, three years before the publication of Darwin's *The Origin of Species*. Darwin's scientific breakthrough invigorated the sciences and influenced popular thinking about religion and politics. Freud grew up in this scientific movement that reshaped the views of self and society—specifically, in a shift away from a Judeo-Christian religious worldview to a scientific worldview. Freud followed these developments closely in high school and then at university.

From April through October 1895, Freud penned an essay titled *Project for a Scientific Psychology* that began with the words "The intention is to furnish a psychology that shall be a *natural science.*" He went on: "that is, to represent psychical processes as quantitatively determinate states of specifiable material particles, thus making those processes perspicuous and free from contradiction" (Freud, 1895/1966, *SE* 1, p. 295). Freud, the neurologist who had stained and studied neurons and explored hysteria through hypnosis with Jean-Martin Charcot, was trying to make sense of it all with his exceptional powers of observation and his synthetic theory-making mind.

As James Strachey (1966) wrote in his introduction to the English translation of Freud's *Project*, "All emphasis in the picture here is upon the environment's impact upon the organism and the organism's reaction to it... The 'instincts' are only shadowy entities, with scarcely even a name" (p. 291). The technique of psychoanalysis is for the most part absent, and free association, interpretation of unconscious material, and transference "are barely hinted at" (p. 291). Freud ultimately threw out this neurological framework, because, as Strachey wrote, "He found that his neuronal machinery had no means of accounting for what, in *The Ego and the Id*, he described as being 'in the last resort our one beacon-light in the darkness of depth-psychology'—namely, 'the property of being conscious or not' " (p. 293). Strachey ended his introduction by saying, "The Project must remain a torso, disavowed by its creator" (p. 293). While Freud dismissed this early work, and we can understand why, I see the *Project* as Freud's Golem, a "being," in a sense, who set the stage for all that was yet to come and was then dismissed.

By 1913 everything had changed. The foundation of psychoanalysis had been established. And then, following the completion of *Totem and Taboo*, Freud wrote a small essay titled *The Claims of Psycho-Analysis to Scientific Interest* (1913/1955a). He did not ask if psychoanalysis was a science but instead demonstrated that other fields, including scientific fields, could be interested in psychoanalysis. In that essay he addressed the following topics:

✻ The Philological Interest of Psycho-Analysis

✻ The Philosophical Interest of Psycho-Analysis

✻ The Biological Interest of Psycho-Analysis

✻ The Interest of Psycho-Analysis from a Developmental Point of View

✻ The Interest of Psycho-Analysis from the Point of View of the History of Civilization

✻ The Interest of Psycho-Analysis from the Point of View of the Science of Aesthetics

✻ The Sociological Interest of Psycho-Analysis

✻ The Educational Interest of Psycho-Analysis

As psychoanalysis gained interested readers and critics, people wondered, Is this "science of the mind" real? Is it even a science? And in some ways, and perhaps more important, *who* should be allowed to practice it? Neurologists? Psychiatrists? Medical doctors? Psychologists? Philosophers? Lawyers? Art historians? School teachers? Artists?

And then it happened: Theodor Reik, a psychoanalyst and close associate of Freud, was charged by Austrian authorities with "quackery"—the practice of medicine without a license.

Theodor Reik was a lay analyst. He held a PhD in psychology, not a medical degree. While Sigmund Freud was himself a physician, many of his colleagues were not medically trained. They were never excluded by him and were, in fact, highly valued for the different perspectives they brought to psychoanalysis. Freud argued vigorously on their behalf and against the officials in Austria who challenged the legitimacy of lay analysis.

When Reik was charged with quackery, an official involved with the legal case called upon Freud to write an opinion on the subject. Freud wrote his opinion in *The Question of Lay Analysis* (1926/1959). Ultimately the charges against Reik were dropped, but Freud did not believe his little book had anything to do with the legal basis for dropping the case.

At that time there were many highly respected lay analysts in Europe, such as Hanns Sachs, Otto Rank, Theodor Reik, Ernst Kris, Melanie Klein, Oskar Pfister, August Aichhorn, Lou Andreas-Salomé, Beate Rank, Siegfried Bernfeld, Geza Róheim, Susan Issacs, Victor Tausk, Robert Waelder, Ella Freeman Sharpe, Marie Bonaparte, and Anna Freud. But lay analysis was still held suspect by the legal authorities in Austria. In the United States, it was legal but seen as unacceptable by most medical analysts, who equated lay analysis with "wild analysis" and quackery.

Freud recognized psychoanalysis as a special kind of conversation that any properly trained analyst, whether medically trained or not, can establish with a patient. While acknowledging the contributions of medical analysts, he also wrote, "In his medical school a doctor receives a training which is more or less the opposite of what he would need as a preparation for psychoanalysis" (Freud, 1926/1959, *SE* 20, p. 228). Freud described a proper analytic training as including indepth coursework in psychology, biology, the science of sex, medical disturbances belonging to the field of psychiatry, the history of civilization, mythology, the psychology of religion, and literature (p. 228).

Although there were a few European analysts opposed to lay analysis, most of them supported it. In the United States, however, the overwhelming majority of analysts were opposed to it. The US colleagues cited the problems of wild analysts, quacks, and charlatans in their country and sought to restrict the practice of psychoanalysis to medically trained analysts. In the *International Journal of Psychoanalysis,* Freud addressed their position by saying, "Our American colleagues' resolution against lay analysts was prompted essentially by practical motives; yet it seems to me unpractical, for it cannot alter any one of the factors which govern the situation. It is in some sort equivalent to an attempt at repression" (Freud, 1927, p. 398).

Thus, behind the question of Is psychoanalysis a science or an art? lurked the question, Who is qualified, and permitted, to practice psychoanalysis? But independent of the lay analysis question, medically trained psychoanalysts were concerned for their own reasons. They were marginalized by other medical specialties and felt called upon to defend their profession as medical and scientific. In the 20th and 21st centuries much of the modern world found, and continues to find, "science" as the most respectable context within which to frame any discipline as "real." But, of course, there is plenty in the world that is real and yet also not science or discoverable by science.

Is dance a science? Are teaching or journalism sciences? How about history or literature or counseling? Speculation, intuition, and clinical judgment are essential in the work of the psychoanalyst, and they can certainly be employed in the scientific process. But are they sciences in and of themselves? Is it possible that parts of psychoanalysis are science, or employ scientific methods, and other parts are not?

In 1952, even before the English publication of the *Project,* the California Institute of Technology sponsored the Hixon Lectures on the *Scientific Status of Psychoanalysis* (Pumpian-Mindlin, 1952), with lectures given by Ernest R. Hilgard, PhD, Lawrence S. Kubie, MD, and Eugene

Pumpian-Mindlin, MD. Hilgard addressed "Experimental Approaches to Psychoanalysis" (p. 2–45), including experimental tests of the validity of psychodynamics and aspects of psychoanalytic theory and techniques. Kubie discussed "Problems and Techniques of Validation in Psychoanalysis" (p. 46–124), starting with a broad review of psychoanalytic observations and a call for help from the exact sciences to make concepts more precise. He also proposed the establishment of a research institute in psychoanalytic psychology with an interdisciplinary team of researchers. Pumpian-Mindlin spoke on "The Position of Psychoanalysis in Relation to the Social and Biological Sciences" and brought into high relief how psychoanalysis straddles biological phenomena and our participation in society. He stated, "Psychoanalysis cannot give the final exact answers that science demands, at this time, but the great question is whether science can afford to exclude such important aspects of human activity as psychoanalysis attempts to investigate" (p. 125–158).

While it might be debatable whether psychoanalysis is a science or not, what is not debatable is whether it is possible to conduct scientific research on psychoanalytic concepts. One need only think of the research on maternal deprivation or projective tests. Once a psychoanalytic concept is operationalized, it is possible to construct a scientific study to examine it. This is the way it is in other social sciences as well. But what about psychoanalysis as a treatment? Is that a science? There, too, researchers have conducted numerous outcome studies in psychoanalysis. One of the common forms of psychotherapy research employs the transcription of analytic sessions. But how does one recognize, in a typed transcript, those words that seemingly leap from the dialogue and become points of analytic orientation. How does one transcribe intuition, or empathy, or being emotionally present? Despite these problems, psychotherapy researchers have a reputation for creativity and compelling conclusions. (For a good overview of this literature, see *An Open Door Review of Outcome Studies in Psychoanalysis* [2002], edited by Peter Fonagy.)

But the question remains, *Is the practice of psychoanalysis itself a science?*

Why do we care if psychoanalysis is a science? Do we diminish what is not scientific and grant reality to what is? Are we chasing after the public's need to recognize psychoanalysis as real and distinguish it from palm reading? Is it a way to elevate the status of psychoanalysis above the offshoot psychologies of Adler, Jung, Reich, Perls, Berne, and others like them? And if so, what of Klein, Kohut, and the relationalists? Who is legitimate or real? What is real? And how can psychoanalysis be real if it isn't science? If it is a science, what kind of a science is it? A hard science? A natural science? A social science? A historical science?

In the 1920s and early '30s there was an effort to anchor psychoanalytic theory in the physical sciences. This led Siegfried Bernfeld, with his background in botany and mathematics, to collaborate with Sergei Feitelberg in a series of physiological studies proposing to measure libido. In 1930 they published *Energie und Trieb* (Energy and Drive). Bernfeld's daughter, Ruth Goldberg, was a subject in her father's libidometry experiments and recalled, "I would sit still and they would have some apparatus to touch the skin to see when I started feeling it…to measure the energy, I suppose, that was needed till the subject would feel it…one of those sensory experiments where some needle came toward the skin and you said when you could feel it" (Goldberg interview, Los Angeles, August 10, 1991). But Bernfeld was not alone in the concrete interpretation of libido as a form of energy. It was seen as a form of real energy by many psychoanalysts and, of course, Wilhelm Reich had his own version, which he called "orgone energy."

George Gero, MD (1901–1993), the Hungarian analyst, said that when Bernfeld told Freud about his project to measure libido, Freud was unimpressed and said, "Well, my friend Bernfeld, I believe I will die with unmeasured libido" (Gero phone interview, April 28, 1992). My understanding is that this effort to measure libido ultimately led Bernfeld and

Feitelberg to a dead end, after which, I presume, the concept of libido was allowed to return to its place as what I would call an "energetic metaphor" for the location, direction, and intensity of desire. Ruth Goldberg recalled, "He didn't pursue it, because it was fruitless. It was just not an approach that gave results." That said, Nathan Adler, a close student of Bernfeld's in San Francisco, laughed at himself when he recalled his own efforts, no doubt under Bernfeld's influence, to measure libido by measuring the strength of the urinary stream (Adler interview, San Francisco, c. November 15, 1990). Ultimately, Bernfeld would say psychoanalysis is a Spurenwissenschaft, a science of traces, referring to the facts of observation in psychoanalysis—that is, the traces of the resistance and transference (Etchegoyen, 1995, pp. 10–12).

Many analysts will be quick to point out the "empirical" nature of their clinical work but may hold back from calling psychoanalysis a science. Psychoanalysis is certainly not a "hard science." It is often difficult to get two observers in the same room to agree on the diagnosis of a given patient. What can we expect of their ability to identify the presence, or lack, of a positive outcome, and how might they recognize the components responsible for therapeutic change? And even if the observers were all properly trained and a respectable scientific study were conducted, what would analysts of another theoretical orientation have to say about their observations and conclusions? We like data to be quantifiable so that we can analyze it, but qualitative research might be more suitable for psychoanalytic research—if the observers can at least agree on what they saw and what they made of what they saw. Questions of repeatability and predictability become difficult if not impossible from one therapeutic pair to the next, but perhaps the attempt itself is worth the effort and may lead to new knowledge.

Eric R. Kandel (1999), Nobel laureate in Physiology or Medicine in 2000, addressed what he felt was the importance of psychoanalysis embedding itself in the sciences of human cognition: "A closer relationship between psychoanalysis and cognitive neuroscience would accomplish two goals for psychoanalysis, one conceptual and the other experimental. From a conceptual point of view, cognitive neuroscience could provide a new foundation for the future growth of psychoanalysis, a foundation that is perhaps more satisfactory than metapsychology... From an experimental point of view, biological insights could serve as a stimulus for research, for testing specific ideas about how the mind works (pp. 505–506)."

"To return to its former vigor and contribute importantly to our future understanding of mind, psychoanalysis needs to examine and restructure the intellectual context in which its scholarly work is done and to develop a more critical way of training the psychoanalysts of the future (p. 522)."

But what is the nature of metapsychology in psychoanalysis? Is the id a thing to be measured? If we operationalize ego functions, can they be usefully measured? Is the unconscious Freudian? Jungian? Embedded in the group? Or just everything beyond the horizon of awareness? Can we measure object relations? Freud spoke of the "I," the "over I," and the "it." It was Strachey who scientificized "I" into "ego," "over I" into "superego," "it" into "id," and, perhaps most fatally, "soul" into "mind." My old mentor Nathan Adler used to say, "There is no ego, only egoing. There is no mind, only minding." But if the ego is not a thing, perhaps it is a way of speaking about something that is difficult to speak of. Perhaps it is an analogy. In *The Question of Lay Analysis*, Freud (1926/1959) confessed, "In psychology we can only describe things by the help of analogies. There is nothing peculiar in this; it is the case elsewhere as well. But we have constantly to keep changing these analogies, for none of them lasts us long enough" (*SE* 20, p. 18). But how do we conduct scientific research on analogies?

Observations of unconscious motivation are fascinating. They are clearly based on empirical data but require analogical thinking and speculation as well. In this regard, they are similar to Freud's psycho-anthropological work *Totem and Taboo* (1913/1955b). Most sciences rely heavily on logical thinking, and psychoanalysis does as well, but the distinctive mode of thought in psychoanalysis is analogical thinking—thinking in analogy, in metaphor, in symbolism.

One of the cornerstones of psychoanalysis is the theory of infantile sexuality, but it has been said that Freud didn't discover anything in this regard that every nanny in a nursery doesn't already know. But seeing the analogues of adult sexuality in the behavior of children and the analogues of infantile sexuality in the behavior of adults is still upsetting, if not subversive, for many.

Paracelsus (1493/94–1541) wrote, "Medicine is not only a science; it is also an art. It does not consist of compounding pills and plasters; it deals with the very processes of life, which must be understood before they may be guided."[1] Writing 500 years ago, Paracelsus seems to suggest that the processes of life are best apprehended by way of art. Is that still the case? Perhaps psychoanalysis is part science and part art. But what kind of art is this?

Is psychoanalysis a hermeneutic art? A literary endeavor? A mode of applied philosophy? A way of looking at the configurations of human behavior? Is psychoanalysis the co-construction of narrative? What might we say about the music of the session or the theater of dream interpretation? How much of clinical work can be described as an aesthetic treatment of erotic and aggressive engagement through the transference and countertransference? How much of the existential engagement of two subjects is science and how much is dance? And how much of the ancient ritual and shamanic healing traditions remains a vital part of modern psychoanalysis?

Freud, citing Leonardo da Vinci, reflected on the art of painting as *per via di porre*, the art of putting paint onto the canvas, and the art of sculpture as *per via di levare*, the art of

---

[1]https://www.brainyquote.com/quotes/paracelsus_170321

removing parts of the matrix to reveal the figure within. He described psychoanalysis as *per via di levare*, because the analyst carefully removes the obstacles to disclosure (interprets the resistance and the transference) thereby making the unconscious conscious (Freud, 1905/1953, *SE* 7, p. 260).

Peter Gay wrote,

One of the Nobel prize winners who refused to support Freud's candidacy was Albert Einstein, who wrote to [Heinrich] Meng on February 15, 1928, that he could not offer any dependable opinion on the truth of Freud's teaching, 'much less offer a verdict that should be authoritative for others.' Moreover, Einstein cautions, it seemed doubtful to him that a psychologist like Freud should really be eligible for the Nobel prize in medicine, 'which is I suppose, the only one that could be considered.' (Gay, 1988, 456n)

And Richard Feynman (1963–1965) wrote, "Psychoanalysis is not a science: it is at best a medical process, and perhaps even more like witch-doctoring."

Much of the concern about whether psychoanalysis is a science or an art pertains to its respectability, perceived reality, professional status, and, of course, the question of who is qualified to practice it. While both Einstein and Feynman expressed serious doubts about the scientific status of psychoanalysis, the theoretical physicist J. Robert Oppenheimer consulted several psychoanalysts for personal concerns in London and Paris in the 1920s and participated in Siegfried Bernfeld's psychoanalytic study group in the late 1930s in San Francisco (Benveniste, 2006). While I have found no reference to Oppenheimer regarding psychoanalysis as either a science or an art, he clearly had a more positive view of the value of psychoanalysis, whether it was a science or not.

In the collection of articles to follow, we will hear from a number of distinguished psychoanalysts who have strong arguments for their differing positions. Following each article, another distinguished author, or authors, will offer discussion allowing us all to witness and share in the debate. The editors of *IJCD* hope that in bringing these authors and their articles and discussions together, we will stimulate further thought and productive debate on this important and controversial topic in psychoanalysis.

References

Benveniste, D. S. (2006). The early history of psychoanalysis in San Francisco. *Psychoanalysis and History*, 8(2), 195–233.

Bernfeld, S., & Feitelberg, S. (1930). *Energie und trieb: Psychoanalitische studien zur psychophysiologie*. Liepzig, Wein, Zurich: Internationaler Psychoanalitischer Verlag.

Darwin, C. (1968). *The origin of species by means of natural selection; or, the preservation of favored races in the struggle for life*. J. W. Burrow (Ed.). Middlesex, Eng.: Penguin. (Original work published 1859)

Etchegoyen, R. H. (1995). The science of the traces, the traces of a master. *International Psychoanalysis: The Newsletter of the International Psychoanalytical Association*, 4(1).

Feynman, R. (1963–1965). *The Feynman Lectures and Physics, Vol. 1*. Pasadena: California Institute of Technology.

Fonagy, P. (2002). *An Open Door Review of Outcome Studies in Psychoanalysis*. London: International Psychoanalytical Association.

Freud, S. (1895/1966). Project for a scientific psychology. In J. Strachey (Ed. & Trans.), *The standard edition of the complete psychological works of Sigmund Freud: Vol. 1. Pre-psychoanalytic publications and unpublished drafts* (pp. 295–397). London: Hogarth Press.

Freud, S. (1905/1953). On psychotherapy. In J. Strachey (Ed. & Trans.), *The standard edition of the complete psychological works of Sigmund Freud: Vol. 7. A case of hysteria, three essays on sexuality and other works* (pp. 257–268). London: Hogarth Press

Freud, S. (1913/1955a). The claims of psycho-analysis to scientific interest. In J. Strachey (Ed. & Trans.), *The standard edition of the complete psychological works of Sigmund Freud: Vol. 13. Totem and taboo and other works (1913–1914)* (pp. 1–161). London: Hogarth Press.

Freud, S. (1913/1955b). Totem and taboo. In James Strachey (Ed. & Trans.), The *standard edition of the complete psychological works of Sigmund Freud: Vol. 13. Totem and taboo and other works (1913–1914)* (pp. 1–161) London: Hogarth Press.

Freud, S. (1926/1959). The question of lay analysis. In James Strachey (Ed. & Trans.), *The standard edition of the complete psychological works of Sigmund Freud: Vol. 20. An autobiographical study, Inhibitions, symptoms and anxiety, Lay analysis and other works (1925–1926)* (pp. 183–258). London: Hogarth Press.

Freud, S. (1927). Concluding remarks on the question of lay analysis. *International Journal of Psychoanalysis, 8,* Part 3, pp. 392–398.

Gay, P. (1988). *Freud: A life for our time.* New York: Anchor Books.

Kandel, E. (1999). Biology and the future of psychoanalysis: A new intellectual framework for psychiatry revisited. *American Journal of Psychiatry, 154*(4), 505–524.

Pumpian-Mindlin, E. (Ed.) (1952). *Psychoanalysis as science.* Stanford, CA: Stanford University Press.

Strachey, J. (1966). Introduction to Project for a scientific psychology. In J. Strachey (Ed. & Trans.), *The standard edition of the complete psychological works of Sigmund Freud: Vol. 1. Pre-psychoanalytic publications and unpublished drafts* (pp. 291–293). London: Hogarth Press.

Our Secular Religion

Robert Bergman

I believe our work, our knowledge, and our theories make use of both science and art but psychoanalysis is neither. It is a religion.

Many years ago, the Vietnam war knocked me out of training in the Chicago Institute. If it were not for the war, I would have spent my life in Hyde Park and on Michigan Avenue. But to stay out of the army, I enlisted in the United States Public Health Service, volunteered for the Division of Indian Health and was sent to the Navajo Nation. I expected to stay two years but was so happy there I stayed ten. Several years earlier, an unfortunate experience with my cousin, the rabbi, completed my disillusionment with Judaism and religion in general.

Back then, most Navajos spoke their own language and only about half of them could speak English, and they valued their traditional medical systems more highly than ours. Intelligent PHS leaders, needing to earn the people's trust, had cultivated cooperative relationships with the medicine people. And, given the task of creating a mental health system, I did the same. I hired hatathli, Navajo Ceremonialists as consultants and ultimately became the one nonnative faculty member of a school for medicine people. In 1967, when I met my first consultant, Tom Largewhiskers, when he was 100, he said, "I don't know what your grandfathers told you, but the most important thing mine taught me is that there is a part of our thoughts that we don't know about." He had a crooked lower leg he had broken in a wagon accident when he was young. The medicine man who had set the fracture told him that besides the splint he needed treatment for the cause of the accident because Tom had unconsciously decided to hurt himself. I figure that conversation took place about a decade before the publication of *Studies in Hysteria*. The hatathli were not only the most learned of the healers but were also the priests of the Navajo religion. The two roles were inseparable; there was no distinction between medicine and religion. (When the medicine person school was established with the support of the NIMH, I worried that we'd get in trouble because the government was supporting a religion, but when a constituent complained about that to a congressman, he dismissed the complaint as ridiculous.)

Besides traditional Navajo religion, the Native American Church, a pan Indian religion had spread to the Navajo and about half the tribe had joined despite the Tribal Council, influenced by white missionaries, having made it illegal when it arrived about twenty-five years earlier. It was legalized in 1970, but in my first years there, I couldn't find anyone who would acknowledge membership to a white government employee like me. I wanted to go to a Peyote Meeting to learn what it was that half my patients believed in and were doing. Finally, a man whose trust I had earned invited me to one. I went as a frightened observer but left the all-night ceremony moved and changed. I kept up the idea that I was going as an observer for another meeting or two and then recognized that I had become a member and asked and received permission to officially join despite not being Native American. The man who had taken me to the meeting, Tom Nez, became my adopted brother. I had dropped back into religion. The NAC, like traditional Navajo medicine was psychologically sophisticated. It also served both the functions of healing and worship. Most meetings are for the purpose of treating a specific person. One night that person was Tom's wife, Carol, who was depressed. There is plenty of time for talking between sundown, when the ritual starts, and sunup, when it ends, and that night, Carol talked about her sadness at reaching menopause and never having any more children. Her husband said that he thought he was also part of the problem because he was so often away running meetings and doing other church business. He said that he had noticed that sometimes he had doubts about the religion and that then he threw himself more heavily into its work to forget those thoughts.

After some years of my going to meetings, Tom told me that it was time for me to take up my training as a road man, the priest who officiates. I was delighted by his confidence and was initially simply happy with the idea. But then I stopped to think that I would never be known as a good or bad roadman but always as the white roadman, my freakiness more important than my dedication or my skill and I decided to study what I would fit into better. I dropped back into psychoanalytic training.

As psychoanalysts, just as our knowledge of the unconscious is not new, our role in people's lives is as old as humanity, and this role is much the same as the one medicine people have always played. We are attentively close to the person so that they are not alone. Tom Largewhiskers said of his schizophrenic patients that they are way out somewhere all by themselves and it's our job to go join them and bring them back. We inform our people that their troubles are understandable and that our understanding will help. We help them to see that their suffering and they themselves have meaning. We have a system of ideas that organizes our relationship with patients and which they can learn. We assist them in finding their way in the family, community and culture. Like hatathli but unlike roadmen, we pretend not to have moral authority but we do, and like the priests and healers of every culture we have a value system. We think knowledge is better than ignorance, that honesty is better than deception, especially self-deception, that independence is better than conformity and that self-respect is better than guilt and shame. Though many of us tend to deny it, our opinion has weight and we counteract other authorities, real or imagined, who scorn, scold or punish. We give permission for activities and thoughts that previously felt forbidden. Our value system is crucially different from that of many other religions in that we believe that actions, but not fantasy and thought, should be evaluated as good or bad.

In that, among other ways, we are an improvement on religions that came before us, and like all religions, we came into being as part of a cultural change and we were more adaptive to new conditions. Usually the religious revolution is led by a prophet who rebels against old beliefs and practices and formulates a new and more adaptive system, which the prophet's followers institutionalize. The prophet's insights and inspirations become dogma. I was lucky to become a member of the Native American Church in its prophetic days when we flocked to meetings because they meant so much, despite the risk of arrest. Fifty years later, alas, lots of people go because it is expected. Young people rejecting rigidity of belief in the Native American Church and psychoanalysis or any system, create schisms if not revolutions and divide the original religion into competing sects.

Martin Luther and the Reformation were part of the end of feudalism, the rise of capitalism and the explosion of technical invention, especially movable type which made it possible for everyone and not just priests to read scripture. In the mid-nineteenth century, much of North America had been lost to the European invaders, and native nations were despairing of being able to save the rest. The Ghost Dance religion arose in response to this. Its main idea was that all natives should cease fighting each other and unite against the common enemy. When that didn't work, one of its leaders, Kwanah Parker, a war chief of the Comanche who had succeeded in holding onto their land for longer than almost any other group, became the prophet who founded the NAC, a redemptive religion that helped mourn the loss and offered solace in the idea, among others, that like the Jews, they were special to the Creator, who gave them the gift of the sacrament, Peyote, and a ritual that made them closer to the divine than other people. "The white man prays to God. We speak with him face to face."

When the NAC reached the Navajo, decades later, it served other purposes. In The Peyote Religion Among the Navajo, David Aberle showed that the NAC redeemed the nation from the destruction of its agrarian economy. What happened was that the growth of the human population in the first part of the twentieth century led to a growth of the sheep population that resulted in the overgrazing that destroyed the grassland. The Bureau of Indian Affairs thought to improve the situation by a program of stock reduction, which was carried out in an authoritarian and humiliating manner. People saw their beloved flocks seized, killed and burned. They didn't lose their land but they lost their livelihood and the organizing principle of their society. Besides its redemptive nature, the religion also provided new social structure as the matrilocal, extended family system broke down, and Peyotists became each other's new extended family by adoption in the way that I became a member of the Nez family and a whole family system of adopted relatives from a number of other regions.

Freud, our psychoanalytic prophet, was brought to the big, sophisticated city from a rural extended family culture when he was a little boy. I think that seeing his mother unclothed on the trip was not only oedipally significant but also a screen memory for the culture shock of his dislocation. His fine secular education, which his parents valued so highly, marked an enormous cultural change in one generation. It gave him the keenness of social vision common among well-informed outsiders and a need to resolve the conflicts resulting from losing old ways and digesting new ones. His replacement for

Judaism was Science, which was a religion for him and for many of his time. His reverence for science and his insistence that he was a scientist was the ultimate origin of this collection of essays. The idea that we are scientists is a religious dogma that still has considerable sway. Many analytic meetings call the sessions where we read papers to each other "Scientific Sessions", a name which makes me, for one, a little queasy. I identify with Mark Twain, who after meeting with Louis Agassiz, said, "Between us we comprehend all of human knowledge. He knows all that can be known, and I know the remainder."

In addition to needing to replace Jewish religious belief, Freud had to bridge the gap between an extended family culture and a nuclear family culture. In the heyday of American psychoanalysis in the mid-twentieth century, analysts thought the main focus of their work was the Oedipus Complex, but the public knew it was separation-individuation, a concept that had only just then been specifically formulated. Everyone knew in those days that you got analyzed to free yourself from your parents, especially your mother. Almost every sketch in Mike Nichols and Elaine May's show about analysis was about a controlling, guilt-inducing mother or, in one case, a controlling guilt-inducing motherly analyst.

When families migrate from an extended family culture to the United States or when the industrial revolution arrives in a new part of the world and the population moves from the country to the city, there is a strain between the generations. Under the old regime, children remained unseparated and it worked all right. In the industrial and post-industrial world, the children see and want separation and, anyway, it is necessary in order for people to be mobile enough to succeed economically and socially. Americans, by and large, don't need help with this problem any more, but millions of Asians do. They, like other ethnic groups before them, are climbing the acculturation and status ladder, and in their turn are subjecting their children to ambitious parental control with the result that the next generation, like Freud no longer fit the extended family system and have to solve the resulting conflicts. The same circumstances are favoring the growth of psychoanalysis in Iran, where it is relatively new and has been growing rapidly. I am fortunate to be a consultant and hear frequently about the struggles of analysands who come from rural traditional families and have become doctors and lawyers in Tehran.

I don't know what comes next, but I feel hopeful we will be relevant for a long time. Buddhism has shown great staying power and I think that in two crucial ways, it's like psychoanalysis. Neither the Buddhists nor we compel belief in a magical explanation for the origin of the universe. The Dalai Lama, asked what Tibetan Cosmology was, said that it evolved as science made new discoveries. Like the Buddhists, our essence is a practice, which I think will remain valuable no matter what else happens.

What Sort of a Thing is Psychoanalysis, Who's to Say, and What of It?

Margaret Crastnopol

Is psychoanalysis an art, a science, or, as Robert Bergman eloquently proposes, a religion? If it partakes of *any* of these, it could arguably just as well be considered a philosophy, a form of spirituality, a moral code, a value system, or, more broadly and simply, its own subculture. So challenging is this attempt to characterize psychoanalysis!

Here I'll offer some loosely linked observations on the question itself and on Dr. Bergman's perspective. From the outset, I find myself in closest agreement with his argument that psychoanalysis is fundamentally a *practice*. It's a mode of treating someone's psyche that's informed by a particular worldview and associated with a particular technique—these elements varying, depending on the practitioner's own character and personality, theoretical affiliation, relevant training and experience, and so forth. Psychoanalysis is one among a slew of self-exploratory, self-healing activities that we've needed to develop throughout the ages, to deal with the impact of the psychic damage we receive, and to grapple with our propensity for psychological and behavioral dysfunction.

For me, Dr. Bergman's commentary points to our being prone to classify psychoanalysis as one thing or another *depending on our socio-political context and the zeitgeist to which we are attuned*. If at a certain place and time science is believed in and prized, we may claim psychoanalytic thinking and therapy as scientific. If art, then we'll emphasize its aesthetic credentials. If religion is what's known and valued, then psychoanalysis will likely register as a form of religion. I'm not saying that characterizing a psychoanalytic process in this fashion is a marketing ploy or some other sort of crassly utilitarian act—whichever value predominates is simply the water that society or sub-society swims in, making it likely we'll identify with it. Calling our field whatever discipline is ascendant is what we *need* to do to invest it with validity and gravitas, and this in turn adds to its potential impactfulness. There's no harm—and can be some good—in this, especially if we periodically take a step back and recognize the factors influencing our characterization of it.

Looking at this the other way around, whatever discipline the culture most closely expresses itself through, is also likely to be put to use addressing its members' psychic and emotional needs.

Now, the above comments speak to how psychoanalysis is broadly conceptualized, and from the perspective of its professional practitioners and fellow travelers (for instance, academics of various stripes, etc.). For patients, and when we ourselves are the patient, psychoanalysis is likely to register in a more personal, specific way. And this idiosyncratic, *experiential* one may be a more meaningful characterization than an overarching conceptual one. Depending on who the patient is—and who the analyst is perceived to be—psychoanalysis and analytic therapy may be for that patient a refuge, confessional, private club, drama, prison, wrestling match, experiment, self-evaluation or prognostication, proving ground, musical performance, or simply a type of higher education in the business of living. I suspect that for some it's primarily a socially acceptable excuse to take prescribed breaks in the workday, for authorized periods of recurrent companionship, and the like. I'm suggesting that the patient, through his or her contribution to the analytic third, *co-determines* what his or her treatment—and therefore, "psychoanalysis"—will be for him or her. That is, the patient shares significantly in shaping its primary function, style, tone, depth—even to some degree the methods the analyst will be able to employ in doing the work. After all, psychoanalysis is a "subjective object" (in Winnicott's terms), not an objective, absolute one. And it is not dictated solely by the analyst's conceptualization of what patient and analyst are doing.[1] How the analytic process is co-created and registered by the patient plays a big role in the outcome of the work. For these reasons, we practitioners do well to avoid over-identifying with what we think—or like to think—we're doing.

I'm arguing for a more local and personalized understanding, from both analyst and patient's perspective, so it probably behooves me to speak to what psychoanalysis is for *me*, as sometime-patient and ongoing analyst. Psychoanalysis feels to me like the all-important container of and channel for my own and others' inherent psychological mindedness. When this proclivity is strong enough in us, it often carries the self-expectation that we *do something meaningful and useful with it*. Ongoing psychological mindedness is both blessing and affliction, guiding force and exacting taskmaster. (The reader likely knows just what I mean.) We don't *choose* to introspect, to ponder our own and others' psychic life—*it* chooses *us*. Psychological mindedness is for many a signature sensibility and—to use a phrase that's unfairly discredited—a means for self-actualization. Psychoanalysis harnesses that sensibility into something that provides purpose and meaning—not to mention, it allows us to earn a living doing a more sophisticated, "accountable" version of what we can't help but do anyway.

Apropos of *it* choosing *us*—contrary to what I'd felt and believed earlier in life, I've come to recognize that a psychoanalytic belief system and psychological mindedness itself are *not* the be-all, end-all, and last word in understanding humans and their functioning. In fact, much as it pains me to say it, their applicability and utility have significant limitations, that show up in both the public and private spheres.

---

[1] That said, to consider more fully the ways the practitioner's professional allegiance does influence the patient's experience of psychoanalysis, see my 1999 article, "The analyst's professional self as a 'third' influence on the dyad: When the analyst writes about the treatment," Psychoanal. Dial., 9(4), 445–470.

As a case in point, most of the analytic practitioners and other mental health professionals I know of[2] view the man currently occupying the role of United States president as being a "malignant narcissist," if not even more disordered.(See, for example, Justin Frank's 2018 book, *Trump on the Couch*, or Bandy X. Lee's 2019 book *The Dangerous Case of Donald Trump*, the 2nd edition). This considered professional judgment apparently matters *not one whit* to the man's party, as evidenced by its decision to back his patently destructive, impulsive actions, and even support his bid for a second term in office. We analysts have to encompass that discordant fact—that is, the incommensurability of our own diagnostic picture and that of a hefty chunk of this country's politicians and overall electorate. A psychoanalytic understanding of the man himself—and even the attempt to understand his supporters—only takes us so far (and not far enough). We have to come to terms with the fact that our power to influence a larger social current is quite restricted. We know that the same is true for other arts, sciences, and religions, but ours is the discipline one would think might have special weight relative to the society's view of their leader's fitness to govern. Yet other factors affecting the populace—socio-economic, educational, racial, and so on—seem to outshout the mental health community's trained judgment. Here psychoanalysis runs up against its limits.

With respect to the personal sphere, many psychodynamically-oriented practitioners have adult offspring or other relatives in fields besides our own, who, through our influence, appear to have embraced a psychoanalytic perspective enough that they choose to plumb its possibilities within their own discipline. (Ok, there's usually a trace of parody in there as well, but that's to be expected.) I think here of remarkable writers like Ben Lerner (see his 2019 novel, *The Topeka School*), Amy Kurzweil (in her 2016 graphic memoir

---

[2]I refer here to the subgroup of those practitioners who feel it's fair to come to a judgment about this particular public figure's character without the benefit of being able to interview him personally.

Flying Couch), and Steve Almond (especially his 2010 short story "Donkey Greedy, Donkey gets Punched," not to mention his 2017–2018 New York Times "radically empathic" advice column.). The two male writers were brought up by a pair of analysts, the female by a therapist-mother who is psychodynamically oriented. What a delight it must be for these people's parents—how satisfying it must be, trading observations (interpretations?) over the holiday dinner table!

But often, our nearest and dearest just don't grasp—or outrightly reject—our psychoanalytic worldview. A probing, reflective exploration of the inner world (theirs, our own) is not welcomed. Closeness between us psychoanalytic clinicians and these loved ones will only emerge if pursued through other channels. Whether psychoanalysis is fish, fowl, or something else entirely, it's not necessarily the royal road to intimacy—or for that matter, comprehensive self-knowledge—I once imagined it to be.

My thoughts circle back to Dr. Bergman's early analytic training in Chicago, its interruption and his engagement with the Navajos, and his return to analytic training, now enriched by the wisdom of his Native American immersion, and ready to pass that on. Dr. Bergman's journey and his reflections on it demonstrate the importance of our working to escape being narrow and reductionistic, of our not being blinded by the biases of our inherent psychic tendencies or standard ideological affiliations.

In conclusion, why get caught up in trying to find the "right" classification for psychoanalysis? What's most significant is to see it for the multifarious thing it is. This means keeping other disciplinary and subcultural viewpoints close at hand, to be drawn on regularly and assiduously as we strive to promote growth in our patients and ourselves, in the context of the ever more daunting socio-psychological and geopolitical forces surrounding us.

Reply to Margaret Crastnopol's Discussion of His Paper

Robert Bergman

I am grateful to Dr. Crastnopol for her thoughtful and helpful discussion. I agree that we tend to classify our profession according to our socio-political context. Our context is not only secular but, in some ways, anti-religious. I think we may lose something essential about what we do by denying religion, and therefore our cultural lineage and one of the essential ways psychoanalysis is experienced.

Seven Basic Emotional Systems in the Brain and Their Implications for the Human Condition

Lucy Biven

Psychoanalysis is certainly an art, but this paper makes a case that it should be more of a science by focusing on a neuroscientific taxonomy of seven basic emotional systems. These emotional systems direct our visceral responses (i.e., blood pressure, pupil dilation, sweating, etc) as well as our behavior (i.e., approaching, smiling, caressing, grimacing, freezing, running away). They also direct our affective responses—our conscious affective feelings of pleasure and pain (Panksepp, 1998a; Damasio, 1999). Jaak Panksepp delineated these seven systems using simple descriptive words for each one, but he wrote the descriptive words in capital letters to highlight the fact that emotional systems are physical entities rather than metaphorical descriptions (Panksepp, 1998a).

Emotional systems are found in and around the brainstem and in midline regions of the cortex. The brain evolved from the bottom up and from midline to more lateral areas, meaning that subcortical structures evolved before the cortex and that midline parts of the cortex evolved before its lateral parts. The position of emotional systems indicates that they evolved a very long time ago. As animal brains have evolved, these ancient systems have been retained. Thus, all mammalian brains contain the seven basic emotional systems and all mammals are affective creatures. The brains of many other vertebrates contain some of these systems—young birds, for example, display distress when separated from their mothers (Panksepp, 1998a).

In contrast, more recently evolved parts of the cortex differ dramatically from one species to another, which is why mammalian species have different perceptual acuities and levels of intelligence. Emotionally however, we are all cousins, which is why research about the emotional life of animals tells us about human emotions (Panksepp, 1998a; Damasio, 1999a).

We will start with a description of each emotional system, followed by a discussion of ten ways that they impact our understanding of human emotions and the practice of psychotherapy.

The seven emotional systems

1. The SEEKING system has been alternately described as a "foraging /exploration /investigation /curiosity/ interest/ expectancy" system (Panksepp, 1998a p 145). SEEKING arousal is characterized by a persistent exploratory inquisitiveness and a willingness to take risks. It engenders energetic forward locomotion—approach and proactive engagement with the world—as an animal probes into the nooks and crannies of interesting places, objects, and events in ways that are characteristic of its species. Rats, for example, typically sniff vigorously when they explore new environments. The SEEKING system holds a special place among emotional systems, because to some extent it supports and attends all of the other emotional systems. When in the service of positive emotions, the SEEKING system engenders a sense of purpose, accompanied by feelings of interest ranging from enthusiasm to euphoria.

For example, when a mother feels the urge to nurture her offspring, the SEEKING system will motivate her to find food and shelter in order to provide this care. The SEEKING system also plays a role in negative emotions, for example providing part of the impetus that prompts a frightened animal to find safety.

2. The FEAR system generates a negative affective state from which all people and animals wish to escape. It engenders tension in the body and a shivery immobility at milder levels of arousal, which can intensify and burst forth into a dynamic flight pattern with chaotic projectile movement to get out of harm's way.

3. The RAGE system causes animals to propel their bodies toward offending objects, and they bite, scratch, and pound with their extremities. Rage is fundamentally a negative affect, but it can become a positive when it results in victory over one's opponents or in the control and subjugation of others.

4. When animals are in the throes of the LUST system they exhibit abundant courting activities culminating in urgent copulation with a receptive mate and ending with orgasm. Arousal of LUST can be pleasurable even when ultimate satisfaction is not obtained, but excessive arousal can result in an unpleasant craving tension. LUST is one of the sources of love.

5. When people and animals are aroused by the CARE system, they have the impulse to envelop loved ones with gentle caresses and tender ministrations. Without this system, taking care of the young would be a burden. Instead, nurturing can be profoundly rewarding. In extreme circumstances, CARE arouses the impulse to protect others even at the expense of one's own safety. Mother's, for example, will sacrifice their lives in order to protect their young. The CARE system is typified by maternal nurturance, but it is not limited to mothers or

to women. For example, soldiers on the battlefield are often willing to sacrifice life and limb for the sake of their comrades in arms. CARE is another source of love.

6. The GRIEF system (which Pankepp sometimes calls the PANIC or SEPARATION DISTRESS system) might be called the GRIEF/SOCIAL BONDING system because it generates feelings that are good as well as bad (Toronchuk & Ellis, 2012). The bad feelings are panicky misery when people and animals are socially isolated or rejected. Social isolation produces stress chemicals like *corticotropin releasing factor (CRF)* that contribute to the feelings of misery.

The negative arm of GRIEF generates a deep psychic wound—an internal psychological experience of pain. When young children and young animals are in the throes of the negative side of GRIEF, their misery reaches a panicky level and they cry insistently, urgently trying to reunite with their caretakers—usually their mothers. If reunion is not achieved, the baby or young child gradually begins to display sorrowful and despairing bodily postures that reflect the brain cascade from panic into a persistent depression.

The same system, however, produces feelings of joyful contentment when people and animals benefit from the affectionate support of family and friends. This sense of social belonging produces comfort chemicals, oxytocin and opioids (endogenous opiate-like brain chemicals), that engender the sense of well-being. The positive side of GRIEF is yet another source of love.

Although the positive arm of GRIEF is actively enjoyable, the negative side helps to cement positive social relationships because close social bonds alleviate the psychic pain that attends negative GRIEF arousal. Thus, positive social bonds are cemented from two directions. The positive side of GRIEF feels good and the negative side, which feels terrible, is assuaged by close and supportive relationships. Close and positive social relationships are especially important early in life, when young children and animals need the protection of their parents in order to survive. Children value their parents and stay close to them because this fosters positive affects and because it avoids the negative affective experience that attends separation from them.

7. The PLAY system is expressed in bouncy and bounding lightness of movement, where participants often poke—or rib—each other in rapidly alternating patterns. At times, PLAY resembles aggression, especially when PLAY takes the form of wrestling. But closer inspection of the behavior reveals that the movements of rough-and-tumble PLAY are different than any form of aggression. Furthermore, both participants enjoy playing. When children or animals play, they usually take turns at assuming dominant and submissive roles. In controlled experiments, researchers found that one animal gradually begins to win over the other (becoming the top dog, so to speak), but the play continues as long as the loser still has a chance to end up on top thirty percent of the time. When both the top dog and the underdog accept this kind of handicapping, the participants continue to have fun and enjoy this social activity. If the top dog wants to win all the time, the behavior approaches bullying. Even rats clearly indicate where they stand in playful activity with their emotional vocalizations: When they are denied the chance to win, their happy laughter-type sounds cease, and emotional complaints begin. PLAY system probably helps young animals to learn basic skills. For example, a kitten chasing a ball or yarn is also developing skills that will eventually enable it to catch mice. Additionally, PLAY provides an arena for learning about social roles (Bekoff and Byers,1998; Brosnan, 2006; Keltner et al., 2006). PLAY amongst human children is crucial to their socialization (Peterson, 2019b). The PLAY system is one of the main sources of friendship. (Panksepp, 1998a; Pankespp & Biven, 2012).

Implications of the seven emotional systems
1. Why free associations tell us so much

Emotional systems respond only to a small repertoire of stimuli. Rats, for example, are inherently afraid of well-lit open spaces, where they are typically vulnerable to predators. They are also innately afraid of the smell of cat fur. If a rat has been raised in captivity and has never before been exposed to a cat, it will become wary if you place a pinch of cat fur into its cage. The rat will not respond to a photograph of a cat or to the sound of a cat's maiow. Only the smell of cat fur will cause the rat's movements to become constricted, cause it to go off its food and off sex (Panksepp, 1998a).

Other stimuli innately engender an emotional response. Human beings and other animals innately fear pain (Panksepp, 1998a) and loud noises (Clasen, M. (2017). Most young animals, including human babies, are innately afraid of heights (Gibson & Walk, 1960) and of spiders and snakes (Pappel, 2017). Other stimuli are species specific. Rodents fear the light, while many human children are afraid of the dark (Panksepp, 1998a).

This small repertoire of stimuli to which we have an innate emotional response expands exponentially mostly because of conditioning experiences that occur on a regular basis throughout life. Suppose that an urban rat lived near a house with a pet cat. The rat would stay away from the cat because it is innately afraid of the cat's smell. If the cat wore a bell around its neck, the rat would soon learn to fear the sound of the bell.

Seminal experiments by Joseph LeDoux provide a template that explains how conditioning happens. LeDoux's experiments, which focused on fear-conditioning, subjected rats to a mild shock to the foot and the simultaneous exposure to an innocuous auditory tone. These experiments demonstrated that the amygdala which lies at the uppermost regions of the FEAR system (Panksepp, 1998a) is essential for fear conditioning. Like most brain structures, the amygdalae are bilateral, and are situated largely in subcortical brain regions just behind the temples (Bourtchouladze, 2004). Each amygdala has 13 sections or nuclei and the "central nucleus" plays a crucial role in generating fear (Maren & Quirk, 2004; LeDoux, 2008).

An innate neural pathway, which encodes the pain of the electric shock, leads to the central nucleus of the rat's amygdala, which generates a fear response. This is why the rat is unconditionally afraid of the shock. Prior to conditioning, the neural pathway encoding the sound of the tone does not lead to the central nucleus. If the tone were to play on its own, the rat would take little notice. However, if the sound of the tone occurs when the rat receives a foot shock, the rat learns to fear the tone.

LeDoux discovered that conditioned learning creates a molecular/chemical process that allows the neural pathway encoding the tone to gain access to the central nucleus of the rat's amygdala. Once the tone-encoding pathway projects into the central nucleus, the rat is afraid of the tone. LeDoux revealed that in addition to learning to fear the tone, the rat learns to fear all manner of contextual stimuli. The neural pathways encoding contextual stimuli take a somewhat different rout within the amygdala, but they too project into the central nucleus. In addition to fearing the sound of the cat's bell, our urban rat might also learn to fear the sound of the cat owner's voice and the sight of the cat's toys, etc. (LeDoux, 1996).

Ordinarily we think that conditioning is a thought or perceptual process. We assume that the rat somehow thinks that the tone heralds the shock or we assume that the rat somehow associates the sight of the cat with the sound of the bell because they occur together. This, however, is not the case. Decorticate animals that have been surgically deprived of their cortex can be successfully conditioned (Kolb & Wishaw, 2009). Without a cortex, people and animals cannot think, nor can they see, hear, taste, smell, or experience touch. Yet decorticate animals like dogs, and children born without a cerebral cortex can be conditioned to associate the unconditioned (i.e., shock) and conditioned (i.e., tone) stimuli (Culler & Mettler, 1934; Bromiley, 1948; Shewmon et al., 1999).

You might wonder how people and animals without a cortex can be conditioned when they cannot perceive or think about anything. Conditioning succeeds because sub-cortical structures can process information about stimuli (Solms, 2012). For example, cortically blind people often avoid objects in their path even though they do not see anything, a phenomenon known as "blindsight" (Weiskrantz, 1986). Neuroscientists believe that the superior colliculus, a subcortical structure found in the brainstem, processes light-wave information that allows blind people to avoid objects in their path (Cowey, 2004; Pessoa, 2005). Similar studies demonstrate subcortical processing of hearing and touch (Garde & Cowley 2000; Rossetti, et al., 1995).

If conditioning is a non-cognitive, non-perceptual process, what is it? What does conditioning achieve? LeDoux demonstrated that conditioning allows people and animals to acquire an emotional response to previously neutral stimuli. When conditioning succeeds, the unconditioned stimulus (the shock) and the conditioned stimulus (the tone, along with contextual stimuli) become associated because they evoke the same emotional response, namely fear. That is the nature of their association (LeDoux, 1996).

Of course, intelligent species like our own have thoughts about conditioning experiences. If I were subjected to a simultaneous foot-shock and auditory tone, I might think that the tone caused the shock. However, the fact that decorticate animals can be conditioned demonstrates that my thought process does not create the association. I associate the tone and the foot shock because I am afraid of them both.

This observation allows us to make sense of the free associative process. As a general principle emotional arousal inhibits cortical activity (Salzman & Fusi, 2010) and the cortex inhibits emotions (Liotti, & Panksepp, 2004). During conditioning experience, when emotions run high, they influence the ideas that the cortex creates. Because human beings are intelligent, we have a host of ideas when we are emotionally aroused and these ideas center around the emotion that we are feeling. We all know this from personal experience. When you are in love, the whole world is beautiful but if you lose love, your thoughts turn dark.

Here is a simple example of my own free associations. Everyone in our family was excited and happy during the days leading up to my daughter's wedding. I recall that she and her fiancé had trouble finding a cake that they liked, that we all arranged flowers the night before the wedding, that her best friend, who got ordained on the Internet, officiated at the ceremony, and that there was a din of conversation during the wedding meal. These associations: cake, flower arrangements, wedding official, and noise may appear to be disparate thoughts, but they are all connected by a central emotion, namely my happiness at my daughter's marriage. When clients talk about different thoughts and ideas that appear to be unconnected, psychoanalysts can be confident that there is an underlying connecting emotion, which is why free associations are so instructive.

2. Panksepp's taxonomy is more complete and scientifically robust than the psychoanalytic drive theory

Freud maintained that libido (LUST) and aggression (RAGE) are basic drives. Bowlby (1969) added the need for attachment (GRIEF) and Kohut (1971) claimed that we also have a need for narcissistic affirmation. The neuroscientific taxonomy provides a much wider repertoire of basic drives than does psychoanalytic theory. Panksepp stipulates that his taxonomy may not be complete and that other emotional systems may be discovered. Some researchers have tentatively proposed the existence of DISGUST and SOCIAL DOMINANCE systems which may eventually be included in the existing taxonomy (Toronchuk & Ellis, 2012). Notwithstanding, the current list is more complete than any other existing taxonomy (Panksepp, 1998a).

Additionally, the psychoanalytic drives are based on behavior and verbal reports, both of which are open to interpretation and subject to disagreement (Killingmo, 1985). Emotional systems, however, consist of identified brain structures that are fuelled by specific chemicals that we can observe and on which we can agree. Thus, Panksepp's taxonomy provides a broad and scientifically credible understanding of our basic motivations.

3. Support for Bowlby

Panksepp's taxonomy resolves a psychoanalytic disagreement about the status of attachment as a drive (Killingmo, 1985). According to Freud's formulation children are attached to their parents because parents meet the child's libidinal needs and are the objects of the child's libidinal desires (Freud, 1926). However, psychoanalytic theorists like Suttie (1935), Fairbairn (1952), and predominantly Bowlby (1969) maintained that the need for attachment and secure object relationships, especially in early childhood, is a drive that is independent of sexuality (Grossman, 1995). Panksepp's neuroscientific emotional taxonomy corroborates Freud's view that libido (LUST) and aggression (RAGE) are basic drives, but it also supports Bowlby's assertion that attachment (GRIEF), especially in early childhood, is a basic non-sexual drive (Panksepp, 1992).

4. Two types of anxiety

Panksepp's taxonomy reveals two types of anxiety, each emanating from different systems. One type of anxiety emanating from the FEAR system concerns any anticipated adverse event. The FEAR system is typically aroused in the face of physical injury or death, but we can also be afraid of a final exam or a tax audit. This type of anticipatory anxiety is attended by arousal of the sympathetic arm of the autonomic nervous system, which speeds up bodily processes critical to survival and shuts down those that are not. Sympathetic arousal is attended by an infusion of stress chemicals which accelerate heart rate and respiration, cause pupil dilation and the release of glucose to fuel muscles. Gastro-intestinal and excretory systems, on the other hand, shut down. Sympathetic arousal also generates the fight/flight response to danger that is typical of FEAR arousal (Lanese, N., 2019).

The GRIEF system generates another type of anxiety that typically occurs when young children or animals are separated from their mothers and cry in distress. GRIEF is also aroused to a lesser extent when adults are deprived of social support and feel lonely, abandoned or rejected (Panksepp, 1998a). The parasympathetic arm of the autonomic nervous system attends this type of anxiety. Parasympathetic arousal causes a slowing of heart rate and respiration, muscle relaxation, and an increase in digestive function. Ordinarily, parasympathetic arousal prompts animals to "feed and breed" (Lanese, 2019). However, extreme parasympathetic arousal can have pathological consequences (Porges, 1997). When people and animals are isolated and lonely, parasympathetic arousal contributes to a sense of weakness and depression along with a tightness in the chest, a lump in the throat and an urge to weep (Panksepp, 1998a).

In addition to the difference in autonomic participation, FEAR and GRIEF respond to different medications. Benzodiazepines like Valium are effective in assuaging FEAR, but they have only a modest effect on quelling panic attacks. The anti-depressant, Imipramine, however, quells panic attacks (Klein, 1964) and separation cries in young animals, but is ineffective in reducing FEAR arousal (Panksepp, 1998a). This indicates that anticipatory anxiety which responds to benzodiazepines is a symptom of FEAR arousal, while panic disorders and separation distress, which respond to imipramine, emanate from the GRIEF system (Panksepp, 1998a).

It is also likely that there are different sub-divisions in emotional systems. For example, as we noted above, rats are inherently afraid of well-lit open spaces. Researchers test anxiety in rodents using an elevated plus-shaped (+) maze, which is an apparatus with two open and two enclosed arms (Pellow et al., 1985). Ordinarily rats stay in the enclosed arms where they are more protected, this being a sign of anxiety. When rats are treated with benzodiazepines they remain in the enclosed arms indicating that they continue to feel anxious. When treated with morphine, however, anxiety abates and they are willing to venture into the open arms of the maze. The fact that different drugs quell different levels of anxiety indicates that there are different neurochemical levels of FEAR (Panksepp, 1998a).

5. Two ways to feel good and bad

The seven systems also highlight a dichotomy of good/bad pairs of affects, each pair stemming from different emotional systems. The positive arm of the GREIF system generates feelings of comfort and joy that we feel in the company of friends and family. Conversely if we are abandoned or betrayed, we endure the misery of loneliness and rejection, emanating from the negative arm of GRIEF (Panksepp, 1998a).

The SEEKING system generates a different pair of good and bad feelings. The good feeling is an energized focus on a goal and a euphoric sense of being an effective agent who can make things happen in the world. However, when SEEKING arousal is at a low ebb, we feel hopeless and depressed.

Thus, we see that depression has two sources, one the miserable sense of isolation stemming from GRIEF arousal and the other a hopelessness emanating from the relative absence of SEEKING arousal (Panksepp, 1998a).

6. The importance of the SEEKING system in mental health

Most psychoanalysts are aware of the importance of secure attachments, particularly in early childhood. However, there has been far less attention on the needs and joys of the SEEKING system. SEEKING arousal imbues people with a euphoric sense of anticipation, a feeling of being able to effect changes in the world, as well as a willingness to take risks (Panksepp, 1998a). The urge for achievement, independence and personal agency might be seen as the opposite of attachment, but it is as important to human fulfilment and happiness (Peterson, 2019a).

7. Emotional neutrality does not exist

Neuroscientific research demonstrates that neutrality on the part of a psychoanalyst should not extend to an emotional neutrality toward the patient. People experience neutral facial expressions as ambiguous (Cooney et al., 2006), resulting in arousal of the amygdala which generates feelings of anxiety (FEAR) (Balderston et al, 2011). In other words, people feel ill at ease when they think that other people do not care about them. An apparently "neutral" psychoanalyst is not neutral at all.

8. Aggression is not pleasurable

Although there has been much disagreement about the role of aggression in psychoanalytic theory (Dennen, 2005), many modern psychoanalysts believe that aggression, like libido, is a source of instinctual pleasure (Hartmann, H., Kris, E., Loewenstein, R. (1949). Neuroscientific research, however, opposes this view. Animals avoid places where their RAGE systems were electrically aroused, indicating that RAGE arousal is an unpleasant experience—except, of course, when one is about to win the day (Panksepp, 1998a). When a client is chronically angry, a therapist can be confident that this is not a wishful pleasant state.

9. A neuroscientific explanation of difficult cases

Psychoanalysis distinguishes between a problem and a conflict. A problem arises when you know the variables involved: do you want to go out for pizza or sushi? You weigh the pros and cons of each and make your decision. Conflict arises when at least one variable is unconscious. Then you cannot make a rational decision.

According to the classical Freudian view, our drives always strive for pleasurable gratification (1923c). Conflict arises when the drives run into opposition either from the demands of reality or the superego (Thornton, 1995). Then the ego institutes defences that keep drives unconscious (A Freud, 1936). The aim of psychotherapy is to remove the defences and thereby reveal hitherto unconscious element(s). When this happens people can make more rational and adaptive decisions (Nagera, 2018).

Rationality, however, is often unattainable due to reasons like secondary gain that clients obtain from their symptoms (Fishbain, 1994) and co-dependent relationships that preserve and/or foster symptoms and pathological attitudes (Cullen & Carr, 1999). Most frequently, however, psychoanalysts fail to successfully treat people with severe personality disorders (Katz, 2003). Neuroscience offers some reasons why such clients are difficult to treat.

We noted above that the neocortex, which roughly corresponds to the psychoanalytic ego (Solms & Panksepp, 2012), generally serves to inhibit emotional systems, while emotional systems generally arouse the neocortex/ego. There are many more connections from emotional systems to the neocortex than there are in the reverse direction, which means that emotions, especially when they run high, control our thoughts and that our neocortices are relatively ineffective in inhibiting emotions (LeDoux, 2013).

As therapists we hope that when an emotion becomes conscious, the client will be able to find a better outlet for its expression or to quell it in other ways. If, for example, a client's envy becomes conscious, he will abandon it, usually because of superego condemnation and find a means of achieving success that will quell the feelings of envy. This kind of solution takes time and involves a measure of cortical inhibition.

Unfortunately, clients with severe personality disorders, tend to be emotionally unstable, impulsive and often suicidal (Paris, 2005). They fail to exhibit a capacity or willingness to inhibit their feelings even when unbridled emotional expression only worsens their plight. In these cases, the revelation of a hitherto unconscious emotion may make matters worse by increasing emotional arousal and exacerbating a client's inability to think rationally (Bateman, 2007). Indeed, one study indicates that 20% of clients deteriorate during psychotherapy (Lambert, 2007). In neuroscientific terms, this happens when emotional systems overwhelm the rational and strategic capacities of the neocortex.

10. Psychoanalysis does not offer a complete cure

Psychoanalytic studies indicate that even when clients improve and therapy is considered to be a success by both client and therapist, cure is incomplete. Although therapy may improve the lives of clients, problems are weakened rather than eradicated (Pfeffer, 1963; Oremland, et al., 1975). Neuroscience offers reasons why psychotherapeutic cure is incomplete.

After fear-conditioning, a rat will be afraid of the conditioned stimulus (i.e., the tone) for the rest of its life. However, conditioning can be extinguished if the rat is repeatedly exposed to the tone without any following shock. Extinction, however, is not the same as forgetting. In order to forget, neural circuitry needs to be destroyed.

Neuroscientific research demonstrates that this does not happen. Following extinction, conditioning circuitry remains intact, which is to say the pathway encoding the conditioned stimulus (the tone) continues to have access to the central nucleus of the amygdala. Why then is the fear extinguished? Extinction is achieved by the creation of new circuitry that is created when the animal learns that a shock does not follow the tone. When people and animals learn anything, the learning process creates new circuitry that encodes the learned information (Kandel, 2006). In the case of FEAR extinction, the new circuitry inhibits the activity of the central nucleus of the amygdala (Amano et al., 2010).

The learning process is inaugurated by circuitry in medial parts of the rat's prefrontal cortex and by circuitry within the amygdala itself. Once created, this new circuitry inhibits the activity of the central nucleus and the rat no longer exhibits FEAR when exposed to the conditioned stimulus (the tone) (Sotres-Bayon, et al., 2004). Instead of erasing conditioning circuitry, extinction is an active form of learning that creates new circuitry.

This new circuitry competes with existing conditioning circuitry (Davis, et al., 2003), and FEAR extinction is rarely permanent. Fear of the conditioned stimulus can re-emerge spontaneously at any time, for example, if the animal is returned to the cage where it was initially conditioned, or if it is subjected to an unexpected presentation of the unconditioned stimulus (i.e. a shock) (Myers & Davis, 2007; Chang, et al., 2009).

People with emotional problems have had conditioning experiences that have caused them to learn maladaptive ways of dealing with their problems. A man with a dictatorial father may learn to hate and oppose his father. In later life this circuitry will cause him to argue with his boss and be fired from a series of jobs. Psychotherapy reveals the client's unconscious anger with his father and helps him to see his irrational opposition to his boss. This is a learning process that is much like extinction because the analytic insights allow the client to learn a new and better way to behave at work. However, because the neural pathways encoding his old ways of behavior still exist, the client remains vulnerable to relapse during periods of stress. Thus, while psychotherapy can be a life-changing and even life-saving experience, it does not eradicate pathological tendencies.

Concluding remarks

I have indicated some of the ways that neuroscience can inform psychotherapy. No doubt there are many more. I hope to have convinced the reader that neuroscience offers objective facts about the ways that the emotional brain functions. These facts allow us to escape from relying so heavily on extrapolation from behavioral and verbal reports, which different clinicians interpret in different ways. Neuroscience is scientifically robust and Panksepp's taxonomy of seven basic emotional systems is a good starting point for understanding the emotional brain.

References

Adamec, R., Berton, O., & Razek, WA. (2009). Viral Vector Induction of CREB Expression in the Periaqueductal Gray Induces a Predator Stress-Like Pattern of Changes in pCREB Expression, Neuroplasticity, and Anxiety in Rodents. Neural Plasticity, Volume 2009. https://www.ncbi.nlm.nih.gov/pmc/articles/PMC2664642/

Balderston, NL., Schultz, DH., & Helmstetter, FJ. (2011). The human amygdala plays a stimulus specific role in the detection of novelty. *Neuroimage., 55(4)*:1889–1898. https://www.ncbi.nlm.nih.gov/pmc/articles/PMC3062695/

Bekoff M., Byers J. A. (1998). Animal Play: Evolutionary, Comparative, and Ecological Perspectives. Cambridge: Cambridge University Press

Bourtchouladze, R. (2004). *Memories Are Made of This: How Memory Works in Humans and Animals.* New York:Columbia University Press

Bowlby, J. (1969). Attachment and Loss, Vol. 1: Attachment. London: Hogarth Press and the Institute of Psycho-Analysis.

Chang, C-h, Knapska, E., Orsini, CA., Rabinak, CA., Zimmerman, JA, & Maren, S. (2009). Fear Extinction in Rodents. *Curr Protoc Neurosci., Unit 8.23* https://www.ncbi.nlm.nih.gov/pmc/articles/PMC2756523/

Clasen, M. (2017). How Evolution Designed Your Fear: The universal grip of Stephen King's personal terrors. *Nautilus.* http://nautil.us/issue/53/monsters/ how-evolution-designed-your-fear

Cooney, RE., Atlas, LY., Fanny, E., & Gotlib, IH. (2006). Amygdala activation in the processing of neutral faces in social anxiety disorder: Is neutral really neutral? Psychiatry Research: *Neuroimaging 148*:55–59. https://web.stanford.edu/group/mood/gotlib_pdfs/cooney_ gotlib_2006.pdf

Cowey, A. (2004). The 30th Sir Frederick Bartlett lecture. Fact, artefact, and myth about blindsight. Quarterly Journal of Experimental Psychology A, 57: 577–609.

Cullen, J & Carr, A. (1999). Co-dependency: an emperical study from a systemic perspective. *Contemporary Family Therapy 21*:505–526 https://www.academia.edu/10492416/Co-dependency_An_empirical_study_from_a_systemic_perspective

Culler, E., & Mettler, F. A. (1934). Conditioned behavior in a decorticate dog. Journal of Comparative Psychology, 18(3), 291–303. http://psycnet.apa.org/record/1935–01728–001

Damasio, A.R., (1999a). The Feeling of What Happens: Body and Emotion in the Making of Consciousness. Harcourt Brace: New York.

Davis, K.L., Panksepp, J. & Normansell, L. (2003). The affective neuroscience personality scales: Normative data and implications. NeuroPsychoanalysis, 5: 21–29.

Dennen, J. M. G. V. D. (2005). Theories of Aggression: Psychoanalytic theories of aggression. Default journal.

Fairbairn, WRD. (1952). An Object Relations Study of the Personality. New York: Basic Books

Fishbain, DA. (1994). Secondary Gain Concept Definition Problems and Its Abuse in Medical Practice. *APS Journal 3(4):* 264–273. https://www.jpain.org/article/S1058–9139(05)80274–8/pdf

Freud, A. (1936). The Ego and the Mechanisms of Defense. New York: I.U.P Nagera, H. (2018). The Psychoanalytic Theory of Conflicts.

Freud, S. (1923c). On: The Theory of Psychoanalysis. Standard Edition

Freud, S. (1926a). Inhibitions, Symptoms and Anxiety Standard Edition 20

Garde, M. & Cowley, A. (2000). "Deaf Hearing": Unacknowledged Detection of Auditory Stimuli in a Patient with Cerebral Deafness. Cortex 36 (1): 71–79.

Gibson EJ, Walk RD. The "visual cliff" Scientific American. 1960;202:64–71

Grossman, KE. (1995). The Evolution and History of Attachment Research and Theory. In *Attachment Theory: Social, Developmental and Clinical Perspectives.* Susal Goldberg, Roy Muir & John Kerr (eds.). Hillsdale NJ: The analytic Press Inc.

Hartmann, H., Kris, E., Loewenstein, R. (1949) Notes on the Theory of Aggression. Psychoanalytic Study of the Child 3:9–34

Hill, C., Spiegel, SB., Hoffman, MA., Kivlighan, DM Jr., Gelso, CJ., (2017). Therapist Expertise in Psychotherapy Revisited. *The Counseling Psychologist:* 1–49. https://www.apa.org/education/ce/therapist-expertise.pdf

Kandel, E. (2006). In Search of Memory—The Emergence of a New Science of Mind. WW Norton & Company, New York.

Katz, W. (2003). Failures in Psychoanalytic Treatment (Book Review). https://www.apadivisions.org/division-39/publications/reviews/failures

Killingmo, B. (1985). Problems in contemporary psycho-analytic theory: 1. Controversial issues. *Scandinavian J of Psychology, vol 26, issue 1.* https://onlinelibrary.wiley.com/doi/abs/10.1111/j.1467–9450.1985.tb01141.x

Klein DF. (1964). Delineation of two drug-responsive anxiety syndromes. *Psychopharmacologia, 5:*397–408.

Kohut, H. (1971) The Analysis of the Self. New York:Int. Univ. Press.

Kolb, B., & Wishaw, IQ. (2009) Fundamentals of Human Neuropsychology: Sixth Edition. New York: Worth Publishers

Lambert, M. (2007). What we have learned from a decade of research aimed at improving psychotherapy outcome in routine care. Psychotherapy Research, 17, 1–14. https://www.researchgate.net/publication/254439590 Presidential Address What we have learned from a decade of research aimed at improving psychotherapy outcome in routine care

LeDoux, J., (1996). The Emotional Brain: The Mysterious Underpinnings of Emotional Life. New York: Simon and Schuster.

LeDoux, J. (2008). Amygdala. Scholarpedia 3(4):2698 http://www.scholarpedia.org/article/Amygdala

LeDoux, J. (2013. The Emotional Brain. https://www.youtube.com/watch?v=8yxgPFXWLJA

Liotti, M. & Panksepp, J. (2004). Imaging human emotions and affective feelings: Implications for biological psychiatry. In J. Panksepp (Ed.), Textbook of Biological Psychiatry, (pp. 33–74). Hoboken, NJ: Wiley

Maren, S., & Quirk, G. J. (2004). Neuronal signaling of fear memory. Nature Reviews Neuroscience, 5, 844–852. http://deepblue.lib.umich.edu/bitstream/2027.42/61954/1/marenNRN04.pdf

Myers, K.M. & Davis, M. (2007). Mechanisms of fear extinction. Molecular Psychiatry 12: 120–150.

Nagera, H. (2018). The Psychoanalytic Theory of Conflicts. https://www.youtube.com/watch?v=ZEfNmEA09ho

Oremland, J. D., Blacker, K. H., & Norman, H. F. (1975). Incompleteness in "Successful" psychoanalyses: A follow-up study. Journal of the American Psychoanalytic Association, 23, 819–844. https://psycnet.apa.org/record/1976–22572–001

Panksepp J (1992). Oxytocin effects on emotional processes: separation distress, social bonding, and relationships to psychiatric disorders. Annnal of the New York Academy of Sciences, 652,243–252. Panksepp, J., (1998a). Affective Neuroscience: The Foundations of Human and Animal Emotions. New York: Oxford University Press

Panksepp, J. and Biven, L. (2012). Archaeology of the Mind. New York: Norton

Papple, D. (2017). Innate Fears: Even Babies Get Stressed When They See Spiders And Snakes. *Inquisitr.* https://www.inquisitr.com/4556275/babies-stressed-spiders-and-snakes/

Pare, D., Quirk, G.J., & LeDoux, J. (2004). New Vistas on Amygdala Newtorks in Conditioned Fear. Journal of Neurophysiology 92: 1–9 http://www.ncbi.nlm.nih.gov/pubmed/15212433

Paris, J. (2005). Borderline Personality Disorder. *CAMJ, 172(12):*1579–1583. https://www.ncbi.nlm.nih.gov/pmc/articles/PMC558173

Pellow, S., Chopin, P., File, SE., & Briley, M. (1985). Validation of open:closed arm entries in an elevated plus-maze as a measure of anxiety in the rat. *Journal of Neuroscience, vol 14, issue 3:*149–167. https://www.ncbi.nlm.nih.gov/pubmed/2864480

Peterson, J (2019b). We Need Play. https://www.youtube.com/watch?v=GKMHN7hICkQ

Pfeffer, AZ., (1963). The meaning of the analyst after analysis—A contribution to the theory of therapeutic results. *Journal of the American Psychoanalytic Association, 11:*229–244. http://www.pep-web.org/document.php?id=apa.011.0229a&type=hitlist&num=14&query=zo

Porges, S. W. (1997). Emotion: an evolutionary by-productof the neural regulation of the autonomic nervous system. Annals of the New York Academy of Science, 807: 62–77.

Rossetti, Y., Rode, G., and Boisson, D. (1995). Implicit processing of somaesthetic information: a dissociation between where and how? NeuroReport, 6: 506–510.

Salzman, CD & Fusi, S. (2010). Emotion, Cognition, and Mental State Representation in Amygdala and Prefrontal Cortex. *Annu Rev Neurosci., 33:*173–202. https://www.ncbi.nlm.nih.gov/pmc/articles/PMC3108339/

Shewmon, D.A., Holmes, D.A. & Byrne, P.A. (1999). Consciousness in congenitally decorticate children: developmental vegetate state as a self-fulfilling prophecy. Developmental Medicine and Child Neurology. 41: 6, 364–374.

Solms, M. (2012). The Conscious Id. https://www.youtube.com/watch?v=s7J1FLZUg3A

Solms, M., & Panksepp, J. (2012) The "Id" Knows More than the "Ego" Admits: Neuropsychoanalytic and Primal Consciousness Perspectives on the Interface Between Affective and Cognitive Neuroscience. *Brain Sci., 2(2):* 147–15. https://www.ncbi.nlm.nih.gov/pmc/articles/PMC4061793/

Sotres-Bayon, F., Bush, DEA & LeDoux, JE. (2004). Emotional Perseveration: An Update on Prefrontal–Amygdala Interactions in Fear Extinction. *Cold Spring Harbor Laboratory Press ISSN: 11:*525–535 http://citeseerx.ist.psu.edu/viewdoc/download?doi=10.1.1.829.1682&rep=rep1&type=pdf

Suttie I (1935). The origins of love and hate. London: Penguin.

Thornton, S. P. (1995–present). Sigmund Freud (1856–1939). Internet Encyclopedia of Philosophy. http://www.iep.utm.edu/freud/

Toronchuk, J.A., & Ellis, G.F.R. (2012). Affective Neuronal Selection: The Nature of the Primordial Emotion Systems. Front Psychol. 3:589. http://www.ncbi.nlm.nih.gov/pmc/articles/PMC3540967/

Weiskrantz, L. (1986). Blindsight: A Case Study and Implications. Oxford University Press.

Yoshihara, K., Tanabe, YH., Kawamichi, H., Koike, T., Yamazaki, M., Sudo, N., & Sadato, N. (2016). Neural correlates of fear-induced sympathetic response associated with the peripheral temperature change rate. *Neurolimage, Volume 134*:522–531.

Discussion of Lucy Biven's Article "Seven Basic Emotional Systems in the Brain and Their Implications for the Human Condition"

Susan Kavaler-Adler

Lucy Biven doesn't mention Psychoanalysis in the title of this paper, which seems appropriate, since the information and opinions she offers in this paper do appear to pertain much more to an overall view of the "Human Condition" than to any clinical practice of Psychoanalysis. Her belief that Psychoanalysis needs to be more scientific, and not primarily artistic, seems like a bias that one might agree or disagree with. In agreement or not, her opening sentence that "Psychoanalysis is certainly an art, but this paper makes a case that it should be more of a science" certainly sets up her paper with her bias, from its inception. As an author who has spent decades writing and publishing books and articles on Psychoanalytic clinical process, and on developmental interactions with long case examples of clinical process, I have felt like a "stranger in a strange land" when entering, reading, and re-reading her paper.

Although I have my own prejudices that might be reflected in how I analyze the shortcomings of her paper, I wish to begin by giving Lucy Biven her due tribute for painstakingly defining and organizing the "seven basic emotional systems in the brain." Her references also reveal the large degree of scholarship that has gone into this paper. Certainly, I believe that what Biven offers in this regard helps all of us to become familiar with the various dimensions of brain activity that stimulate differentiated emotional modes of reaction in us as humans, and which overlap with a broader species of "mammals."

Many of the examples that Biven offers to define the 7 emotional systems of the brain are experimental animal experiments. She defines how we overlap with these rodents and mammals, and how we may differ.

The problems begin I believe when Biven attempts to extrapolate from such "rat" experiments, not only to humans, but to humans in psychoanalysis or psychotherapy. She never seems to make an adequate transition into psychoanalytic thinking. Further, she certainly does not forge a path into the clinical situation, where the development of the subjective self and of symbolic meaning are most relevant. She does not attempt any analogies with the meaning of psychic fantasy, and particularly of unconscious psychic fantasy. In fact, in one attempt to refer to "free association" she speaks of how her own associations to everything in the atmosphere of her daughter's wedding had the same emotional valence of "happiness," even though different thoughts about different things observed were described.

Her point seems to be that the emotion defined how the thoughts of things observed and felt all linked together. The emotional state did the linking. O.K. Fine. But how does that relate to the clinical situation in which "free association" is related to the Internal World, not to the external world, and to the preconscious and unconscious emerging as defenses are surrendered?

Then in an attempt to speak of the shortcomings of Psychoanalytic phenomena for scientific thinking she devalues the analytic patient's expressions as "behaviors and verbal reports."

She says that "behaviors and verbal reports" can be interpreted in different ways—causing controversies--as opposed to a hypothetical communal sharing in "objective" observation of concrete physiological/visceral/emotional reactions to brain systems. I had a strong reaction to her reducing analysands' self and unconscious expressions to "behaviors and verbal reports." As far as I know, when analytic patients only offer behaviors they are acting out, and when they only offer "verbal reports," they are defensively contriving their self-expression, rather than allowing the spontaneous emergence of unconscious feelings and psychic fantasy imagery. "Reports" would be seen as a defensive attempt to limit and control the analytic situation. Such "reports" would imply avoiding being present in the room with the Analyst, and avoiding being in their own minds and selves in the present.

Biven offers one attempt, at the end of the 19-page article, to give an example of psychoanalytic theory only to show the limitations of psychoanalysis or psychoanalytic psychotherapy, where transference is worked with. She speaks generally, and I would propose stereotypically, of a man who acts out self destructively in work situations with "bosses" because he had a "dictatorial" father who he is rebelling against in transference displacement. She says that Psychoanalysis can help such a man to identify his rebellious and self-destructive behavior in the present with bosses, as coming from reactions to his father of his childhood past. She then postulates that this "re-learning" might have a temporary beneficial effect in this man's life, curtailing situations that might lead to him being fired by bosses in work situations. However, she focuses on the limitations of such "re-learning," since renewed stress might again trigger the old reactions that are related to still prevailing old brain circuitry; overcoming the new "brain circuitry" that is built in analysis, as the transference situation becomes conscious. This is the culmination of an argument that aims at defining the limitations of psychoanalysis in general, which she buttresses by citing a research study in which the data supposedly show that 20% of psychotherapy cases fail (Biven, p. 37), and further that the opening of unconscious emotional affect can result in an overwhelming psychic situation that has regressive rather than progressive effects. She never mentions how this would be worked with in a containing psychoanalytic situation, where negative transference is analyzed, and symbolic meaning of the emotions opening up is offered through interpretation. In any case, the example Biven gives totally skips over the analysand having an Internal World, or a transference situation in the session with the analyst, as opposed to just with his bosses. Yes, I agree with Biven that stress, and certainly new trauma, or re-living old trauma, can temporarily wipe out the cognitive and conscious gains that go with making unconscious phenomena conscious. However, the symbolic meaning of the transference can once more emerge into consciousness, as the stress is reduced, and as a new integration process evolves, following the regressive splitting and dissociation.

When Biven speaks about medications having differentiated effects on different emotional brain systems I experience her bias away from being a psychoanalytic practitioner again. Yes, I can agree if her point is to say there really are different emotional systems with different brain chemical reactions. How this relates to the psychoanalytic situation, or psychoanalytic psychotherapy situation, I am at a loss to define.

Specific Emotional Systems: Beyond Freud to Bowlby and Grief, to "Seeking, agency" evolution, and to contrasts between the Sympathetic and Parasympathetic Brain/Body Systems. Also controversies on Aggression re pleasure

The Author's Interest in Human Emotional Life Going Beyond Freud

Lucy Biven is looking for a larger scientific scope and vantage point to understand all the complicated aspects of human motivation. She states that in Psychoanalytic theory only John Bowlby and Heinz Kohut went beyond Freud's view of sexual and aggressive drives. She credits Bowlby with the expansion of human emotional experience (not actually sure she is looking at "motivation") to that of an attachment drive, which is not driven by sexual or libidinal impulses towards pleasure. She credits Bowlby with the positive side of longings for social affiliation and attachments, and with the consequent suffering of grief in loss, as being basic to the human condition. She even sees the grief related to separation from old attachments as being an experience that links to love, as it implies love lost, and I suppose as it renews the capacity to love when grief is tolerated. However, in citing Bowlby and not Melanie Klein (Bowlby's analyst), Biven limits grief to separation in a behavioral sense, because Bowlby's studies were all behavioral while Klein's studies are all clinical. So Biven does not venture into the symbolic meaning of mourning a particular loved one and how this can take place in psychoanalysis (see Kavaler-Adler on "Developmental Mourning," 1992a,1993/2013a, 1995, 1996/2014a, 2003a, 2003b, 2004, 2005, 2006, 2013b, 2014b, 2018). She sees Bowlby mainly as a pioneer in psychoanalytic theory, which goes beyond Freud, and does see Grief as an important category of the emotional brain systems. She credits Heinz Kohut in going beyond Freud in proposing "narcissistic affirmation" (Biven, p. 37) as another avenue of psychoanalytic speculation that bypasses the limits of Freud's two-drive systems.

Nevertheless, Biven's point here is to again point out the limits of psychoanalytic theory. She declares that the neurological theory of emotional brain systems expands our horizons much further than even these later pioneers in psychoanalytic theories. Then she proceeds to valorize specific ones within the overall seven. She thinks psychoanalysts neglect the area of "seeking" that has "euphoric anticipation" at its positive pole, while they have come to acknowledge Bowlby's views on Attachment.

Biven sees the emotional system of seeking as leading to the growth of the brain towards the independence of the self, or what I would call "self agency." I would beg to differ regarding seeing psychoanalysts as neglecting the growth of "agency." Other than the obvious roots of psychoanalytic thinking about "agency" in Margaret Mahler (1971, 1975) in terms of the Practicing Period within the wider scope of "Separation-Individuation," I would point to my own writings on the growth of "Agency," as well as those of Melanie Klein on

61

her theory of Reparation in the Depressive Position (Klein, 1937). In 2006 I published two articles in the *American Journal of Psychoanalysis* entitled "From Neurotic Guilt to Existential Grief: On the Way to Compassion, Agency, and Interiority," Part One and Part Two. I show in these two articles the organic evolution of self agency, along with many other ego functions, as a natural mourning process proceeds in developmental terms during intensive Object Relations psychoanalysis, along with separation-individuation, self integration, and transference analysis. This mourning involves separation grief, but also the abandonment affect states written about by James Masterson (1976, 1981, 1985, 2000), and the depressive position guilt and loss (regret, Kavaler-Adler, 2013) process of Melanie Klein. See also Kavaler-Adler on *The Anatomy of Regret...(2013) and* "The Conflict and Process Theory of Melanie Klein" (1992).

Contradiction of Hartmann, Kris, and Loewenstein on Aggression being Pleasurable

Here again Lucy Biven asserts her critique of the limitations of psychoanalytic theory by speaking of how neuroscientific empirical research has shown that Rage is not inevitably pleasurable, but rather is extremely unpleasant. She cites Hartmann, Kris, and Loewenstein (1949) (Biven, p. 35) as fallaciously declaring aggression to be pleasurable. In contradiction, Biven quotes Panksepp's 1998 research-based observation that "Rage arousal is an unpleasant experience, except of course, when one is about to win the day." Rage is one of the seven emotional brain systems.

I propose that psychoanalytic thinking has progressed beyond Hartmann, Kris and Lowenstein's theory that aggression (rage, sado-masochism) is pleasurable. I think we have more clinical evidence than in the past that aggression is addictive because of its intensity. However, addictive attraction to intensity is not the same as pleasure. Intensity is powerfully addictive, in masochism, as well as in sadism, which is why "Kink" has become a prevalent theory and practice. In fact, today there are even "kink" therapists. Affection is pleasant, but lacks the intensity of sado-masochism. Therefore, it does not seem to have the same addictive magnetism. Also, ego/self contained assertive aggression is not as addictive as sadism and masochism. It can give a sense of power and agency, but it lacks the intensity of Rage and sadism. The growth of self agency and assertion are pleasurable. Still they lack addictive intensity.

The Sympathetic Versus the Para-Sympathetic Neurological Systems

Biven speaks of the sympathetic nervous system as being responsible for fight versus flight self-protective instincts. She also speaks of the paranoid aspects of the psychic reactions that accompany such black and white fight and flight behavior. I propose that this nervous system's reactions can be likened to Melanie Klein's "paranoid-schizoid position" psychodynamics. When Biven offers the example of gastro-intestinal difficulties being body reactions of the fight and flight, black and white, primitive mode of the sympathetic nervous system, I think of a patient's "knots in the stomach." Knots in the stomach can be the body expression of knotty psychic conflicts that haven't made it beyond the visceral level, into consciousness, because of defensive opposition to unconscious rage that threatens self-sabotaging self-destruction. The visceral level symptom is a compromise formation. It is a compromise between expression and total dissociation. The dissociated visceral level psychic conflict can lead to an analytic patient's associating to the internal world Object who their rage is felt toward. I've witnessed the opening of the psychic visceral knots. Consciousness emerges, most frequently, with the expression of anger/resentment towards the analyst in the transference. We can see here the projection, projective-identification, and the splitting of the paranoid-schizoid position (Klein, 1946). Bringing the rage and projection to the conscious level, where symbolic meaning for interpersonal communication can be found modifies the paranoid-schizoid visceral reactivity, and encourages movement into the depressive position conscious affect experience, which articulates the growing dimensions of the evolving subjective self.

Biven describes the Para-sympathetic nervous system as a center for grief and loss, and for affiliation attachment affects that cause physiological arousal. Given this description, I would like to point out the analogy of this neurological system to Melanie Klein's other main psychological position (a position of core anxieties, core defenses, and core affects), the depressive position. In the depressive position the main anxieties are related to fears of losing the object, of losing love, and of losing the Object due to one's own aggression. Consequently, loss and existential guilt—(not Fairbairn's spurious Moral Masochism guilt, 1952)—are felt together, not just as separation loss. Rather, loss is linked to the awareness of one's own aggression destroying relationship. When Biven speaks of the visceral arousal of "a lump in the throat," and an "urge to weep" as related to the grief and loneliness that can be felt in the Para-sympathetic neurological body, she is speaking of someone who may be unconsciously experiencing Melanie Klein's depressive position affect states of "pining for the Object," feeling the loss of the Object, experiencing loneliness without the Object, and possibly the existential grief of regret related to awareness of "hurting the one you love."

The Absence of Melanie Klein's Thinking in this Article!!!

Ironically, Biven has a reference to a Klein in her paper, but it is not a reference to Melanie Klein.

She does have references to Ronald Fairbairn (his 1952 collected papers) and to Bowlby and Kohut. It is not irrelevant that John Bowlby was Melanie Klein's analysand, who went out and did empirical animal research on Melanie Klein's theories of both mourning and of reparation, and who then went back to Klein and said "I have been proving your theories." The fact that Klein was too arrogant to accept this empirical contribution with any grace or gracious thank you—claiming that she didn't need such empirical validation to know it's true—does not detract from the profound bond that Bowlby felt with Melanie Klein in his motivation for his research.

Biven gives a nod to Freud, although mainly focusing on the limitations of his thinking, in relation to what we know today, and to what we know today in neurological research. A majority of Biven's references are to those looking specifically at neurology, and not at psychoanalysis. She totally lacks any reference at all to Melanie Klein's work. To me this is shocking, particularly because Melanie Klein's theory is the strongest theory of affects and affective experience, both conscious and unconscious. Ruth Stein wrote a major paper on this, and then a book containing her study of Klein on affect theory, in 1991, entitled "Psychoanalytic theories of affects." I have written books and articles on my theory of "Developmental Mourning" (Kavaler-Adler, 2007), which always is seen in relation to Melanie Klein's developmental view of affect progression, and accompanying psychic fantasy, going back to "Mourning and Its Relation to Manic Depressive States" in 1940. Melanie Klein's theories of progression from the paranoid-schizoid position to the depressive position, and within the depressive position, speak of the progression towards more refined and differentiated affects, as the psyche progresses developmentally toward self integration.

So how is this not essentially relevant to any discussion of emotional systems in the brain, where affects originate? Also lacking is the abandonment depression affect state theory of James Masterson, with all its developmental understanding of character disorders, which goes back to Melanie Klein and Ronald Fairbairn (1952).

Nevertheless, I believe we owe a debt to Lucy Biven for her forays into the neurological brain psychology that helps us understand the various modes of emotion. I just request she progresses into the area of symbolic meaning, and into the subjective experience of the Self and Other within the

Internal World. To me, these psychological areas characterize the essence of psychoanalysis, as opposed to behavioral
symptomatology. In the end, the brain is a concrete Beta
"thing in itself" (see Ogden on Bion, 1986, Bion, 1963), as
opposed to a psyche employing symbolic level psychological
processing, called "Alpha function" by Wilfred Bion (Bion,
1963). Wilfred Bion was also an analysand of Melanie Klein's,
who extended Klein's theories in many directions, including
into the interpersonal realm of "the container and the contained," for active clinical symbolic meaning processing, on
the part of the psychoanalyst. He also spoke of "the attacks
on linking" (Bion, 1959) that operated in dissociated ways in
the mind to evacuate affects, as well as interpretations from
the analyst, before anything could be felt or communicated in
the symbolic language of words.

www.kavaleradler.com

drkavaleradler@gmail.com

References

Bion, W. R. (1959). Attacks on linking. *International Journal of
Psycho-Analysis, 40:* 308–315.

Bion, W. R. (1963). *Elements of Psychoanalysis.* London: Tavistock.

Bowlby, J. (1969). *Attachment and Loss, Volume 1, Attachment.*
London: Hogarth Press and the Institute of Psychoanalysis.

Bowlby, J. (1980). *Attachment and loss, Volume 3: Sadness
and depression.* London: Hogarth Press and the Institute of
Psychoanalysis.

Fairbairn, R. D. (1952). *Psychoanalytic Studies of the Personality.*
London: Routledge, Kegan, and Paul.

Kavaler-Adler, S. (1992a). Mourning and erotic transference.
International Journal of Psycho-Analysis, Volume 73 (3): 527–531.

Kavaler-Adler, S. (1992b). The conflict and process theory of Melanie Klein. *American Journal of Psychoanalysis, 52 (3):* 187–204.

Kavaler-Adler, S. (1993/2013). *The Compulsion to Create: Women Writers and Their Demon Lovers.* London and New York: Routledge; re-published 2013 by ORI Academic Press, New York.

Kavaler-Adler, S. (1995). Opening up blocked mourning in the preoedipal character. *American Journal of Psychoanalysis 55 (2):* 145–168.

Kavaler-Adler, S. (1996/2014). *The Creative Mystque: From Red Shoes Frenzy to Love and Creativity.* London and New York: Routledge; re-published by ORI Academic Press 2014.

Kavaler-Adler, S. (2003a). *Mourning, Spirituality, and Psychic Change: A New Object Relations View of Psychoanalysis.* London: Routledge (Taylor and Francis).

Kavaler-Adler, S. (2003b). Lesbian homoerotic transference in dialectic with developmental mourning: On the way to symbolism from the protosymbolic. *Psychoanalytic Psychology, 20 (1):* 131–152.

Kavaler-Adler, S. (2004). *Anatomy* of regret: a developmental view of the depressive position and a critical turn toward love and creativity in the transforming schizoid personality. *American Journal of Psychoanalysis, 64 (1):* 39–76.

Kavaler-Adler, S. (2005). The case of David: nine years on the couch for sixty minutes: once a week. *American Journal of Psychoanalysis, 65:* 103–134.

Kavaler-Adler, S. (2006). My graduation is my mother's funeral: transformation from the paranoid-Schizoid to the depressive position in fear of success, and the role of the internal saboteur. *International Forum of Psychoanalysis, 15:* 117–130.

Kavaler-Adler, S. (2007). Pivotal moments of surrender to mourning the parental internal objects. In *Psychoanalytic Review, 94:* 763–789.

Kavaler-Adler, S. (2013). *The Anatomy of Regret: From the Death Instinct to Reparation and Symbolization in Vivid Case Studies.* London: Karnac/Routledge.

Kavaler-Adler, S. (2014). *The Klein-Winnicott Dialectic: New Transformative Metapsychology and Interactive Clinical Theory.* London: Karnac/Routledge.

Kavaler-Adler, S. (2018). The beginning of heartache in character disorders: On the way to relatedness and intimacy through primal affects and symbolization. *International Forum of Psychoanalysis, 17 (4):* 207–218.

Klein, M. (1937). Love, guilt, and reparation. In J. Rickman (ed.) *Love, Hate, and Reparation. Psychoanalytical Epitomes* (No.2), pp. 37–119. London: Hogarth, 1981.

Klein, M. (1940). Mourning and its relation to manic-depressive states. Int. J. of Psycho-Analysis, 21: 125–153 [reprinted in The Writings of Melanie Klein, Volume 1, 1975].

Klein, M. (1946). Notes on some schizoid mechanisms. *International J. of Psycho-Analysis, 27:* 99–110.

Mahler, M.S. (1971). A study of the separation-individuation process and its possible application to Borderline phenomena in the psychoanalytic situation. *Psychoanalytic Study of the Child, 56:*403–424.

Mahler, S. (1975). Mahler, S., Pine, F., and Bergman, A. *The Psychological Birth of the Human Infant.* New York: Jason Aronson.

Masterson, J. F. (1976). *The Borderline Adult.* New York: Brunner Mazel.

Masterson, J. F. (1981). *Narcissistic and Borderline Disorders.* New York: Brunner Mazel.

Masterson, J. F. (1985). *The Real Self: A Developmental Self, and Object Relations Approach.* New York: Brunner Mazel.

Masterson, J. F. (2000). *The Personality Disorders: A New Look at the Developmental Self And Object Relations Approach: Theory, Diagnosis and Treatment.* Phoenix, A.Z.: Zeig, Tucker, and Heisen.

Ogden, T. (1986). *The Matrix of the Mind.* Newvale, New Jersey: Jason Aronson.

Stein, R. (1991). *Psychoanalytic Theories of Affect.* Santa Barbara, Cal.: Praeger, ABC-CLIO Solutions.

Response to Dr. Kavaler-Adler

Lucy Biven

Dr. Kavaler-Adler begins her critique by pointing out that I failed to make adequate links between affective neuroscience and the psychoanalytic process, especially the transference and symbolic meaning. This is a fair point. I should have realized that a paper relying so heavily on neuroscientific research would be alien to most psychoanalytic readers. I had wanted to delineate ways in which neuroscience can inform psychoanalysis and I had expected that readers would make the connections for themselves. In light of Kavaler-Adler's remarks, my expectation was naïve. Dr. Kavaler-Adler also points out my failure to mention Melanie Klein when speaking about psychoanalytic innovators. I apologize for this oversight.

My paper elaborated two points, the first of which is that neuroscientific data is scientifically credible, while psychoanalytic data is less credible because it is based on behavior and verbal reports, both of which are open to interpretation and disagreement. Jaak Panksepp, has delineated a taxonomy of seven basic emotional systems found in all mammalian brains. His taxonomy is more reliable and complete than any provided by psychoanalysis. It is more reliable because it is rooted in brain science, identifying specific brain structures and brain chemicals involved in each system. It is more complete because it offers surprises. For example, the urge to PLAY, especially in young animals, is a basic emotional motivating drive.

It is obvious to me that psychoanalysts gain their understanding from a patient's behavior and verbal reports. How else do we learn about them or about anybody? However, Dr. Kavaler-Adler states that I devalue the analytic patient when I speak about verbal reports and behavior. She also writes, "As far as I know, when analytic patients only offer behaviors they are acting out, and when they only offer 'verbal reports' they are defensively contriving their self expression, rather than allowing the spontaneous emergence of unconscious feelings and psychic fantasy imagery."

I am not sure that I understand her objections. I never meant to devalue patients and I have never encountered any patients who offer only behavior or only verbal reports. It is always an amalgam of both, in my experience. In any case, behavior can sometimes be an instance of acting out, but it is often a spontaneous expression of emotion. For example, a frown might defensively hide a forbidden delight, but it might express genuine irritation or even confusion. The same claim can be made about verbal reports—words too can deceive or reveal.

It is not always easy to discern the true meaning of a person's behavior or to correctly understand the things about which he or she speaks. Brain science, on the other hand, relies on observable physical data and offers greater scientific reliability about the nature of emotion and affect. For example, when Bowlby first wrote about non-sexual attachment as a primary drive, many analysts disagreed, arguing that attachment may seem to be non-sexual, but that it is really a sublimation of the libidinal drive. Although general opinion now favors Bowlby, this does not resolve the controversy scientifically.

Neuroscience does offer resolution. When rat pups are deprived of maternal care, their brains have fewer opiate receptors. Endogenous opiates are comfort chemicals that facilitate positive non-sexual social interactions. Poorly nurtured rats exhibit anxious behavior and the females become inattentive mothers. Chemicals like morphine and heroin, both opiate agonists, do not induce hypersexuality in human beings or in animals. Rather they are powerful anti-depressants.

Therefore, neuroscientific evidence indicates that non-sexual attachments are not basically libidinal as Freud thought.

On the basis of this kind of neuroscientific evidence, Panksepp proposed a GRIEF system consisting of brain structures that include cingulated cortex, septal area, bed nucleus of the stria terminalis, the preoptic area, dorsomedial thalamus and periaqueductal gray, all of which are largely fuelled by endogenous opioids. When we are in the company of friends and family opioids are plentiful and we feel good. But when we are abandoned and lonely, opioids are in short supply and we are miserable. The GRIEF system is Janus-faced but neither face concerns sexuality. This neuroscientific evidence supports Bowlby rather than Freud and it is the kind of physical evidence that is more convincing than are theories based on the things that people say and do.

When elaborating on the seven emotional systems, I wrote about the importance of the SEEKING system, which engenders feelings of euphoric, enthused anticipation along with a sense of agency and a willingness to take risks. I said that while most psychoanalysts accept that attachment (GRIEF) is a basic emotion, the SEEKING system is not fully appreciated. Dr. Kavaler-Adler points out that analysts like Mahler and Klein have highlighted the importance of agency. Dr. Kavaler-Adler herself has written about the role of agency in mourning and development. The SEEKING system, however, encompasses more than agency in the struggle to develop and overcome negative affects of grief and mourning. It is a spontaneous, positive response to life challenges. For example, the SEEKING system is unconditionally aroused when animals are hungry and it spurs them to hunt for food with energy and determination. No doubt Dr. Kavaler-Adler and others appreciate the importance of agency and they may also see the significance of euphoric enthusiasm. However, in my experience, the positive effects of SEEKING arousal remain underappreciated.

The second point of my paper concerned neuroscientific

explanations for psychotherapeutic failure. Neuroscience demonstrates that, in general, the cognitive cortex inhibits emotional arousal, while emotional systems arouse the cortex. For example, if you are frightened by a horror-vampire movie, you can regain your composure by telling yourself that vampires do not exist. Conversely, if you are robbed at gunpoint, your FEAR system will be aroused, and you might experience worrying thoughts, bad dreams or even PTSD. Neuroscience demonstrates that more neural connections lead from emotional systems up to the cognitive cortex than in the reverse downward direction. This means that emotions have more power to arouse the cortex than the cortex has to quell emotional arousal.

Psychoanalysis relies on the power of cognitive understanding and the inequality of influence between emotional systems and the cognitive cortex offers a credible explanation for psychoanalytic failure. This evidence does not undermine the value of psychoanalysis, which is often effective. However, every psychoanalyst knows that treatment has limitations. Nobody has a 100% success rate. We should try to understand when and why psychoanalysis fails.

Dr. Kavaler-Adler, seems to have more confidence in psychoanalysis than do I. She agrees that psychoanalytic gains can be lost during periods of stress, but she believes that analytic insights can redress the balance. Later in her critique she writes about the addictive power of intense emotion, which she distinguishes from pleasure. Most addicts feel better when they take drugs or drink alcohol. They are addicted to the affective pleasure which temporarily replaces and eradicates their misery. If one is addicted to an intense emotion that does not provide pleasure, what motivates such addictions? Such non-pleasurable "addictions" indicate that a person is in the grip of overpowering emotions. I gather that Dr. Kavaler-Adler believes that therapy can address and overcome such unpleasurable addictions. On both points I am not as sanguine. In my experience, even after relatively successful therapy, severe stress, such as bereavement or physical illness, can set in motion a regressive process that is difficult to ameliorate. Similarly, some patients are resistant from the start. Sometimes patients abandon therapy early on, and in other cases, treatment drags on but does not help. The inequality between emotional systems and the cognitive cortex may explain these sad outcomes.

These disagreements notwithstanding, Dr. Kavaler-Adler and I might see eye-to-eye on some issues were we to engage in a conversation rather than in the formal setting of paper-critique-reply. I liked her comments about knots in the stomach reflecting a knotty psychic conflict, and I would like to talk more with her about the mind/body relationship. Likewise, I found her links between parasympathetic arousal and the depressive position persuasive, and, again, I would like to discuss these ideas further. I also thank her for criticizing my failure to make adequate connections between neuroscientific research and the psychoanalytic situation. In contemplating her remarks, I think I might find ways to do better.

Psychoanalysis: Art and/or Science? A Brief Contribution from Quantum Mechanics

Gerald J. Gargiulo

Imagination is more important than knowledge. For Knowledge is limited, whereas imagination embraces the entire world, stimulating progress, giving birth to evolution.

–Albert Einstein

One of the fallouts from living in a world where Newtonian physics colors our everyday experience—observation, measure, and, most importantly, replication (repeatability)—is that it promotes the distinction between what is art and what is science. Art is, by definition, unique. Its tools are many, e.g., metaphor, color, movement, mystery—which are not realties we necessarily associate with Newtonian scientific observations. Newtonian physics commands attention not only because in our macro world it works, and works very well, but because its repeatability gives it an exact stability, which is a necessary experience in our everyday life. Freud tried to make his theoretical understanding and models of the mind universal and verifiable, knowing that without such a perspective his science would be suspect. His theoretical models are, ultimately, just that, i.e., models—a fact that some psychoanalysts have difficulty accepting.

The clinical practice of psychoanalysis is, by definition, not exactly repeatable, given the individuality of the parties involved. Consequently, psychoanalytic clinical interventions have been criticized for not being scientific. Their individuality suggests an art rather than science. I have obviously summarized this critique of psychoanalysis from the perspective of a Newtonian worldview.

I might add, also, that the religious denominational aspect of the various theoretical psychoanalytic schools has not helped present psychoanalysis as a scientific discipline. A scientific mode of operation is dedicated to pursuing truth—but such a quest is, by necessity, an ever open and ongoing question. Truth, in a scientific framework, has more to do with process than possession.

It is very difficult to briefly summarize even a few of the findings of quantum physics, even after nearly a hundred years of discovery and exploration. Having said that, let me try. One of the most basic findings is the conclusion, to Einstein's disbelief, that God (or, *the Ancient One* —Einstein's designation) does play dice with the world. That is to say that from quantum findings there is no possibility of exact repeatability; rather we live in a world of high probability and not the exact repeatability evidenced in Newtonian experience. Such a finding of high probability vis-à-vis strict determinism is basic and should modify our understanding of free association and dream interpretation.

Turning to clinical practice, I would like to offer a brief overview of how some of the basic findings of quantum thought can be of help in our understanding of psychoanalysis. Each quantum observation—that is, interaction—is necessarily unique although following a prescribed protocol. An observation, for example, of a proton—relative to its location and momentum—is necessarily individualized. By very force of its nature, it is not exactly repeatable but only generically so. Part of the mystery of quantum findings is that each observation of a proton, for example, creates the proton, although it is always waiting to be created—so to speak. (D. W. Winnicott's reflections might be of help here). A proton always exists as an excitation in an energy field and it is simultaneously created by observation. (Similarly, light is both a wave and a particle, as the double-slit experiment established). I would like to ask the reader to see a parallel here with clinical interventions, e.g., interpretations. There are of course a set of procedures and protocols for a quantum observation as there are valid guidelines which any analyst follows in formulating interpretations and/or interventions.

Of course we are talking analogy here; but analogy in the quantum world is what we have. All we understand of the quantum world, as Niels Bohr reminds us, are our mental concepts, not the quantum world itself. In terms of process, each quantum observation is necessarily unique. Just as each psychoanalytic intervention is unique. Just as each work of art is unique. The reality of the necessary individuality of each quantum observation has, I believe, bearing on the practice of clinical interpretations and interventions. That is, individuality is not per se unscientific. It has a valid reflection in quantum observations.

Additionally, one of the more profound mysteries of quantum findings is the reversibility of cause and effect. John Wheeler, from Princeton University, demonstrated how changing an effect can change a cause—something we are not familiar with in our macro world. By way of analogy, a patient telling and retelling his or her thoughts, phantasies, dreams and/or hopes does, in fact, change his/her history. When patients experience that the past is likewise the present and that the present re-creates the past, they are creatively mirroring Wheeler's findings. Richard Fenyman, speaking to this past/present experience, named the process whereby a proton takes every possible route—even backward in time—"sum over histories." That psychoanalytic technique necessarily demands a high degree of creativity is obvious; that psychoanalysis itself is an exercise in creativity is obvious.

Is psychoanalysis an art or a science reflects a question mirroring macro consciousness. It is simultaneously both. Just as, by way of comparison, a proton is both created by observation and also always exists.

Quantum mechanics findings have been repeatedly validated – just pick up your cell phone and you will appreciate what quantum mechanics has made possible. And, as I have briefly outlined, there is more than an interesting parallel between quantum mechanics experience and psychoanalytic practice.[1]

Such a conclusion does no violence to the reality that psychoanalysis is a profoundly human enterprise. That is, one pained human being listening to another as Bion reminds us; one particularly sensitive and introspective clinician listening to his/her unconscious in order to hear another, as Reik depicts. I used the above quote from Einstein as a reminder to myself and others that true scientific growth comes from the imagination as much as from measurable procedures.

Psychoanalysis is a science of the mind; it proposes certain models to understand the complexity of human experience— as does any science. What I am proposing is that its clinical procedures are more understandable using quantum models rather than Newtonian models. In its best moments psychoanalysis offers models of understanding—not concrete existent realities—similar to quantum mechanics postulates. A scientific mindset is more than comfortable with usable but simultaneously changeable models. A willingness as well as a dependency upon testing models, and retesting, is evidence of a scientific mindset just as an appreciation and experience of creativity in responding to individuality is a mark of art.

---

[1]Anyone interested in exploring the contributions of quantum mechanics should read any of the works of Brian Greene. My own text *Quantum Psychoanalysis* develops many of themes I have mentioned here.

A willingness to examine what one is doing—be it scientific and/or artistic or both—necessarily is basic to any pursuit of who we are.

Response to Gerald Gargiulo's article, "Psychoanalysis: Art and/or Science? A Brief Contribution from Quantum Mechanics"

Merle Molofsky

Gerald Gargiulo is the author of *Quantum Psychoanalysis: Essays on Physics, Mind, and Psychoanalysis Today*, International Psychoanalysis Press, 2016, and his deep knowledge of quantum physics and its relevance to, and affinity with, psychoanalysis permeates his discussion of whether psychoanalysis is an art or a science. He also is an accomplished poet, and thus, in reading his discussion whether psychoanalysis is an art or a science, we encounter a sensibility that embraces both artistry and science as elements of psychoanalytic theory and practice.

Gargiulo introduces his article with a quotation from Albert Einstein: "Imagination is more important than knowledge. For Knowledge is limited, whereas imagination embraces the entire world, stimulating progress, giving birth to evolution." With this quotation, he demonstrates and defends his approach to the question, for imagination is necessary both for art and for science.

Further, he immediately questions assumptions we form when using the easily recognized concepts of science represented by Newtonian physics. He points out that Newtonian physics describes what he calls our "macro world," a world which can be observed and measured, the results of such operations resulting in replication. When he introduces the term "repeatability" as a substitute for "replication," he leads us to contrast the uniqueness of art and quantum observations with the Newtonian physics.

Since I was a poor science student in my formal education, and would still be so were I still a student in an educational institution, I immediately began to assume that Gargiulo was going to share my perspective, that psychoanalysis is more of an art than a science. Gargiulo, however, does not do so. Rather, he speaks to Freud's desire to establish psychoanalysis as scientifically valid, and his desire for his "theoretical models of mind to be accepted as "universal and verifiable." Gargiulo then pointed out that the clinical practice is not repeatable, due to the unique individuality of each person in psychoanalysis and compares that to the uniqueness of each quantum observation. We recognize that science always entails a search for truth.

Given his knowledge of quantum physics, and applying some of its findings to psychoanalysis, Gargiulo wittily and wisely turns any assumptions a reader may make on their head. In introducing quantum physics into his discourse, he focuses on the fact that "there is no possibility of exact repeatability; rather we live in a world of high probability; not the exact repeatability evidenced in Newtonian experience." Also, he notes that such a finding "vis-à-vis strict determinism should modify our understanding of free association and dream interpretation."

Gargiulo leads the reader into making a quantum leap into new possibilities in the psychoanalytic situation. Since imagination is a common necessity in both art and science, since psychoanalysis addresses the particular needs of the unique individual, our curiosity is piqued. While perhaps we may agree with Gargiulo that the flexibility of "high probability" may better describe our understanding of basic psychoanalytic concepts such as free association and dream interpretation than "strict determinism" does, what does this freedom imply?

Imagination and artistry: Gargiulo becomes somewhat playful. His article invites us into a quantum world of intriguing proton behaviors. Even someone who struggles with science, someone like me, can be engaged and fascinated. Even more so, when he points out that each observation of a proton creates a proton, a perfect example of the Heisenberg uncertainty principle, which states that if we know the speed of a proton, we cannot at the same time know its location. It does imply that the proton becomes observable by observation! This extends to research occasions in which the very act of measurement or observation directly alters the phenomenon under investigation. What are the implications for the psychoanalytic encounter?

I actually learned about the Heisenberg effect, a quantum theory principle, nearly 40 years ago, in a psychoanalytic course early in my psychoanalytic education! I didn't know then that it was a scientific principle, advanced science, quantum physics! I heard words. They seemed poetic to me. I didn't see a mathematical equation, which is how a physicist would express it. I believed it. My gut reaction was that of course it was true.

Gargiulo emphasizes that the telling and retelling of thoughts, phantasies, dreams, and hopes in the psychoanalytic situation "does in fact change his/her history." How? That, in his wisdom, Gargiulo leaves up to our imagination.

Leaving the question up to our imagination leads to his once again posing the question—"is psychoanalysis an art or a science?"—and his answer is that it is "a question mirroring a macro consciousness. It is simultaneously both. Just as, by way of comparison, a proton is both created and always exists."

I am grateful that in this article, Gerald Gargiulo gave me the opportunity to recognize the wider scope of science, the role of imagination in science, and a new way to think about the psychoanalytic endeavor.

Merle Molofsky

mmpsya@gmail.com

Response to Merle Molofsky

Gerald J. Gargiulo

I want to thank Merle Molofsky for her generous response to my article. Let me say at the beginning that I myself am not a scientist. My point in bringing some of what we have learned from quantum findings is that, by analogy, we might better understand the clinical process of psychoanalytic therapy. One need not know physics, in this discussion, to appreciate the role of analogy in gaining a deeper appreciation of psychoanalytic experience.

I quote Einstein, as Molofsky approvingly notes, since he affirmed the role of imagination and creativity in aiding our search for a deeper understanding of reality. It's interesting that Einstein greatly appreciated Freud's writing style—which he conveyed in their numerous letter exchanges—but was not a follower of his theories. Perhaps his focus was so centered on the outer world that the world within him held less interest. This is a bit puzzling, nevertheless, since his undying commitment to determinism would be consonant with many of Freud's assumptions.

Of course, as therapist and patient interact, they necessarily change what is experienced—another analogy with quantum findings. An analogy that I have found deepens my appreciation of clinical experience. My point in making such an analogy is simply to say that there is no need to be defensive and say psychoanalysis is just an art; unique interventions are not per se, unscientific. What my readings in quantum theory have made clear is that psychoanalysis is both an art and a science…at the same moment. And that is the point.

Finally, Molofsky playfully notes that she leaves it to the

reader's imagination to decipher what I mean when I note that a good analysis, following Paul Ricoeur, changes a person's history. Change the effect, as John Wheeler established, and you can change the cause, literally in quantum observations, symbolically in therapy. To re-experience and revisit childhood events, memories, and phantasies, now with mature understanding, is no longer to be the victim of events but to be the conveyer, now with insight and, whenever possible, compassion. That gives one a new childhood.

What has been singularly unscientific about psychoanalysis has been the behavior of many of its practitioners. For too many years, again as Molofsky conveys, analysts from different perspectives, have assumed that unchanging truth has been found; that technique was codified and that theory was no longer theory but fact. That is, that models of the mind, particularly the model of a psychoanalytic unconscious, somehow reflected an unchanging reality. Needless to say, such beliefs are the ground space of religion and not the home of either science or art.

Is Psychoanalysis a Science or an Art?

Jeff Golland

Leo Rangell (2007) pointed out the need for replacing either/or thinking with both/and formulations to better advance our field. We should apply his recommendation to the science/art binary. Psychoanalysis not only defies such binaries, it goes beyond hybridization. Psychoanalysis is both scientific and artistic, yet it does not fit comfortably with either science or art.

Science makes use of empiricism and rationality to understand reality, and to discover laws of nature. Art makes skillful use of a variety of materials and methods, aiming for originality and an enhanced sense of wonder and beauty. Science also relies on original thinking for solutions to empirical problems. Among the defining elements of psychoanalysis is that much mental functioning is out of awareness, and involves non-rational mental operations.

British scientist and novelist C.P. Snow's 1959 Rede Lecture had as its thesis that "the intellectual life of the whole of western society" was split into two cultures—the sciences and the humanities; he claimed that this split was a major hindrance to solving the world's problems. In 2008, The (London) *Times Literary Supplement* included Snow's *The Two Cultures and the Scientific Revolution* on its list of the 100 books that most influenced Western public discourse since World War II. We might expect that six decades of influence would have made for some reconciliation, but Snow's thesis has been both elaborated and disputed, while science and the humanities (including the arts) are still considered in many quarters to be antimonies. The theme of this initial issue of *The International Journal of Controversial Discussions* addresses this vexing post-Snow state of affairs.

Jaak Panksepp (2012) counted curiosity as one of seven inherent human drives, not merely a sublimated sexual voyeurism. The science or art question addresses psychoanalytic epistemology: how do we slake curiosity and come to know anything? Knowledge acquisition began prehistorically, and led to the survival and dominance of our species. Like the Tower of Babel story, a pluralism of epistemologies ensued, with intuition and revelation the first of these, and shamans and priests the earliest non-warrior tribal leaders. The 18th Century Enlightenment and the technology revolution of the last 140 years defined distinct disciplines to expand knowledge and appreciation of the world: theology, philosophy, history, biography, linguistics, mathematics, natural sciences and the arts among them. Advancement and refinements generated subspecialties within each discipline, seeking more nuanced means of increasing human understanding, adaptation and control of natural events. Psychoanalysis emerged from the creative mind of a single genius, claiming as its domain a heretofore little known or dismissed realm of human nature. Freud's ambition went beyond therapeutics; he sought a complete theory of mind and its products. His limitations have provided opportunities for his successors to correct, modify, redirect and expand upon his work.

As Freud (1923) wrote of the Ego, psychoanalysis itself serves three masters. It is a treatment method (in fact the theory informs several related treatment methods usually referred to as "psychodynamic"). In the eyes of its founder and of many contemporaries it is a natural science. It is also recognized as a contribution to the history of ideas, that status marked by inclusion in the *Great Books of the Western World* (1952). These disciplines—therapeutics, science, and intellectual history—differ in their criteria for disciplinary membership; psychoanalysis has aspirations in each, but does not fit easily within them. In a voice recording made in his final year of life, Freud stated that psychoanalysis is "a part of psychology, not medical psychology." I will argue that psychoanalysis is unlike other sciences, but is and must be scientific. Nor is psychoanalysis art, as that term is commonly and sometimes disparagingly understood, but it includes a central therapeutic enterprise that relies on the creative intuition of clinicians and theorists: its practice is artistic!

Like medical treatment, the practice of psychoanalytic psychotherapies is informed by best evidence. For psychoanalysis, the treatment situation is exquisitely individualized, relying nonetheless on tentative generalizations about the mind's regularities and variations. As a scientific discipline, psychoanalysis rests on a systematic observational methodology that does not lend itself to rigorously-controlled experimental design. Its primary database is comprised of 125 years of clinical reportage, and attempts at theoretical integration. There is however a vast literature (hundreds of thousands of Google hits) for "psychoanalytic research" that tests hypotheses within and outside the confidential clinical situation. Its scientific aims include validation of therapeutic work, and testing and refining psychological propositions and the general theory of mind. The work of the late Sidney Blatt, commemorated in a special issue of *Psychoanalytic Psychology* (Auerbach, 2019), underscores the essential privacy of the clinical situation, which makes extra-clinical validation essential for scientific acceptance.

Those who dismiss psychoanalysis as unscientific use a narrow definition of science, limited to methodologies that would exclude Darwin and Einstein as well as Freud. I prefer the definition offered by philosopher Francis Bacon (1561–1626), the father of empiricism, cited by Brenner (2006).

Bacon spoke of science as "an attitude toward the universe in which observations are made using the best methods available; logic is employed; and contradictions or magical, supernatural, and *ad hoc* solutions are rejected." Brenner added that all sciences are inferential and influenced by the observer's psychology, but "facts must rule." Experimentation may be employed but is not required (e.g., Galileo's astronomy); quantification is a tool of science, not its essence. Two additional principles: scientific conclusions are tentative, and although "psychological reality" is rife with contradiction and paradox, as Freud (1900) showed in his dream book, its methods are rational and empirical. Scientific advances may occur without scientific methods, as with Kekule's dreaming discovery of the benzene ring, and Fleming's incidental observation of the anti-bacterial effects of penicillin.

A clear definition of art is harder to come by. Definitions are verbal; art is not limited to—or by—language. When poets are asked to explain their work, they typically decline, saying the poem speaks for itself. Art history reveals great variety of forms and subject matter, and striking cultural differences. And art forms evolve: the invention of photography led to obsolescence of still life painting and portraiture. Non-representational art forms emerged early in the 20th Century, with visual aesthetics redefined by Picasso and others. Music also underwent changes in the last century, from tonality to atonality, to jazz and rap, among other new genres. Art exceeds its limits through the creative imagination of those who become recognized as artists, often with delay and sometimes posthumously. "Fine" art came to share the word with commercial art and graffiti. Literature evolved to include violation of rigid grammars and "stream of consciousness." Craft is considered essential, but the forms art takes seem limitless. Art is created to express and evoke an experience of beauty. Great artists change the world by expanding collective aesthetic experience.

While the term "applied psychoanalysis" has traditionally been reserved for non-clinical realms, primarily the arts and humanities, therapeutics still comprise the best known applications of the psychoanalytic paradigm. Scientific applications extend their effectiveness with standardization and generalization, while recognizing the probabilistic and tentative nature of scientific findings.

As with medical applications of science, practice—especially the exquisitely individualized practice of psychoanalytic therapeutics—can only approximate what theory suggests. Jerome Groupman, in a *New Yorker* essay reviewing "psychiatry's fraught history" (2019), states, "For a psychiatrist, writing a prescription remains as much an art as a science (p.68)." Thomas Insel, on retiring from his long-term position as NIMH director, stated: "I spent 13 years at NIMH really pushing on neuroscience.... I don't think we moved the needle in reducing suicide, reducing hospitalizations, improving recovery for the tens of millions of people who have mental illness. I hold myself accountable for that."

Marvin Goldfried (2019), a prominent psychotherapy researcher, considers the lack of consensus after over a century to indicate that psychotherapy is "pre-paradigmatic" in Kuhnian (1963) terms. Irwin Z. Hoffman (2009), to great applause at a plenary session of the American Psychoanalytic Association, disparaged the entire research enterprise within psychoanalysis. Others demean psychoanalysis as *merely* an art, unacceptable therefore as a clinical treatment.

Yet applications of an evolving body of scientific understanding must be as incomplete and inexact as the state of the science; psychoanalytic practice calls for a talent beyond programmatic skills. Since individual talent is involved, psychoanalysis is artistic. In Insel's judgment, a biological focus reached a dead end: narrow scientism is a premature confidence in current findings, even risking a dystopic and dehumanizing Brave New World.

Arlow (1979) discussed the creative phase of interpretive work, which was to be followed by a reflective, thoughtfully-focused phase, in order to lead to the fashioning of an intervention. Bion famously described psychoanalytic listening as without memory or desire; the Kleinian psycho-analytic tradition emphasizes the countertransference as experience generating thoughts and feelings in the analyst that can help the patient in the moment. Athletes and actors speak of being "in the zone," where focused thinking seems to disappear, but with effective result. Poser (2019), in a recent presentation, played several recordings based on Debussy's *Reverie* to demonstrate a theme heard differently. He then showed an interview with Jazz saxophonist Sonny Rollins, who described his music-making as without focus, but using what he calls his "subconscious experience" of the music to determine what emerges from his instrument. Rollins has surely mastered his craft—the melodies, chords, and scales, without which he could not perform—but the performance itself, like the authentic communication of a psychoanalyst in the immediacy of the moment, does not arise solely from focused, evidence-based rationality.

The application of psychoanalysis as paradigm to therapeutics can be described as artful in the same way that mathematical propositions can be considered things of beauty. Freud's Goethe Prize treated his writing as highly artistic literature. The art of Freud's writing is discussed by Blass (2019), commenting on a paper by Joan Riviere (1958). The artful work of clinical psychoanalysis refers to authentic, spontaneous interactions with patients that turn out, though not necessarily immediately, to be helpful.

The curiosity drive (the Kleinian epistemophelic instinct) is renewed with each human birth. We cannot know who will be the next Mozart or Einstein, advancing the range of human experience and knowledge. Curiosity is not to be sated; humans remain novelty-seeking and curious; we become bored with sameness. A Grand Unifying Theory is likely to remain elusive. If there is a god's-eye view of the universe, we lack the capacity to see it; human limitation must be acknowledged by the godless as well. Ignorance is often motivating, and can lead to exploration and discovery. Advancing knowledge requires originality, unbound from contemporary methods. Psychoanalysis is not medicine, nor is it science. Psychoanalysis is a set of ideas, a paradigm, not a fixed entity or restricted domain. The study of the human mind and its products is limitless, and subject to ongoing indeterminacy and generative controversy.

Each new patient presents a challenge to a therapist's knowledge, skill and talent. Stone's (1962) "physicianly attitude" does not require a medical education. Despite all prior experience, therapists are ignorant when meeting a new person. We are also ignorant as to what the next meeting will reveal. We must accept Keats's "negative capability" (rather than philosophical certainty) as essential to achieving understanding that will enhance the adaptation, creativity and joy of the patient. Ulric Neisser (1958), the psychologist who coined the term "cognitive psychology," taught that, while the brain has a finite number of synapses, billions, the mind's ability to generate thought is infinite.

Artists may promote art for art's sake; it is its own explanation, ultimately inexplicable but central to the good life. Psychoanalysis is neither science nor art *per se*, but both scientific and artistic, and its clinical applications are often effective. Yet an art whose claims are more than aesthetic needs more than claims to affirm its value (Golland, 2016). Psychotherapy must be more than an art.

Engaging in psychoanalytic practice enhances knowledge and creativity, and can also provide joy for the practitioner. The quest to satisfy curiosity is incomplete but gratifying, and involves debunking false antimonies while providing better resolutions of inner conflict. Irving Steingart (1977) saw the psychoanalytic relationship as "a thing apart," a special case in which the more we learn, the more we recognize the complexity and paradoxical nature of its subject matter. Neither science nor art, but both scientific and artistic, psychoanalysis is itself "a thing apart."

References

Auerbach, J. (2019). Sidney J. Blatt's contribution to psychoanalytic psychology. *Psychoanalytic Psychology*, 36:287–290

Arlow, J. (1979). The genesis of interpretation. *J. Amer. Psychoanalytic Assn.*, 27 (Supplement):193–206

Blass, R. (2019). Freud's writing as a living creative presence in our minds. *Int. J. Psa.*, 100:635–636

Brenner, C. (2006). *Psychoanalysis or Mind and Meaning*. NY: Psychoanalytic Quarterly

Freud, S. (1900). *The Interpretation of Dreams*. In Standard Edition (SE) 3,4

Freud, S. (1923). The Ego and the Id. SE 19: 3–66

Goldfried. M. (2019). Obtaining Consensus in Psychotherapy: What holds us back? *American Psychologist,* 74: 484–496

Golland, J. (2016). Psychoanalysis is Scientific! *Division/Review Forum,* 7/20/16 http://www.div39members.wildapricot.org/DR-Home/4898328

Groopman, J. (2019). Medicine in mind: Psychiatry's fraught history. *The New Yorker*, 5/27/19

Hutchens, R.M. & Adler, M. eds. (1952). *Great Books of the Western World*, vol. 54, Chicago: University of Chicago Press

Neisser, U. (1958). "Memory," an undergraduate course at Brandeis University

Panksepp, J., & Biven, L. (2012). *The archaeology of mind: Neuro-evolutionary origins of human emotion.* New York, NY, US: W. W. Norton & Company

Poser, S. (2019). *Debussy Comes to Harlem.* Presented to the Group and Family Therapy Conference, Mount Sinai School of Medicine, 10/24/19

Rangell, L. (2007). *The Road to Unity in Psychoanalytic Theory.* NY: Jason Aronson

Riviere, J. (2019). A character trait of Freud's by Joan Riviere (1958). *Int. J. Psycho-Anal.*, 100(4):637–639

Snow, C.P. (1959). *The Two Cultures and the Scientific Revolution*, Oxford University Press

Steingart, A. (1977) *A Thing Apart: Love and Reality in the Therapeutic Relationship.* NY: Jason Aronson

Stone, Leo. (1961). *The Psychoanalytic Situation.* New York: International Universities Press.

Discussion of "Is Psychoanalysis a Science or an Art?" by Jeffrey H. Golland

Leonie Sullivan

The title of this article is a question "Is Psychoanalysis a Science or an Art?" The author starts by saying, "Psychoanalysis is both scientific and artistic, yet it does not fit comfortably with either science or art." Whilst in agreement that psychoanalysis defies such binary organization, I think it is also useful to return to what Freud said originally. Freud defined psychoanalysis as being a method of investigation of the mind, especially the unconscious mind, a body of knowledge and mode of treatment based on his method of investigation, He saw this as a new self-standing discipline based on the knowledge gained from the application of the investigation method in work with patients. In other words, he proposed both a method of research and of treatment based on the ongoing research findings from each unique treatment. This research implied making use of the individual observations in each treatment. As such, it is more than a sum of any two parts. In the everyday work in the consulting room this can be witnessed by patient and analyst.

I will describe how this works in terms of investigation, treatment and research in the consulting room. This will of course not lend itself to a meta-analysis of the effectiveness of psychoanalytic psychotherapy and leave us with the basic conclusion that questions the empirical evidence. There is evidence that therapy is effective but the lack of comparisons with control treatments limits the interpretation of the results (Shedler, 2010, de Maat et al, 2013, Gaskin, 2014). Better controlled studies are required to verify the evidence base for the effectiveness of psychoanalytic psychotherapy (de Maat, 20123). However, for clinicians and patients, the psychoanalytic method provides convincing experience of an improved quality of life and capacity to bear their emotional suffering and to think creatively (Shedler, 2010).

Bion made use of the expression "the selected fact" (an expression used in 1908 by the French mathematician Henri Poincare who was referring to the element that makes it possible to give coherence to a group of scattered data. It was used to refer to the "selection of facts" that enabled science to discover laws of general validity—that is, facts that introduce order and coherence into the complexity of the world). In psychoanalytic work the selected fact, serves as a starting point for interpretation by the psychoanalyst, who becomes aware that a multitude of aspects of the patient's material come together and make sense, beginning with a given element of the transference. Bion borrows the notion of the selected fact from scientific methodology, however he establishes an essential difference between the scientific approach that seeks the laws of nature and the psychoanalyst exploring the psychic reality of their patient. The scientist is searching for logical connections among the objective data collected, whereas the psychoanalyst is interested in the emotional links that seem both to dominate the transference relationship and to create interconnections among the disparate elements of associative material. Bion also noted that it is the preconception of the analyst that has to act as a container for the realization and not the other way around. Bion states that in analysis it is both the patient and analyst who have to face periods of disintegration as new experiences are confronted before they are digested or understood (Bion, 1970).

To say psychoanalysis needs to belong to art or science in an "either or way," would seem to be a misrepresentation of both science and art. The debate on art and science goes back to the Greek philosophers and is referenced in the author's other work (Golland, 2016). In the Oxford dictionary the term *binary* is stated as coming from Middle English usage, to denote a duality or pair. The middle English usage came originally from the Latin "binaries" or "bini," two together. I note this with reference to the author's quoting Irving Steingart (1977) who saw the psychoanalytic relationship as "a thing apart," a special case in which the more we learn, the more we recognize the complexity and paradoxical nature of its subject matter. Neither science nor art, but both scientific and artistic, psychoanalysis is itself "a thing apart." I am in agreement with this statement and will expand further on two points.

One is the capacity to observe and make use of such observations, this technique being a valuable one in both science and art. In respect to the carrying out of psychoanalytic work, the British psychoanalyst Wilfred Bion is referred to briefly by the author and I will expand on this. My reason for doing is that I think it will demonstrate the use of a specific technique and what it can offer in each unique treatment. Psychoanalytic listening as being without memory or desire is mentioned and I will add how I think this assists in the technique of the psychoanalyst making use of the method of investigation or observational stance in each session. There is a paradox here. Bion wrote "A desire for cure or results must be left aside, as well as any deliberate attempt to remember past sessions. Instead of that, every session should be seen as complete, not only as a part of the psychoanalytic process but also as a process in itself. This means that the patient develops not only over a period of time but within every session. Therefore, the analyst should aim at achieving a state of mind so that, at every session, he feels he has not seen the patient before" (Bion, 1967 p. 18). I wish to expand further on this point, where the author refers to the much-misused concept of "without memory or desire," which was central to Bion's own analytic method. Joan and Neville Symington point out that Bion makes it clear that it is not the memory as such that blocks our understanding in the work with patients, but rather our attachment to it (Symington and Symington, 1996). This can impede the development of new ways of thinking.

Francesca Bion wrote the following about this method that

Bion used in an account of his life that she gave in Canada, in 1994:

> It is hard to know why this recommendation—to all appearances one of obvious common sense—should have been adversely criticised and, one suspects, wilfully misunderstood. Bion knew that it is extremely difficult to achieve and can at first arouse fear and anxiety in the analyst, but he also knew from experience and perseverance, that it makes possible what he called 'at-one-ment' with the patient. By divesting the mind of these temptations, 'the noise made by learning, training and past experience is at a minimum.' Those who have succeeded in putting this technique into practice have found it profoundly beneficial. I know that it was central to Bion's own analytic method. (Bion, 1994).

My second point relates to the mention by the author of the notion of negative capability. He notes, "despite all prior experience, therapists are ignorant when meeting a new person. We are also ignorant as to what the next meeting will reveal. We must accept Keats' "negative capability" (rather than philosophical certainty) as essential to achieving understanding that will enhance the adaptation, creativity and joy of the patient." The term was used in a letter from Keats to his two brothers, when he was making a criticism of the poet Coleridge, who he thought sought knowledge over beauty.

This concept in relation to psychoanalysis was first mentioned in 1970 by Wilfred Bion in his book *Attention and Interpretation*. In the introduction, Bion reminds the reader that in a session: "what matters is both the communication and the use to which it is being put."

> Psycho-analysts must be able to tolerate the differences or the difficulties of the analysand long enough to recognize what they are. If psychoanalysts are able to interpret what the analysand says, they must have a great capacity for tolerating their analysands' statements without rushing

to the conclusion that they know the interpretations. This is what I think Keats meant when he said Shakespeare must have been able to tolerate negative capability. (Bion, 1970)

Bion applied the term used by John Keats to illustrate an analytic attitude of openness of mind. He thought this attitude was of central importance not just to psychoanalytic work, but in life as well. Bion saw this concept as an ability to tolerate the pain and confusion of "not knowing," rather than foreclosing knowledge with certainty based on resolving the emotional challenge of ambiguity. Bion, having discovered the importance of the mother's (and by association, the analyst's) capacity to tolerate the infant's (and patient's) projective identifications, sought a source for this tolerance. Bion was suggesting that the analyst must be able to foreswear knowing or having to know so that he can be free to intuit and ultimately to realize. In this state the analyst, has more open access to his own psychic reality. He wrote that in analysis, the analyst must possess the capacity for patience and be able to have faith that in time he will be able to find the selected fact, which unites the apparent randomness of the analysand's associations. The possible origins of this term are not really known, but Keats may have been using his knowledge of medicine and chemistry to refer to the negative pole of an electric current, which is passive and receptive. In the same way that the negative pole receives the current from the positive pole, the poet receives impulses from a world that is full of mystery and doubt, which cannot be explained but which the poet can translate into art (Bion, 1970).

In addition to this concept's application to the individual session, this attitude or openness to any an ongoing question, such as the one raised in the title of this article can also apply. I believe that science and art share this capacity, to not need to prematurely conclude any question out of a need for a finished piece of work or to deal with ambiguity. Many great art works and scientific findings have this in common.

In respect to any evaluation of psychoanalysis, where it is mentioned that there are "those who dismiss psychoanalysis as unscientific" I would add as part of any such evaluation, that the nature of the relationship of the "Those" be fully disclosed so that their underlying assumptions are clear as in any other scientific evaluation and that any conscious conflict of interest in the investigation/discussion can be stated clearly and also observed.

In terms of ethics perhaps the question should be, to what purpose is any comparison being made between art or science? If it is to promote a questioning and growth of creative capacity there can be a generative cross-fertilization between different disciplines. Ferro and Nicoli's view, stated in *The New Analysts Guide to the Galaxy: Questions about Contemporary Psychoanalysis*, is that psychoanalysis cannot be an abstract intellectual, scientific or artistic endeavor, as it is grounded in the reality of the mental suffering dealt with in the consulting room and the role of the psychoanalyst in healing mental suffering (Ferro and Ncoli, 2017). In my view this takes me in my own work back to the original notion that psychoanalysis is a self-standing discipline based on the knowledge gained from the application of the investigation method in work with patients.

References

Bion. April 1994 in Toronto and Montreal, Canada. Published in The Journal of the Melanie Klein & Object Relations, Vol 13, No.1, 1995.

Bion, W. R. 1967 Notes on Memory and Desire in The Psychoanalytic Forum, 2:272–3, 279–80.

Bion, W. R. (1970). Attention and Interpretation. London: Tavistock Publications.

de Maat, S., de Jonghe, F., de Kraker, R., Leichsenring, F., Abbass, A., Luyten, p., Barber, J.P., Rein, Van., Dekker, J. (2013). The current state of the empirical evidence for psychoanalysis: a meta-analysis approach. Harv Rev Psychiatry 21, 107–137.

Ferro, A., Nicoli, L. (eds) The New Analysts Guide to the Galaxy: Questions about Contemporary Psychoanalysis Karnac books. London 2017

Gaskin, C. (2014). The effectiveness of psychoanalysis and psychoanalytic psychotherapy: A literature review of recent international and Australian research. Melbourne: PACFA.

Golland, J. (2016). Psychoanalysis is Scientific! *Division/Review Forum*, 7/20/16

Shedler, J. (2010). The efficiency of psychodynamic psychotherapy. American Psychologist. 65, 98–109.

Symington J. & Symington N. 1996, The Clinical Thinking of Wilfred Bion. Routledge.

Psychoanalysis: Science or Art

Rómulo Lander

To answer this complex question, I will organize the response in two parts. **First**, I will consider psychoanalysis as a *social science*. It is a science because it has *[1] Data Collection [2] Experimental Procedures [3] Logical Reasoning* based on *Psychoanalytic Theory*. This theory also presents organized ideas regarding a model of the human mind with a proposal for its *mental structure* and corresponding *mental mechanisms*. This theory presents a proposal for the *formation, development* and *functioning of the mind*. **In the second part** I will consider the practice of psychoanalysis as an *Art*. I say this, because it is possible that the *analytic act* done by a qualified psychoanalyst may *create new ideas*. Since this analytic act may produce new ideas, this new knowledge may be a revelation for that particular individual. That is, this knowledge may have not existed before the analytic act was performed. Also, sometimes these *new ideas* are new for the *psychoanalytic theory*. This is something that may happen in all sciences, which are all of them under constant development. When the new idea appears, we may say that a *creative act* had happened. If we define *Art* as the performance of a creative act, then the practice of psychoanalysis is also the exercise of an art: The art of listening. Here I am referring to a special kind of listening, which is performed without *prejudice* and above all without any *moral judgment*. This listening seeks to understand the functioning of a particular mind without prejudice of any kind. It is a kind of pure scientific observation through a special form of listening.

In this text, which respectfully I present here, I will show more detailed arguments with the intention to support these two ideas.

1. Psychoanalysis as a Science

In my opinion science refers to an ordered set of knowledge that can be verified. This scientific knowledge is obtained by *data collection, experimental procedures and logical reasoning*. This will allow the verification of any new scientific proposal. Scientific knowledge is organized on the basis of complex theoretical principles. Those principles have their corresponding *logical reasoning*. From this scientific knowledge all sciences build up new theories, models, and systems. Training for these scientific specialties are obtained when engaging in advanced studies which will produce experts in each corresponding scientific field. Being an expert with a proper knowledge will permit professional observation and the proper recollection of data. This data collected will be organized in a logical, useful and productive manner, which will permit the expert to understand this particular and specialized information.

It is clear that all this knowledge in science takes place at the level of *consciousness*. The activity of *consciousness* will give *validity* to this new scientific knowledge. The importance of consciousness has its root in *logical reasoning* that tries to understand these new ideas that have arisen from observations and experimental procedures. Thus, the *logical conscious awareness* offers a scientific sense of *conviction* steaming from the revealing power of *evidence*. The *logic of evidence* raised by the philosopher René Descartes in the middle of the seventeenth century caused an accelerated development of Sciences.

Science can be divided arbitrarily into three groups:

* Pure Sciences [Basic sciences], which include: Geometry, Mathematics, Physics, Astrophysics, Chemistry, Trigonometry, Quantum physics, etc.

* Natural Sciences [Biological sciences], which include Biology, Biophysics, Botany, Veterinary Medicine, Medicine [in all its specialties], Geology, Mineralogy, etc.

* Social Sciences [Human Sciences], including Sociology, Anthropology, Psychology, Psychoanalysis, etc.

As proposed already, science has its foundations in the *logic of evidence*. This *evidence* is something *conscious* in nature. This *evidence* is regarded as *something with a true-value,* therefore is considered something *valid*. From this argument René Descartes had proposed his famous statement the so-called Cógito, which says: *"I think, therefore I exist."* In this way *consciousness,* according to Descartes, gives validity to the *existence of being*. Here it is necessary to say that this statement by Descartes applies only to the world of *consciousness*.

The Psychoanalytic theory, as we all know, is not based *on certainty* nor is it is based *on evidence*. It is necessary to affirm that the psychoanalytic proposal is not based on *conscious processes*. However, the knowledge derived from Psychoanalytic Research, ends up being something that inhabits the *world of consciousness*. So, it is *"we know, that we know."* But that is not all. Since the very end of the 19th century, we know that there is a world *beyond consciousness*.

In the late 19th century Sigmund Freud introduces the idea of the *existence of unconscious* and says the contrary of the statement proposed by René Descartes in the 17th century. Sigmund Freud had said *"I exist, where I don't think,"* referring to the self that exists in *the unconscious*. Freud proposes in his first topic, published at the very end of the 19th century, a *model* of a *mental apparatus*. In fact, this model was the first model of the mind that ever existed in history. In this model Freud proposes the mind is divided in three instances: *conscious, preconscious, and unconscious*. The *unconscious* instance was the largest one. So large that it was called oceanic. This unconscious cannot be known directly. Sigmund Freud proposes and establishes that the most important part of *Self* resides in the *unconscious*. There in the unconscious, in German and English called the Id, reside, among other things, *desire* and *drive*. The term *drive* refers to an *Energy* that drives us to life. Thus, the *unconscious* is known only by its *effects*, such as dreams, symptoms, hallucinations, delusions, jokes, common errors of daily life, psychosomatic illnesses, bodily posture, etc.

Let me step back a moment to something I already said: *Evidence* is based on *conscious processes*. Thus, *scientific evidence* should be, and can be, subject to *verification*. An example of the need to *verify evidence* and *review* it periodically may be found in scientific astronomical observations. For example, we know thanks to Herodotus and Plutarch, that 250 years before Christ, an astronomer and Greek mathematician, Aristarchus of Samos, made a heliocentric model of our Solar System. In his day he declared in writing that the earth revolves around the Sun, and managed to assert that the Sun was bigger than Earth. His writings rested for years in the ancient library of Alexandria. We all know the rugged evolution over the centuries of this heliocentric proposal. The idea traveled long [centuries] up to Copernicus in the 15th century and then later to Galileo, who presented it as something new. Despite all that, the idea was strongly rejected by the authorities of the Church, who defended the opposite idea. Then, when it got to the middle of the 17th century, this heliocentric astronomy was accepted by the scientific community and then accepted by the culture as scientific truth. So, *certainties of science* are always in constant evolution. New discoveries force us to review and validate the *existing knowledge* of all sciences.

2. Psychoanalysis as Art

An artist is someone who performs a *creative act*. A *creative act* is any act that produces something new. I mean something that did not exist before being created. So, the artist with his *creative act* creates a new thing. The *created product* can be varied. Therefore, the artists will be of different types. Thus, we have the possibility of having plastic artists [painters, sculptors], musician artists [composers, performers], scenic artists [drama, ballet dancers, and modern dancers], gastronomy artist, carpenter artists, artists of poetry, literature, philosophy, and artists in the field of Psychoanalysis. We also have artists in Chemistry, as it happens with Dmitri Mendeléyev, that Russian chemist, who discovered and presented for the first time the idea of the Periodic Table of Elements. Or, as it happens with August Kekulé, that German chemist, who solved for the first time the mystery of benzene chemical structure. Or Charles Darwin, the Englishman who first introduced the idea and presented evidence for the Theory of Evolution. Or, the American and English researches Watson and Crick, who introduced the idea of a double helix in the chemical structural model of DNA. All of them had their creative moment. All of them created something new, something that did not exist before they were revealed. At that precise moment they are artists, creators of a new idea.

Something additional happens with inventors. The inventor develops an original idea, his idea or an idea from another person. The inventor further develops the idea and uses his intelligence and creativity to build a machine. This happened to Thomas Alva Edison who, based on somebody else's idea, industrially developed mass production of electricity. He acted based on the original idea of Nicolas Tesla, a Croatian electro-magnetic engineer who was the first to reveal the secrets of electricity. Tesla had his *creative act*. Edison was the meritorious inventor who developed electricity producing plants. These engines would produce electricity for industry and for society, as shown in the 1900 World Fair in Paris.

The *act of making crafts* defines a craftsman. The work of craftsman does not imply a *creative act*. A craftsman with his/her craftsmanship makes beautiful things, but they are not unprecedented. They are not original. They are variations of something already created. A very distinguished artist [a creator] can also be a *craftsman*. A very distinguished psychoanalyst [a creator] can also be a *craftsman*. This means that the psychoanalyst can work with the mind of a person being analyzed using the *Psychoanalytic dialogue* without creating a new idea. At that moment this analyst is working as a *craftsman*. This craftsman's work is valid, is useful and is honorable. No problem with that.

The verbal interventions of the analyst do not always reveal something new. Something that, prior to being said by the analyst, did not exist for the analysand. Therefore, the psychoanalyst has their moments as an *artist* and their moments as a *craftsman*. It is appropriate to insist here that *the analyst's thoughts and proposals* are scientific. This is so because they rely on a psychoanalytic theory of mind and on a psychoanalytic theory of technique. Both theories have a scientific, logical reasoning and they are based on scientific observation through the data collected in *the act of listening*. The analyst has *training to listen* to the productions of the analysand attentively *without prejudice* and without *moral judgment*. The analysand presents his productions through *spoken language, behavior, and affect*. In a spoken language *the unconscious truths* are hiding between the lines, as metaphors, and in the presence of certain silences that are full of meanings. It is the work of the psychoanalyst to be able first to detect them and then to decipher them. Then the analyst has to decide if it is the proper time to reveal this *unconscious truth* to the owner, the analysand.

It is necessary to be trained to perform this special *analytical listening* which requires working analytically with *the other*. This work has to be done with this particular other based on *asymmetry*. This *asymmetry* refers to the concept of *alterity*. This *alterity* refers to the relationship with the other based on the "I-am-not-you" and "you-are-not-me."

For psychoanalysis, working with the analysand in asymmetry is something basic. At the same time, it is difficult to install this capacity in the mind of the future analyst. When the candidate of psychoanalysis acquires that capacity to listen in alterity [asymmetry], then he or she is ready to practice successfully *analytic listening*.

To achieve the capacity for *analytic listening* the future analyst must be previously analyzed for several years. When he or she is analyzed and acquires the *capacity for alterity*, then the candidate can legitimately occupy the chair of the analyst. It is fair to say, of all of us qualified analysts, when working analytically with an analysand, that we may lose momentarily the capacity for alterity. We have to learn to identify those episodes of identification with the other [that produce loss of alterity]. And then rescue ourselves from that moment of symmetry.

There is something else. I refer to the capacity to understand "behavior and emotions." That is not a simple thing. I may say the analyst must be capable of deciphering both. In order to do that, the qualified analysts must know, as much as possible, the working of the human mind. The important thing is to be able to understand it and to communicate it to the analysand, whom at the end is the legitimate owner of this alleged truth.

For all these reasons we may say that *psychoanalytic theory* is organized as a *"Science* and the *practice of psychoanalysis"* is performed as a *"Art."*

www.romulolander.org

rlander39@gmail.com

Bibliography

DESCARTES, R. [1637]: Discourse on the Method
Encyclopedia Britannica, Volume 31. 1952

DESCARTES, R. [1637] : Discourse on the Method
Madrid: Biblioteca Nueva, 2010.

FREUD, S. [1895]: Studies on hysteria
Complete works, Hogarth Press London 1967

FERRATER-MORA, José [1994]: DESCARTES
Dictionary of Philosophy. Editorial Ariel, Barcelona, 2004

LANDER, R [2019]: Some philosophy and theoretical physics for
psychoanalysts. Free circulation digital edition, 807 pages. Spanish
edition.

Discussion of Psychoanalysis: Science or Art by Rómulo Lander

Arthur Leonoff

Rómulo's thesis: Art or Science

Rómulo's formulation centers on the distinction between theory and practice. He notes that psychoanalytic theory is organized as a science whereas psychoanalytic practice is performed as an art. There is the notion that artistry creates *ex nihilo* whereas science discovers what can be tested and, most importantly, verified. The analyst, according to Lander, integrates both polarities. True artistry, however, is rarer than good craftsmanship, he observes.

It is certainly true that moments of creativity within the analytic relationship are often treasured for their significance to the analysand. These new discoveries leverage change and nourish the analytic identity of the analyst.

Not everyone, however, would accept these clear polarities between art and science or theory and practice for that matter. Moreover, using Rómulo's example of heliocentrism and its acceptance, knowledge in science cannot be separated from human culture, tradition and belief structures. This is the hermeneutics of human knowing in which we are always historically situated and comprehended through the lens of culture and traditional ways of organizing experience. The earth always rotated about the sun but it took more than 1500 years before this would be 'known' even after it was discovered.

Rómulo's clear definition of science as "an ordered set of knowledge that can be verified," helps us situate psychoanalysis in what Freud called "a science of the mind" (1925, p.46) or "the science of unconscious mental processes" (p.70). Unlike Rómulo, who locates psychoanalysis in the social science domain, Freud insisted that psychoanalysis was a natural science. This began even before he founded psychoanalysis *per se* in his *Project for a Scientific Psychology* (1895). It was essential for Freud that the drive was deemed the point of intersection between body and mind. He was at home in the in-between.

This link to the body was as elemental for Freud as thoughts were to Bion. The psyche evolves, said Freud, to contend with the demand of the drives as much as it must contend with the constraints of family and society.

Those voices that refute psychoanalysis' credibility reduce science to empiricism in which it fares relatively poorly because it is so broadly explanatory and linked with therapeutic relationships. If by science, rather, we understand its roots to be in the desire to know (Latin *scire*), then psychoanalysis is profoundly scientific. Hypotheses are tested and verification is instrumental through the increase in rapport, ready access to other psychic material, and the self-report of the patient. Efficacy studies confirm the benefit of psychoanalytic treatment and this adds further verification that a psychoanalytic process has real value to people in their lives. Neuro-psychoanalytic formulations and imaging studies can address the brain correlates of change, which is another framework of verification. Viewing mind and brain as two essential vantage points of the same phenomena, needing each other to make sense of the person, frees both neuroscience and psychoanalysis from an artificial and limiting dualism.

Part of the problem between psychoanalysis and science stems from historical beginnings when it was unclear what was verified knowledge in psychoanalysis and what was simply dogmatic conviction. The depth of the leap that Freud fashioned in 1900 with the *Interpretation of Dreams* in which he listened to the patient's associations to apprehend the personal meaning cannot be underestimated. This was observational science at its best. Freud, for one, was acutely aware of the laws of evidence.

On the other hand, grand theories in his burgeoning science of the unconscious could take on a life of their own—becoming a coherent explanatory model from which there could be no deviance. Forbidden sexual wishes and an Oedipal template were often a bias that needed to be confirmed in order for the Freudian structure to stand as well as Freudian authority over the nascent science. It was an authority that derived from men who wore the same ring and formed a tight inner council that controlled analytic truth. More than 100 years later, we are still laden with this legacy.

The analyst who listens without presupposition is very much aligned with Freud's advice if not his conflicted method. He wrote in 1912 in his *Recommendations to Physicians Practising Psycho-analysis*:

> *The correct behaviour for an analyst lies...in avoiding speculation or brooding over cases while they are in analysis, and in submitting the material obtained to a synthetic process of thought only after the analysis is concluded.* (p. 113)

It would seem that psychoanalysis has gradually come to embrace a science of meaning, as an alternative to any set metapsychology. Transference and occasional, disruptive countertransference have given way to a more inclusive fluid intersubjective field model where meaning is constructed in real time, subject to a dynamic après coup. It is a living, breathing psychoanalysis as compared to an archeological one founded on repression. Art and science merge in a scene of mutuality with both participants observing, testing and verifying to find a narrative truth that is truly healing.

The construction of meaning itself has also undergone transformation from a study of repressed ideas and unconscious conflict to the formation of thought itself. Bion's notion of the thinking apparatus as a necessity of thoughts turned the science of psychoanalysis decisively towards the way that mind itself evolves. The intrapsychic and interpersonal have merged into the intersubjective and, with this inflection, psychoanalysis has taken a decisive hermeneutic turn.

Using this model then, it would be unclear who is the scientist and who is the artist in the analytic couple. Even the notion of interpretation has deflected towards the mutuality of the process—two artists engaging scientifically with each other. There is not much room anymore for Cartesian dualism, the cogito of conscious thought and positivism that sets art in opposition to science.

Reflections

It was a psychology lecture offered to senior secondary school students that nudged me in the scientific direction. The lecturer presented data from an experiment in which flat worms learned a skill, were sacrificed, ground up and fed to other flatworms. These untrained worms somehow acquired the skill. The lecturer spoke of "Messenger RNA" and I was transfixed.

This was likely not long before my parents requested that I convince my younger adolescent sister that "free love" might not be the optimal way to express herself. They were confident that I could master the art of persuasion. In the end, I suppose, both aspects were indispensable to my becoming a psychoanalyst.

Consider for a moment the caricature of the analyst, the dream reader, as compared to the stage hypnotist and mindreader. The analyst stereotype is the reasoned doctor who has assiduously learned the roadmap of the mind, especially the avenue to the unconscious. This is the scientist. The other is the mental manipulator who sows confusion, disorientation, and within the agnosia of the moment achieves a sleight of hand. This is the artist. Of course, the stereotype sorely underestimates the artistry of the analytic practitioner whose empathy and attuned listening, skilled understanding of the mind, and well-timed interpretations foster change. In turn, the mind-reader is certainly an artist who uses the subject's mind as a tableau while relying on a precise fund of knowledge and techniques. Art and science describe two indispensable sides in a holistic equation. It is how we make essential contact with patients and how we work to understand. Sometimes it can feel like magic.

It is not clear to me though that, as Rómulo states, psychoanalysis is very much a "social science." It certainly has had cross-disciplinary applications in studies of literature, mythology and cultural history but it is optimally suited more to understanding individuals in their own terms than society at large. It was the overreach of psychoanalysis, its excessive confidence and blurring of distinctions between individual and society, that eventually diminished its reputation.

Psychoanalysis does not fare any better if it tries to position itself as a biological science. What might be correlative with brain function and neurophysiology will not likely help the practitioner very much, although it could definitely support the discipline's stature. Psychoanalysis is best served when it is allowed to occupy a transitional arena, somewhere between brain and psyche, art and science, conscious and unconscious, self and other, known and unknown. In my view, this transitional status, made explicit by Winnicott, is the most extraordinary Freudian discovery.

As a science of the transitional, there is no analysand without the analyst, and the analyst is implicated in everything that the analysand comes to know. This underscores that science in psychoanalysis includes subjectivity and the mutual construction of meaning. The art of psychoanalysis is thus also tied up closely with mutuality. Every session like every treatment is its own canvas that needs to be created anew. When Bion articulated his advice to practitioners to meet the patient without memory or desire, he was speaking to the creative element (see Tobias, 2013). There has to be a freshness to the process that allows for creativity and surprise. The analyst's desire is no less potentially oppressive than meta-psychology, imposing on the patient what the analyst wants, expects, demands, believes or needs in order to make sense of the patient's discourse.

Conclusion

Art and science are two sides of the same coin. My impression is that the further we advance as a profession in our knowledge and its application, the less theory-bound we will become, the more confident in understanding the patient's discourse in the patient's own terms. This does not mean that we will stop theorizing or seeking more powerful explanatory models. It just means that we will have the confidence not to put these theories between us and the patient in a way that distorts the process and limits our capacity to listen. Of course, this is the art of the métier as well as its science—how to know and not know, how to interpret and still inquire, how to form common cause through human mutuality while guiding a process that is distinctly psychoanalytic.

Finally, I would like to thank Rómulo for his stimulating thoughts and the clear writing for which he has always been known.

———

Respectfully submitted
Arthur Leonoff

Bibliography

Freud, S (1895: 1950). *Project for a Scientific Psychology*. SE 1: 281–391.

–(1900). *The Interpretation of dreams*. SE 4, ix–627.

–(1912). *Recommendations to Physicians Practising Psychoanalysis*. SE 12: 109–120.

–(1925.) *An Autobiographical Study*. SE 20: 1–74.

Tobias, L. (2013). Memory and Desire, Tension and Conflict in 'Late' Bion. *Int. J. Psycho-Anal.*, 94(6):1175–1177

Reply to Arthur Leonoff's Discussion

Rómulo Lander

I would like to express my gratitude to Arthur Leonoff for his discussion of my paper. He is an analyst of great capacity and experience and his paper has inspired me to make the following comments in reply.

1. It is true, I insist, that psychoanalysis is located more on the side of the social sciences. I say this because of the effects that the bond with the other has on the subject.

2. This is a dynamic phenomenon, not biological phenomena.

3. The formation of the psychic apparatus depends on the personal relationships within the family. These are dynamic relationships and will affect the other of the unconscious.

4. On the other hand, the biological sciences, in this aspect of mental functioning, are strongly influenced by neurosciences. It has a reasoning.

5. I consider brain functioning as corresponding to the neurosciences, and not (corresponding) with the functioning of the psyche.

6. In this sense, it is clear that the brain is not the psyche.

7. With regard to the analytical process, I fully agree with Arthur Leonoff when he says that the analyst's work occurs in a "field" where analyst and analysand interact subjectively.

8. What the analysand says is subjectively heard and assimilated by the analyst. The analyst listens with his subjectivity.

9. In turn, when the analyst speaks and interprets, it is heard by the analysand in an exclusive way, determined by the subjectivity of the analysand.

10. In the end, the analysand constructs his own interpretation. And it's okay that it is this way because it can't be in any other way.

Hysteria: from Hystera to Histrio

Henry Zvi Lothane

The story starts with a physiological allegory of sexual excitement leading to the act of procreation in Plato's *Timaeus*:

> And the seed, having life and becoming endowed with respiration, produces in that part in which it respires a lively desire for emission, and thus creates in us the love of procreation. Wherefore also in men the organ of generation becoming rebellious and masterful, like an animal disobedient to reason, and maddened with the sting of lust, seeks to gain absolute sway, and the same is the case with the so-called womb or matrix in women. The animal within them is desirous of procreating children, and when remaining unfruitful long beyond its proper time, gets discontented and angry, and wandering in every direction through the body, closes up the passages of the breath, and, by obstructing respiration, drives them to extremity, causing all varieties of disease, until at length the desire and love of the man and the woman, bringing them together and as it were plucking the fruit from the tree, sow in the womb, as in a field, animals unseen by reason of their smallness and without form; these again are separated and matured

within; they are then finally brought out into the light and thus the generation of animals is completed (p. 1210).

This is a poetic mythical personification of the sexual instinct in both genders driving the urge to procreate and the propulsive sexual tension of the instinct in both men and women. But it is only in women that the inhibition of this mighty instinct causes a curious disease: what it does to men had to wait for Freud's formulating two actual-neuroses, anxiety neurosis and neurasthenia. Furthermore, Plato did not cite the noun "hysteria" or disease called hysteria but only pointed to an excited male organ desiring to have an emission into womb, *hystera* in Greek, desiring to be impregnated. There is of course a legitimate and genuine use of the womb in medicine when a surgeon performs a hysterectomy. On the other hand, the Leipzig psychiatry professor Paul Flechsig, immortalized by Freud as the doctor of Paul Schreber, literalized the metaphorical womb-disease and prescribed surgery as a treatment for an imaginary disease hysteria.

This history clearly shows that a disease called hysteria does not exist, that there are only women and men called hysterics or hysterical. Furthermore, there was no clearly defined disease hysteria in the Hippocratic works either, but only an adjective of a condition called *hysterike pnix*, i.e., uterine suffocation (Gilman et al. 1993). According to the *Oxford English Dictionary* (OED) the word hysteria was first cited in 1801 as an abstract noun and has been employed ever since as a code word, label, and pathologizing libel of varieties of feminine and masculine conduct; however, for many years it was anathema among doctors to speak of male hysteria because, obviously, they had no womb!

In 1965 the medical historian Ilza Veith created a stir with her book *Hysteria The History of a Disease,* "in essence an expression of awareness of the malign effect of disordered sexual activity on emotional stability" (p. 2). Veith elaborated: "the connection of the uterus (*hystera*) resulting from its disturbances is first expressed by the term "hysteria"...in the thirty-fifth aphorism which reads "when a woman suffers from hysteria or difficult labor an attack of sneezing is beneficial" (p. 10). I checked aphorism XXXV and the word hysteria is explained in footnote 3: "Said by some commentators to refer to retention of the placenta. Galen rejects this interpretation, but Littré seems to accept it" (p. 167). Emile Littré was the famous 19th century lexicographer who also propagated the noun hysteria. Thus, a fictional disorder got adorned by Veith with a fancy Freudian interpretation.

While Plato's fable is one sort of fiction and Veith's is another, as compared to the fact of sex in procreation, both the tropes of Plato and the tricks of Veith have their usefulness: they provide an easy tag, hysteria, for visualizing the picture or image of kinds of conduct. The words hysteria and hysterical have become naturalized in common parlance as indicating a person whose conduct is wildly emotional, excited, uncontrolled and exaggerated, in a word, histrionic. Another usage is to speak of the excited behavior of a crowd, or a mass of people, as hysteria. On the other hand, the word *histrionic* derives from the Latin word *histrio*, a theatre actor, thus hysterical and histrionic are synonyms as well. Hysteria was the name of a faux disease that the young doctors at the Salpêtrière hospital *rehearsed and staged* as a dramatic performance for the benefit of Professor Charcot, the Napoleon of the neuroses, during his legendary public lectures that were attended by the Parisian elite and the young Sigmund Freud and immortalized in the famous 1887 etching by A. Brouillet that hung in Freud's office. The etching shows a swooning Blanche Wittman falling into the arms of Dr. Joseph Babinski which Freud feared might be perceived as "theatrical by ill-disposed strangers" (Freud, 1893a, p. 18) (Lothane, 2009).

To summarize: hysteria is an abstract noun, a myth, what exists and is observed are people and conducts labeled hysterical. Like gravitation, which cannot be seen, for only falling things can be seen, so hysteria is utilized as pointing to forms of conduct along a continuum from common to clinically pathologized. In the wake of Charcot, Josef Breuer and

Sigmund Freud, solved the two thousand years old conundrum of hysteria by describing disorders they called, in the wake of Charcot, *traumatic neuroses*: reactions to traumatic life events, in their epochal 1895 *Studies on Hysteria*. The first case of a traumatic neurosis was Breuer's Anna O, the other women were patients of Freud.

Rereading that book around 2007, when I was visiting professor at the Heidelberg Institute for the History of Medicine directed by Prof. Wolfgang Eckart, I made a discovery: Strachey did not fully understand the meaning of a word used by Breuer to describe the conduct of Anna O., aka Bertha Pappenheim, the co-discoverer of psychoanalysis. The word in question, used in the 19th century and since obsolete, was the verb *tragieren* meaning to act and to perform a role.

Breuer offered this general observation of Anna O.:

> With her puritanically-minded family, this girl of overflowing mental vitality led a most monotonous existence, although she probably exaggerated it to an excessive degree for her illness. She systematically nurtured day-dreaming, which she called her "private *theater*" (Breuer and Freud, 1909b, italics added, p. 14).

Her illness was a syndrome of withdrawal from her family life due to the trauma of having been roped into the role of caring for a moribund father while the day-dream-dreaming was a mode of surviving under these conditions and Breuer's almost daily visits kept her from being hospitalized.

Breuer described the following event:

> Unfortunately, I had to leave the city the same evening, and when I returned after many days, I found that the patient's condition was markedly aggravated. Throughout the whole time she was entirely absentminded and full of anxiety. Her hallucinatory absences were filled with terrifying images of skulls and skeletons. As she lived through these things and *dramatized* them partially in speech,

the people around her could understand most of the content of her hallucinations. In the afternoon she remained somnolent, and at sunset in a deep hypnosis, for which she coined in English the name of "clouds" (italics added p.18).

Freud focused on two kinds of dramatization: (A) dreaming of scenes while asleep, (B) fantasizing in waking day-dreams and noted in the 1900 *The Interpretation of Dreams* that "phantasies or day-dreams are the immediate forerunners of hysterical symptoms" (p. 491).

A. Dramatization in dreams:

Dreams then think predominantly in visual images, but not exclusively. They use auditory images as well...The transformation of ideas into hallucinations is not the only respect in which dreams differ from waking life. Dreams construct a *situation* out of these images, represent something as an event happening in the present,...they *'dramatize'* an idea ... [I]n dreams ... we appear not to *think* but to *experience* ... we attach complete belief to the hallucinations. Not until we wake up does the critical comment arise that ... we have merely been thinking in a particular way" (Freud, 1900, pp. 49–50; three italics by Strachey, the second in the German original and without single quotations marks) (cited in Lothane, 2009).

Freud quotes Hildebrandt on "the dramatic representation mode *[Darstellungsweise]* in dreams" (1900b, p. 72). In a later text Freud defines again: "the transformation of thoughts into situations ('dramatization') is the most peculiar and important characteristic of dream work" (Freud, 1900, p. 653).

B. Dramatization in act as described in the aforementioned vignette by Breuer.

Dramatization in act and in dramatic monologue or dialogue is the very essence of the art form called drama, a word derived from the Greek root *dran* = 'to do,' thus doing versus dreaming. Drama was invented in Greece as *dramaturgy*, i.e., the art of composing dramas and performing dramas in a theater, e.g., the tragedies by Aeschylus, Sophocles, and Euripides, which were analyzed by Aristotle. But life itself was the source of these invented dramas, as it is today for the dramas of theater plays, television plays, and films. There is a need for a domain to accommodate both real life and invented dramas for which I proposed the term dramatology (Lothane, 2009), a word still not found in the dictionaries.

Moreover, the aforementioned Breuer's interaction with Anna O. pointed to the fact that the treatment situation was a drama, too, a *dramatic* conversation and interaction between the patient and the doctor. Breuer employed Aristotle's idea of catharsis, purging the emotions of pity and terror for the spectators, to call his treatment of trauma as cathartic purging, also called *abreaction*, of strangulated emotions. Freud defined psychological treatment as an interaction with "words…the essential tool of mental treatment [having] magical power" (Freud, 1905, p. 283). As I showed, this essay was written by Freud in 1892 (Lothane, 2014), which I discussed in 2007, a foreshadowing of dramatology in 2009.

In that essay Freud described "what is known as the 'expression of the emotions' ":

> A man's states of mind are manifested, almost without exception, in the tensions and relaxations of his facial muscles, in the adaptation of his eyes, in the amount of blood in the vessels of his skin, in the modifications in his vocal apparatus and in the movements of his limbs and in particular his hands (p. 286).

Freud's keen interest in drama was described in his 1942 essay on psychopathic characters on the stage. Drama was also an interest of the American neurologist, psychiatrist and psychoanalyst Smith Ely Jelliffe in the first chapter "The drama and psychotherapy" of his 1934 monograph:

> The drama has always been an important handmaid of

culture, and in every age of human history its develop-ment has kept pace with that of culture. Its direct appeal to the senses, as well as its growing intellectual and ar-tistic value, have made it always a leader of the thought of the race and of its form of expression. It has stimu-lated the people, educated them, directed their religious aspirations, and has served for their amusement and recreation. So well has it done the latter that the dan-ger has increased of forgetting that these in themselves are conventional terms for something deeper and more significant. This is something that lies in the mental life below the surface and ·gives to the drama in its very function of amusement and recreation a far more serious purpose for which it intrinsically stands... It also permits a constructive representation of the emotions (pp. 1–2).

In 1979 the Swedish professor of the history of literature Gunnar Brandell documented Freud's interest in drama but was unaware of Freud's 1942 essay.

Back to Breuer: he not only participated in and observed Anna O.'s dramatizations (and those belonged to dramatol-ogy, a word not yet found in dictionaries), Breuer also trans-formed the dramatic situations into a story, a narrative (and narratives belong to a domain called narratology, a word that is found in dictionaries). What then is the domain of dramati-zation? Dramatology and narratology are thus the two com-plementary sides of the same coin: one represents a life story in action and the other in story-making and story-telling.

Trauma as drama

In the aforecited Freud's remark about dreams, that "phanta-sies or day-dreams are the immediate forerunners of hyster-ical symptoms," the word *symptom* is a medical coinage. But phantasies and day dreams are not really forerunners, they *are* the so-called hysterical symptoms themselves. Hallowed by the medical model, we speak of 'symptoms' of paranoia the way we speak of the symptoms of pneumonia. But pneu-monia is monadic, it takes one to develop pneumonia but paranoia is dyadic, it takes two to develop paranoia. But it was Freud himself who redefined neurosis psychologically and sociologically as action, or drama, as a continuum of health and disease:

> Symptoms—and of course we are dealing with psychical (or psychogenic) symptoms and psychical illness—are *acts* detrimental, or at least useless, to the subject's life as a whole . . .*'being ill'* is in its essence a practical concept...you might well say that we are *all* ill—that is, neurotic, since the preconditions for the formation of symptoms can also be observed in normal people" (Freud, 1916–1917, 358; my italics).

Eventually Freud emphasized the *sociological* dimension of interpersonal conduct: "in the individual's mental life someone else is invariably involved, as a model, as an object, as a helper, as an opponent; and so from the very first individual psychology ... is at the same time social psychology as well" (Freud, 1921, p. 69), all this having dramatological implications.

It should be helpful to show how Breuer and Freud solved the 2500 years old enigma of hysteria: having "[investigated] over a number of years [its] many forms and symptoms... with a view to discovering the precipitating cause—the *event* which provoked its *first* occurrence" (*Preliminary Communication*, 1893, p. 3; italics added). The precipitating causal event turned out to be "*a precipitating trauma*...a girl, watching beside a sick-bed in a torment of anxiety fell into a twilight state and had a terrifying hallucination" (p. 4). The event was a historical fact with time and place and person(s), it was a scene, a situation, with a monologue or a dialogue, and as such could fairly be called a drama. And they concluded: "*Observations such as these seem to us to establish an analogy between the pathogenesis of common hysteria and that of traumatic neuroses and to justify the extension of the concept of traumatic hysteria*" (p. 5, their italics). On an analogy with Charcot's neurological neuroses caused by train accidents, Breuer and Freud described reactions to interpersonal traumatic events and faute de mieux, for lack of something better, called it traumatic hysteria. Today we have a different label for a reaction to trauma: post-traumatic stress disorder. Therefore, I submit, there is good reason to cancel continuing to use the convenient cliché hysteria, one can instead speak of traumatic reactions.

Two more matters were found relevant: not only the nature of the precipitating event, sometimes quite "trifling, but the affect of fright—the psychical trauma" (p. 6), both the stimulus and the response. And it is this psychic trauma that persisted long after the event: "the psychical pain that is remembered in waking consciousness still provokes a lachrymal secretion after the event. *Hysterics suffer mainly from reminiscences*" (p. 7, their italics). And there are sufferers from posttraumatic stress reactions, both civilian and veterans.

Another matter not dealt with in the *Preliminary Communication* was the pejorative use of the label hysteria to characterize imaginary illness of the mind, as in Molière's *Malade Imaginaire*, versus the real—and respectable—organic illness of the body. In 1893 Freud made the distinction between organic paralyses and hysterical paralyses, the latter "completely independent of the anatomy of the nervous system, since *in its paralyses and other manifestations hysteria behaves as though anatomy did not exist or a though he had no knowledge of it*" (1893, p. 169). Note Freud's allegorically personifying hysteria as a female entity or essence, fit for Occam's razor. For in fact there is no such thing as non-organic paralysis, what exists are persons imitating, enacting and playing the part of a patients afflicted with an organic paralysis who simply will not raise their arms or use their legs to walk.

Ideas can be likened to seeds planted in mind and memory that may lie dormant for years until they sprout one day to yield the fruit of previous insights. When I was a resident in psychiatry in Rochester, NY I heard and read my teacher

George Engel (1962) comparing a "conversion reaction to the game of charades. In this game one is asked to translate a verbal (cognitive) message into bodily terms, as pantomime, as gestures or other bodily movements. They are meant symbolically to represent the cognitive content the player had in mind" (p. 369). Conversion reactions, Engel taught, "are most common in and characteristic of hysteria, a condition in which there is a predilection for the use of the body for expression of feelings, wishes, and ideas, but it is not correct to equate the conversion reaction with hysteria, as has been customary in the past" (p. 369), without saying why this is so. But the inescapable conclusion back then was that hysteria is not a condition, that it is conduct and as such no different from ordinary people expressing their emotions with their bodies in gestures, tone and volume of voice, let alone pantomime, grimace, laughter, and tears, as did Freud in the aforementioned 1905 essay. Thus, conversion failed as an adequate explanation as indicated by Engel himself: "a forbidden wish is kept out of consciousness but at the same time is translated ("converted"), not into words, but into some bodily activity or sensation which suitably represents it in a symbolic form" (p. 369). Putting conversion in quotation marks and adding the synonym of translation suggested that hysteria, too, was nothing but "hysteria," a façon de parler, a turn of phrase. In retrospect Engel's teaching was the seed of my dramatology.

Now dramatology is not a *theory* to explain a disease labeled hysteria but a *method* to understand the person, however labeled, the person's character and conflicts, the person's outward appearance and inward thoughts, feelings, and motives of acting. Consider the example of the only male case of a traumatic reaction in the *Studies on Hysteria*:

> An employee who had become a hysteric as a result of being ill-treated by his superior, suffered from attacks in which he collapsed and fell into a frenzy of rage, but without uttering a word or giving any sign of a hallucination. It was possible to provoke an attack under hypnosis and the patient then revealed that he was living through the

scene in which his employer had abused him in the street and hit him with a stick. A few days later the patient came back and complained of having another attack of the same kind. On this occasion it turned out under hypnosis that he had been re-living the scene to which the actual onset of the illness was related: the scene in the law-court when he failed to obtain satisfaction for his maltreatment (1893, p. 14, italics added).

With or without the word, hysteria would enable a writer like Chekhov or Maupassant to compose a short story built on these same scenes.

Another example is the case of Dora, aka Ida Bauer, whom Freud treated in 1900, wrote up mostly in 1901, and published in 1905. Dora's family and family drama were replete with scenes of seduction, sexual manipulation, intrigues of infidelity, love barters, and betrayals so that Freud wished he could write her story more as "a man of letters engaged in the creation of a mental state like this for a short story, instead of being a medical man engaged upon its dissection" (Freud, 1905b, p. 59). But at this point in his life Freud did not listen to Dora, as he did to his patients who were his teachers prior to 1895, but used her as a test case to prove his oedipal theory of hysteria (p. 56) and a sexual theory of hysteria, bombarding her with interpretations which resulted in dramatic verbal duels. Seeing Dora as "a girl of intelligent and engaging looks" (p. 23), "sharp-sighted" (p. 34) and firing "arguments," "rejoinders," "objections," and "contradictions," Freud, was just as sharp in his rejoinders; while not feeling justified "to attack" her thoughts, he nevertheless repeatedly confronted Dora, for "to make an omelet you have to break the eggs" (p. 49). However, the main reason for Dora's breaking off her treatment after three months, I submit, was that Freud was not loyal to her rebuffing a sexually exploitive and unscrupulous adult like Herr K. and others but was siding with them and critical of the patient. And Freud admitted himself: "Might I perhaps have kept the girl under my treatment if I myself had acted a part, if I had exaggerated the importance to me of her staying on, and had shown a warm personal interest in her—a course which, even after allowing for my position as her physician, would have been tantamount to providing her with a substitute for the affection she longed for? I do not know" (p.109).

Proceeding to rationalize the termination Freud argued: "the factor of 'transference' did not come up for discussion during the short treatment" (p. 13). Only after Dora left him did Freud realize that "the transference took [him] unawares" (p. 118) and got dramatic: "She took her revenge on me as she wanted to take her revenge on [Herr K.], and deserted me as she believed herself to have been deceived and deserted by him. Thus, she *acted out* [*sie agierte*] an essential part of her recollections and fantasies instead of reproducing it in treatment" (p.119; italic Freud's), self-pityingly "demonstrating the helplessness and incapacity of the physician" (p. 120). '*Agieren*,' from the Latin *agere*, to act, does in German mean both doing and acting a role in a play, reverberating with Breuer's '*tragieren*,' and thus overdetermined consciously and unconsciously. Dora's termination was not just acting out but her own decisive action to stop treatment and was blessed by Freud: "You know that you are free to stop the treatment at any time" (p. 105), showing that Freud conflated acting out with action. Moreover, Freud viewed acting out as an antonym of remembering, for acting out *is* an unconscious enactment of a memory of a past event. I recall a point made by Brenner in a presentation in 1968 that it is not only in dreams, enactments can also be a royal road to the unconscious.

But there was a silver lining to Freud's lament:

Dora dramatized her conflict with Freud, as other women before her; but here confrontation, contest (*agon*), and combat occupied center stage: she acted and—[according to Freud]—she acted out. Hence the new conception of analysis as a transference drama played out between two protagonists turned antagonists, in which "this latest creation of the disease must be *combated* like the earlier ones. This happens, however, to be by far the hardest part of the whole task. It is easy to learn how to interpret dreams, to extract from the patient's associations his unconscious thoughts and memories, and to *practice similar explanatory arts*: for these the patient will always provide the text" (1905, p. 116; my italics). Interpretation alone is no longer sufficient: "since a whole series of psychological experiences are revived not as belonging to the past but as applying to the physician at the present moment" (p. 116), since "all the patient's tendencies, including hostile ones, are aroused" (p.117), explanation needs to be amplified by confrontation. In this way, "transference, which seems ordained to be the greatest obstacle of psycho-analysis" (p. 117), became a crisis, a challenge, and an opportunity (Lothane, 2009, p.141).

Here, too, dramatology, in agreement with Freud's confrontational approach, makes a contribution to the tradition of psychoanalytically-oriented psychotherapy.

So far dramatology has been cited positively by Philip Bromberg (personal communication), James Grotstein (Brown, 2011, p xvii), Galit Atlas and the late Lewis Aron (2018, p. 47, 54, 84). New ideas tend to arouse suspicion: *if it is true, it is not new* is a common reaction. Dramatology is both old and new and calls for a rediscovery and a reaffirmation.

Some objections to dramatology as method might be raised in the spirit of entries in the psychoanalytic dictionary of Moore and Fine (1990). The author of the entry "Hysteria," citing four references (the *Studies*, the Dora case, Fenichel's *The Psychoanalytic Theory of Neurosis*, and a paper by Rangell on conversion), does not mention the word trauma and starts by claiming that "involved in psychic mechanisms in hysteria [Freud] discovered unconscious fantasy, conflict, repression, identification, and transference, marking the beginning of psycho-analysis" (p. 89). This heterogeneous list is incorrect: psychoanalysis began with the Preliminary

Communication and *The Studies on Hysteria*. One statement seems to support the idea of dramatization: "The hysterical spells often pantomime complicated fantasy stories that can be analyzed in the same way as can the elements of the manifest dream, both phenomena are products of the distortion resulting from mechanisms of the primary process" (p. 90). But this correct insight is immediately vitiated by claiming that "the bodily symptoms of hysteria involve motor, sensory, or visceral phenomena—anesthesia, pain, paralysis, tremors, deafness, blindness, vomiting, hiccoughing, and so on" but also that "the symptoms therefore represent an expression in "body language" of specific unconscious fantasies" (p. 90). This is another mixture of quasi-neurological descriptions of physiological sequelae of strong emotions and the symbolic nature of body language (see chapter 32 and 33 on compensated and uncompensated states). The term *acting out* is often used colloquially as a synonym for *acting up*, to behave in an unruly or capricious manner.

Finally, the author of the entry "action" claims that "analysts think of action as something opposing the psychoanalytic process, for example when psychopathology takes the form of disruptive, maladaptive, or inappropriate behavior" (p. 3). I disagree: action is not inimical to psychoanalysis; any action or enactment can be grist to the mill. Here Wilhelm Reich's character analysis of identifying and confronting habitual character attitudes, both traits and states (Lothane, 2009, p. 146), and dramatology offer an approach and a method: all forms of action can benefit from applying the psychoanalytic method of analyzing enactments the way one analyzes dreams, that is with the help of free association (Lothane, 2018).

References

Atlas, G. and Aron, L. (2018). *Dramatic dialogue Contemporary clinical practice*. London: Routledge.

Brandell, G. (1979[1976]). *Freud A man of his century*. Sussex: Harvester Press; New Jersey: Humanities Press.

Breuer, J., & Freud, S. (1893–1895). *Studies on hysteria. Standard Edition*, volume 2.

Breuer, J., & Freud, S. (1909a). *Studien* über *Hysterie*. Leipzig u. Wien: Franz Deuticke.

Breuer, J. & Freud, S. (1909b). Studies on hysteria. Mental of Nervous and Mental Disease Monograph # 5.

Brown, L. J. (2011). *Intersubjective processes and the unconscious. An integration of Freudian, Kleinian and Bionian perspectives.* London: Routledge.

Engel, G. L. (1962). *Psychological development in health and disease*. Philadelphia: W.B. Saunders Company.

Freud, S. (1893a). Charcot. *Standard Edition*, 3:11–23.

Freud, S. (1893b). Some points for a comparative study of organic and hysterical motor paralyses. Standard Edition, 1:160–172.

Freud, S. (1900). *The interpretation of dreams. Standard Edition*, volumes 4, 5.

Freud, S. (1905a[1892]. Psychical (or mental) treatment. *Standard Edition*, 7:283–302.

Freud, S. (1905b). Fragment of an analysis of a case of hysteria. *Standard Edition*, 7:7–122.

Freud, S. (1916–1917). *Introductory lectures to psycho-analysis.* Standard Edition, volume 15, 16.

Freud, S. (1921). *Group psychology and analysis of the ego. Standard Edition*, volume 18.

Freud, S. (1942[1905 or 1906]). Psychopathic characters on the stage. *Standard Edition* 7:305–310.

Gilman, S. et al. (1993). *Hysteria beyond Freud*. Berkeley, CA: University of California Press, chapter by Helen King, "Once upon a Text Hysteria from Hippocrates," pp. 3–90.

Hippocrates. Volume IV The Loeb Classical Library. London: William Heinemann LTD. https://ryanfb.github.io/loebolus-data/L150.pdf

Jelliffe, S.E. M.D. & Brink, L., A.B. of New York (1934). *Psychoanalysis and drama*. Mental of Nervous and Mental Disease Monograph # 34.

Lothane, Z. (2007). The power of the spoken word in life, psychiatry and psychoanalysis—a contribution to interpersonal psychoanalysis. *American Journal of Psychoanalysis*, 67:260–274.

Lothane, Z. (2009). Dramatology in life, disorder, and psychoanalytic therapy: a further contribution to interpersonal psychoanalysis. *International Forum of Psychoanalysis*, 18(3):135–148.

Lothane, H.Z. (2014). Letter to the Editor On: From psychical treatment to psychoanalysis. *International Journal of Psychoanalysis*, 95:1007–1008.

Lothane, H. Z. (2018). Free association as the foundation of the psychoanalytic method and psychoanalysis as a historical science. *Psychoanalytic Inquiry*, 38(6):416–434. Issue theme: Free Association; Issue Editor: Henry Z. Lothane, M.D.

Moore, B. E. and Fine, B.D., eds. (1990). *Psychoanalytic terms & concepts*. The American Psychoanalytic Association and New Haven: Yale University Press.

Plato, *Timaeus. The collected dialogues* of, Bollingen Series LXXI. Princeton, NJ: Princeton University Press.

Veith, I. (1993[1965]). *Hysteria the history of a disease*. Northvale, NJ: Jason Aronson.

Discussion of Article by Zvi Lothane, MD

Mehmet Sagman Kayatekin and Zerrin Emel Kayatekin

This is a wonderful and evocative article.

The author has a deep scholarly familiarity with the Oeuvre of Freud as it is biblically edified in the twenty plus volumes of painstaking translation by James Strachey. And through his comments, the author provides us with a mastery of the Oeuvre of the founder of Psychoanalysis with occasional Talmudic interpretation of the text.

As one reads the article, one can't help but feel admiration with the author's mastery of the writings of Freud, and, at the same time, there is perhaps an inescapable but neverthe-less a pervasive sense of frustration. This probably emanates from what feels like a difficulty in finding a tie between his theorizing and ordinary clinical experience and expertise. In sum, it is an impression, perhaps ill-founded, that the author has chosen for the sake of this paper, to remove himself from experience-near clinical practice and has instead empha-sized a literary critique perspective on "hysterical/histrionic" phenomenon as it is depicted in various texts.

I am tempted to see the author's vision as a revolt. Psychoanalysis was, and quite likely, still is a revolt to the mainstream thinking. Further, in the recent history of psy-choanalysis and psychiatry, there are quite established mini revolts against the dogma; like Szasz, anti-psychiatry, Laing, many of whom I am quite familiar with and feel a kinship towards, but at the same time, was inescapably, sadly disillu-sioned with these revolutionary heroes of mine over a short period of time.

On the one hand, the concept of "disease" as the author defines it, is bewilderingly simplistic, and, on the other hand, as the author suggests wisely, there is not an individual, but to paraphrase, as Winnicott suggested, there is a mother and a baby. This recognition that we are born into small and large groups sounded extraordinary in the dominating world of ossified psychoanalytic ego psychology theorizing.

These interpersonal dynamics were known for millennia and were forgotten, remembered and re-brought to our attention by many, amongst whom were Freud, Winnicott, Fairbairn as persons of high-level theorizing and many schools of psychoanalysis like, Kleinians, Kohutians, Object Relations theorists and intersubjectivists etc., supported it through their work.

In other words, to counter the author's otherwise bold ideas, we are reminded that psychiatric illness is always in relation to an "other/others" and is partly shaped in the audience of the other(s). Just as transference, countertransference is evoked by and shaped by at least a twosome. As my teacher Martin Cooperman said, the building block of human psyche is not the individual person but the twosome, parent and child, therapist and patient. In the author's shorthand, psychopathology, and thus humans are not monadic but dyadic.

Within this larger context, we have the following comments on hysteria as it is depicted in this article. First, the clinical phenomenon of what is called "hysteria" or "histrionic" exists across many cultures in very similar forms. And it exists, probably for some millennia no matter what coinage we use to name and define the "symptoms" observed. We have a long companionship with "hysteria" as an illness and its appearance in relatively familiar forms.

It is not as different as the differences that the following genres depict; Kabuki theater, mime, puppeteering or a grand theatrical production of Les Misérables. So there must be a common human denominator of certain basic aspects of how we use nonverbal, bodily action and non-action cross culturally if the hysteria of a Turkish village in rural Anatolia and the hysteria of fin de siècle, relatively isolated, self-sufficient cities of Europe; Paris and Vienna have some profound similarities. They are closed in economies and cultures, villages with differing expansions.

But let us go back to our development as psychiatrists and therapists. When we entered the practice of psychodynamic psychiatry in Ankara, Turkey during the late 1970s, we had seen many patients who would come with hysterical paralyses of limbs, aphonias, fugues, arc de cercles, multiple personalities as described by European psychiatrists and neurologists in wondrous detail in the 19th century and early 20th century. We would use a wide range of methods of treatment, including galvanic faradization for hysterical paralysis of extremities, hypnosis, barbiturate analyses and psychodynamic therapy.

None of these were on the stages of fin de siecles theatre/auditorium of Salpetrier under the directorship of charismatic masters like Charcot. But there was clearly a mime-like quality i.e., the actions or inactions, words or the lack thereof, of the patients could easily be interpreted along the lines of some activated conflicts or split off parts of the psyche, defensive constellations around centrally important affects of shame and guilt amongst others. So where was the stage?

The widely known phrase of "It takes a village to raise a child" has another, closely tied side to it—that villages, human ecologies we grow with the help, nurturing and boundary negotiations of a multitude of others are small theaters, where every person is being closely watched by all members of his immediate family and of the literal village as sources of pride, shame, envy and gratitude. So, one is on the stage and in the audience at the same time and all the time. Thus, it is a fertile ground for a mime-like hysterical illness to develop and be displayed on this stage of the village. Smaller Turkish towns were similar, perhaps the main difference was instead of the village being the stage, now neighborhoods were acting as the stage for the actor-audiences.

It was of interest that as the country became more urbanized in the globalizing 20th century world, as the local, self-sufficient, closed-in economies of villages and small towns were integrated into the market of the country and the country integrated with the global economy, hysteria slowly disappeared. With the risk of taking a tangent, one also wonders whether there is a parallel between the disappearance of hysteria and the fate of small traveling show troupes who would visit these small villages and towns and put on some short plays and puppetry and would occasionally display a few esoteric animals like a monkey or a python to the amazed eyes of the villagers.

Whatever we attribute to the causes of this sad phenomenon of attrition, in a similar and parallel way, the dramas of these tiny mobile theater troupes and dramas of hysteria slowly disappeared. It was stunning to note that with the increased availability of local clinics that delivered modern medical care, patients with similar intrapsychic-interpersonal constellations began exhibiting classical depressive symptomatology. To expand the metaphor of the village as a stage —perhaps now there was no central stage to act on. It was gone for hysteria as it was for the small traveling troupes, and thus patients perhaps learned to talk.

It is an interesting fact that many years later, Lacan would hold similar demonstrations, not in action but more around the narrative of the patient in a verbal way in his weekly seminars in Paris. There was a shift from the theater of Charcot to literary analysis and the critique of narrative. Yet the demonstration of madness in visual or verbal forms to educated masses is perhaps a French tradition par excellence.

In the earlier phases of psychoanalytic theorizing, we had a concept of "transference neurosis"—which meant that the central conflicts, defenses, split off aspects of the intrapsychic organization of the patient were replicated in the relationship between the patient and therapist dyad. When the transference neurosis had fully evolved, the psychoanalyst was not just a transference figure but had become a real figure for his/her own sake and was a source of conflict and taking sides in the conflicts the patient had regenerated in the treatment situation.

Thus, the terms of transference; the brilliantly articulated countertransference possibilities by Racker; the idea of projection; the Kleinian concept of projective identification; and role responsiveness of Sandler. All of these describe a series of phenomenon of attribution of the roles from the story of the patient to therapist and the therapist joining the major scripts of the patient and vice versa to a degree. All of which are in sync with drama, theater, acting and enacting and the concept of dramaturgy.

The treatment of what we decided to refer to as severe pathology, after Kernberg, mainly goes through actions, counter actions, enactments, interpretations of actions. Not necessarily just interpreting words or narratives or resistances. As the work in psychotherapeutic hospitals, like Austen Riggs Center and Menninger where there is an abundance of patients with "severe pathology," clearly demonstrates the therapeutic task is to translate the meaningful, communicative behaviors of the patients to words. And we must say "unconscious communication" which is sorely lacking in the author's paper.

But this doesn't mean that hysteria is not an illness or that it is just an illness. In fact, it beautifully overlaps with the dilemma about the nature of psychoanalysis. Is psychoanalysis a medical science, where we have the algorithm of etiology that leads to illness, or is it a hermeneutic field, where human motivation and human communication, be it through words or actions, is essential? These, in my opinion, are not necessarily exclusive positions. Psychoanalysis straddles science and hermeneutics. So does Hysteria as a hybrid of illness and a script originated by the patient in his/her interpersonal and historical context.

Response to Professors M. Sagman Kayatekin and Z. Emel Kayatekin

Henry Zvi Lothane

Psychiatry Professor M. Sagman Kayatekin of the Department of Psychiatry and Behavioral Sciences of Baylor College damns me with florid praise but misses the heart of my article on hysteria as histrionics and sees it as "a revolt"—part of a mixed bag of all kinds of revolts, including Thomas Szasz, allegedly a representative of anti-psychiatry. But I did not bring up Szasz, even though I knew him personally and co-authored a book about him: "Thomas Szasz: The Man and his Ideas."

Breuer and Freud clearly stated their intention in the title of their introduction to *The Studies on Hysteria*: "On the psychical mechanism of hysterical phenomena: preliminary communication." Mark well: hysterical phenomena. They first used the adjective hysterical and not the noun hysteria, and there was a good reason for that: hysterical phenomena applied to a wide range of observations, from "hysterical epileptoid convulsions" to "vomiting and anorexia" to "visual hallucinations"; "...what we are accustomed to find in traumatic neuroses" (*Standard Edition*, 2:6). True, their synonym for "traumatic neurosis" was "traumatic hysteria," but the main phenomenon was "the affect of fright—the psychical trauma... Any experience which calls up distressing affects—such as those of fright, anxiety, shame, or physical pain—may operate as trauma" (p. 6). However, hysterical phenomena occur in everyday life, no matter whether the patients do or don't end up in the hothouse of a psychiatric hospital. David Shapiro also made this clear in his 1965 book *Neurotic Styles*, in which he defined neurotic styles as "a form or mode of functioning—the way or manner of a given area of behavior—that is identifiable, in an individual, through a range of his specific acts" (p. 2). True, Shapiro also meant "the characteristics of various neurotic conditions" (p. 2). But 'neurotic' is also used in common parlance to refer to an "emotionally unstable person" and 'hysterical' to mean "unrestrained emotionalism" (both in the Third New International Dictionary). There was no noun 'hysteria' in the Hippocratic canon, only the adjective *hysterike*, as in *hysterike pnix*, a uterine strangulation probably referring to the retention of the placenta. The famous British doctor Sydenham translated it as suffocations of the mother. The adjective hysterical was coined as a noun in the 19th century (Oxford English Dictionary On Historical Principles), a cause of many sins of reification, including those in diagnostic classifications. In DSM-5 the word *hysteria* is gone and replaced with "Dissociative, Conversion, and Somatoform Disorders." But all this is meant to prove an even more important fact: the most revolutionary consequence of Breuer and Freud describing traumatic reactions was the further extension of the concept of a traumatic neurosis to PTSD, as I stated: "Today we have a different label for a reaction to trauma: post-traumatic stress disorder. Therefore, I submit, there is good reason to cancel the use of the convenient cliché *hysteria*, one can instead speak of traumatic reactions." In fact, we see PTSD in war and in civilian accidents, with or without bodily traumas, and in the survivors of the genocide of the Jews called the Holocaust and in a variety of individual metaphorical holocausts, at times called soul murder, who come to speak with us.

The other major miss of Professor Kayatekin is misunderstanding my concept of dramatology. In fact, he sums up his lengthy discussion of dramatic phenomena as follows: "All of which are in sync with drama, theater, acting and enacting and the concept of *dramaturgy*" (the italics are mine). Clearly, he did not take the trouble to read my paper on *dramatology* in which I distinguish dramatology from dramaturgy: the former referring to hysterical phenomena in real life events or dramas, the latter referring to those depicted in stage dramas created by the great dramaturgs like Sophocles or Shakespeare, showing how art imitates life. This I can forgive. But I cannot forgive without getting a retraction of this statement by him: "In sum, it is an impression, perhaps ill-founded, that the author has chosen for the sake of this paper, *to remove himself from experience-near clinical practice* and has instead emphasized a literary critique perspective on "hysterical/histrionic" phenomenon as it is depicted in various texts" (I added italics). Yes, Professor Kayatekin, this impression is ill-founded: I did not remove myself from anything experience-near, I practice interpersonal drama therapy (IDT)—not psychodrama which is also an invention situation—and confront my patients with the drama happening between them and me during the session and which we are both witnessing, and make them aware of their resistances, transferences, and neurotic habits. It is not transference that explains the here-and-now drama, it is the dramatic here-and-now drama that helps us understand transference as a compulsion to repeat and as neurotic character styles and habits.

Three Analysts, Five Opinions

Merle Molofsky

In contemplating the question, is psychoanalysis a science or an art, and its amplification, or a philosophy, I find myself shrugging, shaking my head in dismay, and wondering, why are we mired in the muck of an old culture war? I thought immediately of the 1959 book, *The Two Cultures and the Scientific Revolution*, by C.P. Snow, which described a face-off between two perspectives, where a humanist would challenge a scientist about what the scientist knew of the humanities, and the scientist would ask the humanities expert what the humanities expert knew of science.

Why would the psychoanalytic community be compelled to compartmentalize, categorize, or divide ways of knowing, in order to frame an understanding of psychoanalysis? Are we somewhat addicted to the excitement of continuing one culture war after another, with the ecstatic possibility of prevailing, winning the battle?

Psychoanalysis has a long history of internal culture wars, beginning with the rifts Sigmund Freud had with Alfred Adler and with Carl Gustav Jung. Once upon a time, in a paradise far away, psychoanalysis was psychoanalysis. The first schism occurred over an understanding of aggression. How fitting! Adler had been invited to join Freud's Wednesday group in 1902, and did so. In 1908 he offered his own theory about aggression, and the hounds of war pricked up their ears. Two capable, thoughtful men had an intellectual interest in the secrets of the human mind, a theory of aggression became the focus of disagreement, a bone of contention, and Adler left Freud's inner circle in 1911. They both elaborated a theory of aggression as years went by, and Freud contended that his theory of aggression was different from Adler's.

In 1914, perhaps paralleling the war breaking out in Europe, World War I, Freud and Jung, his beloved "crown prince," Jung" had a falling out.

Freud and Jung had a close, fraught relationship—fraught because of the fantasies each had of the significance of their relationship, what each wanted from the other. Whatever personal dependencies and wishes emerged, a theoretical disagreement about the nature of the unconscious caused their final break, and that disagreement has in it the components and structure of the question we are contemplating: is psychoanalysis a science or an art?

Freud's work focused on his concept of an individual unconscious, which manifests as symptoms, as defenses, emotions and wishes that can neither be acknowledged nor fulfilled. Jung focused on two aspects of the unconscious, the individual unconscious, which he called the personal unconscious, and the collective unconscious, a vast repository of human culture manifesting as archetypes. Jung was enamored of the manifestations of mind in myth and religion, and Freud, who considered himself a scientist, rejected the emphasis on these "superstitions" as unscientific. Thus, the framework of our culture war in psychoanalysis emerged, similar to the culture war that C.P. Snow identified in academia and among the intelligentsia, emerged. Is psychoanalysis a science, to be conducted scientifically, or is there a whole other element of meaning in psychoanalysis, resonant with mythology, religion, and the arts? It would take decade after decade before psychoanalysts would frame the divide we contemplate now—Is psychoanalysis a science or an art? Yet the foundation for the question emerged with the schism between Freud and Jung.

In those ensuing decades, new schisms arose, as new theories were offered. I remember being so grateful when Fred Pine published a book that seemed to offer the possibility of healing the new tendency toward fragmentation, *Drive, Ego, Object, and Self: A Synthesis for Clinical Work* (1990). Indeed, his book synthesized what had become fractured psychoanalytic theorizing, by postulating that psychoanalytic work, drawing on clinical observation, should integrate the understanding of the human mind, that the human mind reflected human drives, ego functions, representations of object relations, and a sense of self. Thus drive theory, ego psychology, object relations theory, and self psychology all had something to offer to psychoanalysis, and to clinicians who work psychodynamically.

While psychoanalysis was still a young discipline, it became contentious, and riven into factions—Freudian, Adlerian, Jungian. There were distinct theoretical differences and concerns among the three factions, and strong feelings of animosity between Freud and the other two. Yet these emerging culture wars were only a beginning. Is the human mind so fractured within itself that a new, exciting discipline that studies that very human mind also is prone to fracturing, fragmenting, falling to pieces?

Freud actually was the original psychoanalyst, offering a complex theory of the unconscious, encompassing conflict, anxiety, drives, defenses, internalizations.

He also was the first to offer a theory of ego psychology, the first to offer a theory of object relations, the first to conceptualize the concept of self.

Freud's tripartite structural description of the mind—id, ego, superego—gave psychoanalysis its first ego psychology, acknowledging the ego mediating between the pressures and demands of the id and the pressures and demands of the superego, the tensions between desire and conscience.

Freud offered two essays that were insightful descriptions of the relationship of self to internal objects, "On Narcissism" (1914), and "Mourning and Melancholia" (1917). He conceived of the self as an object of one's own drives, in relation to others, who also are objects of one's drives.

In "On Narcissism," Freud introduces the concept of the ego ideal, the self that one expects one's self to be. He describes an original narcissism of libido directed toward the self, taking the self as one's first object. Self-esteem begins with a satisfaction with one's self, fulfilling one's ego ideal. The idealization of the self is reflected in the idealization of others, the love and need for an idealized other.

In "Mourning and Melancholia," Freud differentiates between mourning, grieving for an actual person, a truly lost object, and melancholia, a sense of loss based on internal psychic events. He postulates that the aspect of self that is experienced as superego and ego ideal is formed in large part from internalizations of a desired object, and when the ego ideal is unmet, the superego berates the self, and the self feels bereft and unworthy. Thus, mourning is self-attack, and the beloved object that should love the self is experienced as lost.

These two essays encompass the first object relations theory, and the first theory of self. Self and object are mental constructs, internal representations, in relation to one another.

Subsequently, creative and thoughtful psychoanalytic theorists elaborated in depth aspects of ego, object, and self, and gave the discipline meaningful theories that are components of psychoanalytic understanding. Yet, unfortunately, eventually proponents of each elaborated theory found themselves in opposition to each other. In cathecting the theory they most identified with and admired, they rejected other theories.

154

Perhaps most regrettably, the most egregious fracturing began in Britain, with adherents of Anna Freud and adherents of Melanie Klein quarreling, dividing practitioners into ego psychologists and object relations theorists. Each line of thinking led to creative and original contributions from outstanding theorists in the United States and in Britain, and some theorists, including Michael Balint and D.W. Winnicott, encouraged a "middle school" way of thinking that embraced all possibilities.

I attended the institute from which I graduated in the 1980's in New York City, well after the divisive fracturing in Britain in the 1940's and 1950's, and the arguments that raged in the 1980's New York City halls of psychoanalysis were just as virulent. People expected each other to announce their "theoretical orientation," to adhere to it, and to defend it. I was absolutely bewildered. I was grateful when I came across and read *Object Relations in Psychoanalytic Theory*, by Jay Greenberg and Steve Mitchell, in 1983, when it was first published. The two authors provided a coherent, in-depth history of the evolution of psychoanalytic thought, which allowed me to recognize that the seemingly antithetical theories of the building blocks of the human mind—the same drive, ego, object, self that Fred Pine would later address in 1990—were part of an evolution of psychoanalytic thought. I determined that these theories do not cancel each other out, but rather could lead to integration. That was not the conclusion that Greenberg and Mitchell reached, but I needed to make sense of disparate claims, and integration helped make sense of all claims without privileging any particular one.

When people asked me my theoretical orientation, I answered, "psychoanalytic," and I meant it. I still do. In my teens and in my twenties, long before I began to consider a career as a psychoanalyst, long before I even considered any career path, I had read Freud and Jung. My working-class parents, neither of whom had attended college, both of whom were highly cultured and self-educated, had in their library *The Basic Writings of Sigmund Freud* edited by A. A. Brill, and *Man and His Symbols* by Jung and others. I read these books without any knowledge of any dissent between Freud and Jung or any knowledge of the politics of psychoanalysis, and valued what I was reading.

Perhaps what underlies these fracturings is the need to believe in, and trust, authority. When I first read *Psychoanalytic Treatment: An Intersubjective Approach* (1987), by Atwood, Brandschaft, and Stolorow, I felt a great sense of relief, true illumination. I didn't have to accept some final authority. Rather, I was liberated, in that I could value my own thoughts, my own insights, and, therefore, trust my sense that psychoanalytic work is a partnership with the people with whom I was working.

The culture wars that raise the question of whether psychoanalysis is a science, an art, or a philosophy, dismay me because I know my own strengths and weaknesses. I have always been a poor science and math student, and since I first learned to read and write, I always have been a poet and fiction writer, and a devotee of literature and the arts. I know people who resonate with, and excel equally in, the sciences and humanities, but I am not one of them. I would prefer to stay safe in my own cocoon, claiming that psychoanalysis is an art, but I don't want to impose my insecurities on others in the guise of intellectual belief.

In 2015, I was greatly honored when I was asked to participate in the 2015 Symposium in New York City, on the theme "Brain, Mind, & Body." I was asked to present on "mind." I most assuredly could not have presented on "brain." I drew on the work of D.W. Winnicott, "The Location of Cultural Experience," in *Playing and Reality* (1971), where he said "cultural experience is located in the *potential space* between the individual and the environment (originally the object). The same can be said of playing. Cultural experience begins with creative living first manifested in play."

Science and art are part of our cultural experience, and both involve creativity manifesting in play. Serious play.

I also cited Gerald Gargiulo, who said, in "Inner Mind/Outer Mind and the Quest for an 'I'," *Soul on the Couch* (1997), "mind resides in all the cultural bridges we have built: language, art, philosophy, religion and psychoanalysis to name a few".

Gargiulo is quite at home in both the humanities and the sciences. He is a psychoanalyst, a poet, and he recently published *Quantum Psychoanalysis: Essays on Physics, Mind, and Analysis Today.*

Following Gargiulo, I hope for bridges.

Ofra Eshel, in her book *The Emergence of Analytic Oneness: Into the Heart of Psychoanalysis* (2019), has a chapter, "From extension to revolutionary change in clinical psychoanalysis: The radical influence of Bion and Winnicott," where she talks of "a transition from *extension to scientific revolution* and *paradigm shift (or paradigm change)* in psychoanalysis" (p.237), using terms derived from Thomas Kuhn's discussion of the evolution of science. Continuing with Kuhn's terminology, she speaks of a paradigm in a crisis-transition period, with old and new paradigms each having their adherents, resulting in a communication breakdown. What is needed is translation that results in better communication. She draws on Vermote's concept of integrative modeling, and cites Bion's concepts of K and O as a major paradigm shift in psychoanalysis.

Is psychoanalysis in crisis? Are we witnessing a new paradigm emerging? Or is this the same old, same old paradigm crisis and communication breakdown?

Again, when I was a candidate in the 1980s, the president of my institute, who was committed to drive theory, tried to establish a protocol in which candidates presenting their final case to qualify for graduation would have to present their case using drive theory. If they had used any other theoretical approach to conduct the analysis, they would be required to "translate" their case and use drive theory language only. Fortunately, he did not prevail. But I did know of one candidate, who had used an object relations approach primarily, being counseled by her control supervisor to present in drive theory terms, nonetheless. And she did.

Is our work doomed to be "lost in translation" if we continue fighting useless culture wars?

I am grateful that I have a psyche, that I have a mind, that I have a brain, that I have a body, and that I had the opportunity to become a psychoanalyst. I am indebted to everyone who taught me. I have learned about the human mind, the human experience, from psychoanalytic writings and from literature, from the people in my practice, from my own life experience.

Perhaps we will be fortunate enough to learn from the fractures and fragmentations in the history of psychoanalytic thought.

How can we learn?

In conclusion, I offer two quotes:

> "There is a crack in everything, that's how the light gets in"
> Leonard Cohen, "Anthem" (1992)

> "The Wound is the place where light enters you"
> Rumi, 13th century CE Persian Sufi poet

Merle Molofsky
26 West Ninth Street
Suite 2B
New York, NY 10011–8923

212–982–1054

mmpsya@gmail.com

Discussion of Three Analysts, Five Opinions by Merle Molofsky

Kimberly Kleinman

Merle Molofsky frames the question "Is Psychoanalysis an Art or Science?" as regressive, as a return to a culture war. She connects the frame of the question (is Psychoanalysis this or that), with the presence of dichotomous rifts that started almost as soon a Psychoanalysis was born, starting with Jung and Freud. Jung's theories were regarded as superstitious; Freud was the scientist, his theories were scientific.

Molofsky briefly describes rifts in Europe and the USA that had an impact on training and the field in general. She locates herself outside of these rifts and describes welcoming Fred Pine's work that focused on integrating drive, ego, object and self theory. She posits that some of the "fracturings" are a reaction to authority. Some people need to believe in authority. Molofsky describes liberation in reading Psychoanalytic Treatment: An Intersubjective Approach (1987), by Atwood, Brandschaft, and Stolorow. to quote her: *"I didn't have to accept some final authority. Rather, I was liberated, in that I could value my own thoughts, my own insights, and, therefore, trust my sense that psychoanalytic work is a partnership with the people with whom I was working."*

When Molofsky describes feeling liberated to value her own thoughts, is she voicing the complaints that those who resist the scientific have? She sounds like she is setting up a dichotomy between scientific believers who accept authority, and free liberated artists. But then she walks us through her integration of art and science, which includes describing Gerald Gargiulo's work, including a mention of his book: *Quantum*

Psychoanalysis: Essays on Physics, Mind, and Analysis Today.

Molofsky also raises the impact that theory wars have on psychoanalytic candidates. Included in this is a question of how work is described: In the mother tongue, or the archaic lingua franca?

I think that the scientific method was the first psychological theory. Based on untested theories of mind, the scientific method attempts to remove subjectivity from observation, and the resulting objective observations are then considered scientific. Our postmodern colleagues and physicists seem to agree that observation itself has an effect on the observed and have grave doubts about the effectiveness of any method to create a singular theory with "lawlike patterns." But this does not become a license to abandon empirical research. Our patients deserve a disciplined informed psychoanalyst.

Perhaps what Molofsky does not say explicitly is that the question of art or science itself pulls for a categorization that does not promote a synthetic conceptualization. Quantum Psychoanalysis probably offers the most useful metaphor for integrating the art/science binary. Psychoanalysis can exist in both spaces simultaneously.

Written by Kimberly Kleinman

kim@kskleinman.com

646–942–8716

Georg Groddeck and the Interrelation of Art and Science in Psychoanalysis

Austin Ratner

"Art versus Science" is a false dichotomy that has harmed psychoanalysis. The case of Georg Groddeck, father of psychosomatic medicine, illustrates in concrete terms the problematic consequences of this false dichotomy: a missed opportunity for psychoanalysts to treat prevalent psychosomatic illnesses.

Psychoanalysts and critics of psychoanalysis alike often claim that psychoanalysis is different from other sciences, or even that psychoanalysis does not qualify as a science at all. In making this case, proponents and critics sometimes characterize psychoanalysis as an art rather than a science. One such argument goes: Psychoanalysis attempts to understand human beings' subjective experiences, just as novels and films do; in this sense, it pursues an artistic form of knowledge—what literary critic A.D. Nuttall has called "experiential knowledge."[1] Similarly, psychoanalysts will point out that

---

[1]Nuttall: "By 'experiential knowledge' I mean connaître rather than *savoir*, *Erleben* rather than Wissen, the way you know your sister rather than the way you know DNA theory." (Nuttall 2007, pp. 74–75)

patients suffering from subjective experiences cannot be successfully treated according to protocol, in the way one treats, say, a sinus infection. Freud himself often made the case that the intimate nature of subjective experiences makes it impossible to study them using the methods of experimental psychology—especially when repression actively hides certain thoughts and feelings from both the investigator and the subjects themselves. Postmodern analysts like Paul Ricoeur celebrate psychoanalysis as a form of "storytelling" or "narrative intelligibility." "Psychoanalytic reports are kinds of biographies and autobiographies," Ricoeur writes, "whose literary history is a part of the long tradition emerging from the oral epic tradition of the Greeks, the Celts, and the Germans." (Ricoeur 1977, p. 869) And then there are critics like Allen Esterson or Paul McHugh who agree that Freud was a storyteller, but consider it a vice, not a virtue. They denigrate Freud's theories as spurious, unbelievable products of his "romantic" imagination. (Esterson 2001; McHugh 2006) Every one of these attempts to designate psychoanalysis as an "Art" reflects an underlying conviction that psychoanalytic knowledge differs from scientific knowledge.

Such attempts to polarize knowledge in this way overlook the fundamental interrelationship of art and science. "Art versus Science" is a false dichotomy. Successful scientists incorporate artistry and creativity into their work; successful artists likewise bring technical knowledge to their craft and a scientific dedication to the accurate depiction of reality. Art and science are not mutually exclusive products of the human mind, one fantastical and false, the other clear-eyed and true. Rather, they are distinct but often compatible attributes of human activity. Even a "hard" science like paleontology demands artistry and imagination. Thus Richard K. Stucky, a paleontologist and former curator of the Denver Museum of Nature and Science, had no hesitation in declaring that "Paleontology is art, science, and imagination." (Stucky 2000)

Consider, for example, the intangible skills required to find fossils. Paleontologist Steve Brusatte depicts the hunt for fossils as a matter of luck and intuition, passion and persistence. More than a few of the successful fossil hunters who appear in his book *The Rise and Fall of the Dinosaurs* are not in fact scientists, but hobbyists and adventurers. Helmuth Redschlag, for instance, is an architect. In 2005, he discovered a juvenile triceratops skeleton in the Hell Creek formation in Montana. The celebrated skeleton has been named Homer and stands in the Burpee Museum of Natural History in Rockford, Illinois. Redschlag's artistic "attention to the details of shapes and textures," Brusatte writes, is what makes him "a very good fossil hunter." (Brusatte 2018, p. 237)

Paleontologists not only rely on artistry and "feel" in their fieldwork but also rely on imagination in the genesis of their theories. They have always told imaginative stories of how it might have been with the dinosaurs, and their visions of the remote past have necessarily stretched beyond what could be proven at the time. In the late 19th century, for example, Thomas Huxley proposed that birds evolved from dinosaurs. Many doubted the theory, and it was only in 1995, more than a hundred years later, that the first feathered dinosaur fossil turned up. (p. 275) Paleontologists like Huxley and others persist in their sometimes eccentric notions, Brusatte notes, despite such dry spells in the evidentiary record. They live according to the hopeful maxim, "Absence of evidence is not always evidence of absence." (p. 59)

How about an even "harder" science like physics? According to Albert Einstein, intuition outweighs empirical observation in the formulation of physics theories. In a 1919 essay entitled "Induction and Deduction in Physics," Einstein wrote: "The truly great advances in our understanding of nature originated in a way almost diametrically opposed to induction. The intuitive grasp of the essentials of a large complex of facts leads the scientist to the postulation of a hypothetical basic law or laws." (Quoted in Isaacson 2007, p. 118) Moreover, Einstein depended not only on deduction and intuition, but on imagination. His special theory of relativity, for instance, drew inspiration from the fanciful popular-science writer Aaron Bernstein, who led his readers on a "fantasy trip through space" ("*Eine Phantasie-Reise im Weltall*") riding on an electrical impulse in a telegraph wire. Einstein took that journey in his mind and reconceived of time and space. (Isaacson 2007, pp. 18–19; Canales 2015)

Is psychoanalysis any different from paleontology or physics when it comes to its uses of art and science? Yes, but it needn't be. Sigmund Freud wrote eloquently about the interrelation of art and science in an April 8, 1915 letter to Sandor Ferenczi. In it, Freud described the secret of productivity as "the succession of daringly playful fantasy and relentlessly realistic criticism." (Freud 1915) The description could be applied to all scientific work, and for that matter to every art.

Anna Freud lived her father's creed as a psychoanalyst who could be both artful and scientific. She was herself an innovator who described original defense mechanisms like "altruistic surrender" and "identification with the aggressor," she enlarged our theoretical understanding of the defenses involved in grief, and she founded the discipline of child analysis as a field with its own separate practices and views of child development. "[S]he also could regress creatively," writes her biographer Elisabeth Young-Bruehl, "enjoying what Ernst Kris called 'regression in the service of the ego.'" (Young-Bruehl 1988, p. 380) On the other hand, she collaborated much more closely with experimental psychologists than her father ever did. The collaboration yielded the first psychoanalytic diagnostic questionnaire and the Hampstead Index, the first organized compendium of psychoanalytic case studies. Anna Freud had this to say about Liselotte Frankl, one of the experimental psychologists with whom she worked at the Hampstead Clinic:

> She does not paint pictures (as we more daring people do), she builds with bricks (which is probably much less pleasure). She is a very good teacher when she is alone with the students and, I believe, the Clinic feels that her need for solid structures serves as a very good counterweight

against my quicker flights of imagination... I value her very much as a coworker. (Quoted in Young-Bruehl 1988, pp. 373–374)

In practice, however, most psychoanalysts have excelled at the artistry of therapy and at creative theorizing more than they have at "relentlessly realistic criticism," which in other sciences usually means testing one's hypotheses through experiment and meticulous data collection. I have suggested previously that emotional factors have long interfered with psychoanalysts' efforts to test and prove their hypotheses. (Ratner 2018, 2019) I would argue that this aversion to proof underlies some analysts' inclinations to view psychoanalysis as art, not science.

To illustrate the problematic consequences of this false dichotomy between art and science in psychoanalysis, I would like to consider the case of Georg Groddeck, the physician and novelist who first coined the term "*Es*" or "Id." In 1923 Freud borrowed the term from Groddeck, who had used it somewhat differently in his own writing, and repurposed it for his classic tripartite *Id-Ego-Superego* picture of the personality. But Groddeck made another, more critical contribution to science than naming the Id. "There can be few doubts," writes Lazslo Antonio Avila, "that Groddeck was the founder of modern psychosomatic medicine." (Avila 2003, p. 97) Just as hysteria and neurosis could be explained by unconscious, irrational emotion and relieved by conscious, rational recognition of it, Groddeck argued, so could physical syndromes like chronic pain. Groddeck wrote in *Imago* in 1922, "The symptom of *neurosis*—and I personally believe the same thing is true of *organic* symptoms—express symbolically a tendency of the unconscious." (Quoted in Grotjahn 1945, p. 16)

Martin Grotjahn has suggested that Groddeck epitomized the "intuitive" type of analyst, versus the "more learned" or scientific type. (Grotjahn 1945, p. 22) Groddeck never formally trained as an analyst, but he read Freud's work and applied it to the treatment of psychosomatic illnesses at his clinic in Baden Baden. He published in psychoanalytic journals and also published fantastical novels. Hristeva and Poster tell us that "Groddeck was not part of a group, he never established a school, and he introduced himself as a 'wild analyst' at the 6th International Psychoanalytic Congress in The Hague in 1920 in spite of the fact that he had been accepted and welcomed by Freud." (Hristeva and Poster 2013, p. 250) He empathized so deeply with his patients' irrational ideations, rooted in the magical thinking of their childhoods and the dream-logic of their defense mechanisms, that he came to prize fluency in the irrational language of the unconscious over fluency in the rhetoric of science, as if the two were incompatible:

> If I then were told that all this is nonsense, I must take it, but I keep on believing in it even without proof. Yes, perhaps *because* there is no proof. The longer one concerns oneself with proof, the more suspicious one becomes of it. If someone should tell me: "You indulge in fantasies"—I would reply, "Yes, and I thank God for it." (Quoted in Grotjahn 1945, p. 16)

Making such colorful and provocative statements in defiance of conservative scientific mores may have earned him Freud's respect, but it unsettled many other leaders of the psychoanalytic movement who were fighting to establish the credibility of their new field. (Avila 2003, pp. 95–96; Bos 1992, p. 435)

Having rejected science and critical thinking, Groddeck could be over-reaching and reductive. "In Groddeck's psychosomatics," Avila writes, "intentionality can be found behind all disease." (Avila 2003, p. 89) Such a notion sweeps aside shelves full of pathophysiology with startling naïveté, and furthermore embarrasses Freudian interpretation with its cavalier and distorted uses of it. When Groddeck for example diagnosed the presbyopia of middle age as the expression of an unconscious wish not to see, he was ignoring the material reality of the eye, which obeys natural laws of its own; we now understand presbyopia as a stiffening of the lens with age, which hampers changes of focus. Alas, entropy is no product of psychology, but a feature of the physical universe that does not respect human intentions, whether conscious or unconscious. Groddeck's way of practicing medicine and psychoanalysis could be reckless.

His idea, however, that a physical symptom could be "a kind of speech" (quoted in Avila 2003, p. 90) expressing an unconscious emotion, was a valuable insight if applied more judiciously. Many experts now agree that psychosomatic factors should be considered, for example, in cases of chronic low back pain, a condition which affects as much as 10% of the U.S. population and whose prevalence may still be rising. (Freburger et al. 2009). Physician John Sarno, a specialist in rehabilitation medicine, has described his success treating chronic low back pain with a simple psychotherapeutic intervention: urging patients to consider a psychosomatic explanation instead of a structural explanation. Merely considering the possibility relieved many patients of pain. (Sarno 2007)

Sarno cites Freud as an influence, but the literature on psychosomatic medicine generally makes little use of Freudian psychology and the field is in any case very young. Only in the last 20 years have subspecialties in psychosomatic medicine been recognized by accrediting bodies. Consequently, low back pain continues to be treated with drugs and surgery at a high rate, despite changes in published treatment guidelines, which now urge that "a biopsychosocial framework should guide management of low back pain" with "less emphasis on pharmacological and surgical treatments." In 2011, for example, Americans spent $13 billion on spinal fusion surgeries, which amounted to the "highest aggregate hospital costs of any surgical procedure" that year. (Foster et al. 2018, pp. 2369, 2375) Meanwhile, we're in the middle of an opioid crisis spurred in part by a general problem with pain and a hunger for anesthesia. (Stoicea et al. 2019) More psychotherapy and less opioids would benefit millions of people.

What if Groddeck had more carefully observed Freud's productivity credo and followed his "daringly playful fantasy" with some "relentlessly realistic criticism"? Perhaps more psychoanalysts would have listened to him. As it was, they generally did not. Felix Deutsch, Franz Alexander, and a few others continued Groddeck's work on psychosomatic medicine, but the psychoanalytic mainstream ignored him. Over the past 50 years, psychoanalysis itself has been marginalized, putting Groddeck's work at an even farther remove from mainstream medicine. Groddeck's shocking idea—that the unconscious can speak not only in dreams, hysteria, and neurosis but also in real physical symptoms like back pain—remains obscure. From its remote position in the intellectual hills, it cannot reach the millions of sufferers of chronic low back pain.

Even if Groddeck had been better able to merge art and science in his own professional life, however, the failure of the wider psychoanalytic community to embrace experimental science would have limited Groddeck's reach, just as it's ultimately limited Freud's reach. It doesn't necessarily matter how well individual practitioners live up to scientific and artistic ideals, but it does matter how well a community does. The psychopharmacology community has invested so thoroughly in the inductive process that it often neglects creative, theoretical, original thinking and practices a psychiatry barren of insight. The psychoanalytic community's underdeveloped apparatus for testing its assumptions and new ideas, on the other hand, has endangered its theories just as much by failing to nurture them from the critical and empirical side. Instead of looking to evidence, for example, to test and refine Groddeck's psychosomatic theories, the field has taken its usual approach of assigning him a camp. Some might say, "He is an Artist and a wild analyst, not a Scientist, so I needn't pay attention to his flaky ideas." Other analysts meanwhile celebrate him for a postmodern approach "marked by anti-scientism and a more philosophical, speculative attitude than Freud's psychoanalysis." (Hristeva and Poster 2009,

p. 235) Hristeva and Poster attribute to Groddeck a salutary "maternal turn" in the direction of psychoanalysis. Both rejection or celebration of Groddeck as an artist, not a scientist, reflect a defensive attitude of "splitting and avoidance."

There is simply no need to divorce art from science or theory from experiment in psychoanalysis or in any other field. As Grotjahn concludes:

> It would be wrong to call Groddeck an artist—which he was—in opposition to a scientist—which he also was. To differentiate between Art and Science in analysis would be a meaningless undertaking. The question is just as falsely put as the question concerning the Body-Mind problem once was wrongly formulated. The true problem is in both questions the interrelation between the one and the other part. (Grotjahn 1945, p. 22)

The practical consequences of the failure to integrate art and science are huge for both psychoanalysis and for patients who could benefit from a Freudian style of treatment. In the case of chronic low back pain, the U.S. healthcare system wastes vast resources on the wrong treatments, patients suffer, and psychoanalysts forfeit an opportunity to expand their reach and lead the nascent field of psychosomatic medicine.

If the field of psychoanalysis is ever to stop perseverating on whether it is an art or a science and instead wed the two—or *weld* them as the case may require—psychoanalysts will have to recognize the longstanding problem of their aversion to proof, to inductive method, and to academia, an aversion that Groddeck, Freud, and even Anna Freud shared to varying degrees. When I have presented my work on proof aversion to certain analysts they have responded with a yawn and told me they are "bored as can be" with being "lectured" about evidence. Such chaste devotion to an unfertile status quo reminds me of the Protestant sect once known as the Shakers, who advocated celibacy among their members so successfully that they no longer exist.

References

Avila L. (2003). Georg Groddeck: originality and exclusion. *Hist Psychiatry.* 14(1):83–101.

Bos, J. (1992). On the origin of the id (*das Es*). *Int Rev Psycho-Anal.* 19:433–443.

Brusatte, S. (2018). *The Rise and Fall of the Dinosaurs: A New History of a Lost World.* New York: William Morrow.

Canales, J. (2015). Albert Einstein's Sci-Fi Stories. *The New Yorker.* November 20, 2015. https://www.newyorker.com/tech/annals-of-technology/albert-einsteins-sci-fi-stories, accessed July 25, 2019.

Esterson, A. (2001). The mythologizing of psychoanalytic history: deception and self-deception in Freud's accounts of the seduction theory episode. *Hist Psychiatry.* 12(47):329–352.

Foster, N. et al. (2018). Prevention and treatment of low back pain: evidence, challenges, and promising directions. *Lancet.* 391: 2368–83.

Freburger, J. et al. (2009). The rising prevalence of chronic low back pain. *Arch Intern Med.* Feb 9;169(3):251–8.

Freud, S. (1915). Letter from Sigmund Freud to Sándor Ferenczi, April 8, 1915. In: Falzeder, E. and Brabant E., eds. (1996). *The Correspondence of Sigmund Freud and Sandor Ferenczi Volume 2, 1914–1919.* Cambridge: Belknap, 55–57.

Grotjahn, M. (1945). Georg Groddeck and his Teachings about Man's Innate Need for Symbolization: A Contribution to the History of Early Psychoanalytic Psychosomatic Medicine. *Psychoanal Rev.* 32(1):9–24.

Hristeva, G. and Poster, M. (2013). Georg Groddeck's Maternal Turn: Its Evolution and Influence on Early Psychoanalysts. *Am J Psychoanal.* 73(3):228–253.

Isaacson, W. (2007). *Einstein: His Life and Universe.* New York: Simon and Schuster.

McHugh, P. (2006). *The Mind Has Mountains: Reflections on Society and Psychiatry*. Baltimore: Johns Hopkins.

Nuttall, A. (2007 [1983]). *A New Mimesis: Shakespeare and the Representation of Reality*. New Haven: Yale.

Ratner, A. (2018). The Psychoanalyst's Resistance to the Task of Proof. *Psychoanal Rev*. 105(2):157–186.

Ratner, A. (2019). *The Psychoanalyst's Aversion to Proof*. New York: IPBooks.

Sarno, J. (2007). *The Divided Mind*. New York: Harper.

Stoicea, N. et al. (2019). Current perspectives on the opioid crisis in the US healthcare system: A comprehensive literature review. *Medicine*. 2019 May; 98(20):e15425.

Stucky, R. (2000). Paleontology: The Window to Science Education. UC Berkeley Museum of Paleontology. https://ucmp.berkeley.edu/fosrec/Stucky.html, accessed July 24, 2019.

Young-Bruehl, E. (1988). *Anna Freud: A Biography*. New York: Summit.

Review of "Georg Groddeck and the Interrelation of Art and Science in Psychoanalysis"

Mark Poster

Austin Ratner clearly understands, as he states in his first sentence, that "Art versus Science is a false dichotomy." Yet he is preoccupied with a critique of psychoanalysis for failing to carry out sufficient scientific research. In this paper, he lays this critique at the feet of Georg Groddeck, a German physician highly esteemed by Sigmund Freud and mentor to Sandor Ferenczi, Freida Fromm-Reichmann, Erich Fromm and Karen Horney.

In order to better understand the roots of Ratner's critique, I read his book *The Psychoanalyst's Aversion to Proof* (2019). In that book he grounds the same critique at the feet of Sigmund Freud. He cites Freud's personal failings—shame, anxiety and Oedipal guilt about exposing his sexual theory—as the basis for Freud's "inviolate silence" in the face of calls for scientific study of psychoanalysis. He may as well have added Freud's formation of a Secret Committee as a "central committee for polemics." Or, just as well, the formation of the International Psychoanalytic Association wherein only *he* would decide who could be a member. Such "adherents" would publish their names as such and others would be "repudiated" (Freud, 1910). That decision resulted in the loss of Eugen Bleuler, his most esteemed supporter, who left specifically because, as he wrote to Freud, such is the stuff of religion, not science (Alexander and Selesnick, 1966). Indeed, Alfred North Whitehead (1917) warned, "A science which hesitates to forget its founders is lost."

Ratner's critique re: the relative neglect of scientific research in psychoanalysis, starting with Freud and extending through his epigones, is well-researched and well-taken. Ratner admits to having "a decidedly Freudian-rationalist worldview" (p. 186). He further traces what he describes as a postmodern, relational view back to ancient skepticism and the *verum factum* (made truth) of 18th-century philosopher Giambattista Vico (i.e., not a new paradigm shift, but another form of authoritarianism). Nevertheless, there is scientific value in both nomothetic (general laws) and idiographic (specific cases) research.

Ratner generously shares with the reader of his book his personal history of losing his biological father at age 3 and being warmly raised in the Hannah Perkins psychoanalytic nursery in Shaker Heights, Ohio. Accordingly, his attachment to psychoanalysis at its best is personal and emotional. Later, he trained at Johns Hopkins under Paul McHugh and endorsed Eric Kandel's call for the objective study of the psychoanalytic treatment procedure. Perhaps having teachers who do not practice psychoanalysis influenced Ratner's valuing of science over art, even when his premise is that such is a false dichotomy. Ratner's view of both Freud and Groddeck, not to mention psychoanalysis and psychosomatic medicine, seems to be both aggrandized and then subjected to inordinate criticism. Ratner correctly notes that "psychoanalysis itself has been marginalized." However, the reasons for this are much more complex than Freud's personality defects (see Eisold, 2007; Stepansky, 2009). Likewise, psychosomatic medicine has long since been intertwined with and/or superseded by consultation-liaison psychiatry. The reasons for this are also complex and largely related to politics and funding (see Brown, 2000; Lipsett, 2001). Furthermore, while the psychological component of physical illness is very much larger than Ratner suggests, psychoanalysis is a very minor component of the alternative medicine and bodily treatment healthcare industry.

Ratner charges that my co-author Galina Hristeva and I were

"splitting" when we described Groddeck's "maternal turn" (2013). On the contrary, we were noting the important addition that Groddeck (1923; and later Horney, 1926; Gilligan, 1982; Corpt, 2017; and many others) made by adding a maternal perspective to Freud's phallocentric psychoanalytic theory. Indeed, Ratner acknowledged in his book with regard to this very issue that Horney (who credited Groddeck in her landmark 1926 paper challenging Freud's male bias) "was right and Freud was wrong" (p. 156). Just to highlight the complexity, Hristeva herself has written a whole book (2008), available in German, that too was highly critical of Groddeck's anti-scientism.

Freud was actually very interested in maintaining *die Sache* (the cause, or psychoanalytic movement) on a scientific basis. However, he also was highly ambitious (see Breger, 2009). When Freud lost his Aryan hope, Carl Jung, as a successor, he embarked on an authoritarian path (as Ratner properly notes). It can be noted that only months previously Freud had taken an avuncular and humble stance and credited Breuer and his hysterical patient Anna O. (Bertha Pappenheim) with founding psycho-analysis (Freud, 1910a, p. 9).

Ferenczi coined the term *utraquism* (1933a, p. 221) to describe Freud's ability to bridge psychology and medicine, the very linkage of art and science that Ratner espouses. In that paper, titled "Freud's Influence on Medicine" (1933a), Ferenczi wrote that Freud's "intellectual honesty led him to the realization of the fact that the psychic life is only accessible from the subjective side by means of introspective methods...Thus Freud became a dualist, a term that most scientists at that time and even today considered almost shameful. I do not believe that Freud objected to the monistic conception of knowledge. His dualism merely states that this unification will be possible neither at present nor in the near future" (p. 221). To the credit of Ferenczi, he wrote this paper even as Freud was browbeating him about publishing his own trauma theory in what has become a landmark paper in all of traumatology, Ferenczi's *Confusion of Tongues* (1933b).

Groddeck was more comfortable with monism. Ironically, he is credited with being "the father of psychosomatic medicine," a dualistic term of which he would not approve. Nor was he interested in being the father of any theory or movement. As Freud said, Groddeck was "not a propagandist." He was a master clinician who treated patients from all over Europe. Groddeck was steeped in the medical science of Berlin, his own physician father and his mentor Schwenninger, a strict authoritarian physician. But being a clinician, he came to appreciate that all disease had a *causa interna* and a *causa externa*. Groddeck found that listening to and using his concept of *das Es* as an interpersonal, even an inter-psychic, positive construct brought about remarkable therapeutic results, including in patients with physical illness. Freud, however, appropriated Groddeck's *das Es* and turned it into the wild Id of his more scientific appearing tri-partite model. Groddeck was more interested in trying to understand (*verstehen*) the individual case whereas Freud prioritized designing a model of the mind as a scientific explanation (*erklaren*). Freud recognized that Groddeck and Ferenczi shared an "artistico-intuive" bent. That is why Freud immediately referred his "loyal son" Sandor Ferenczi to Groddeck, and they became great friends (Poster, 2009). They analyzed each other (certainly not a scientific undertaking in the strict sense, but very much so in the sense of trial-and-error experimentation). Ferenczi wrote to Freud that Groddeck was the "master of psychoanalysis *in organicis*" (Poster et al, 2016).

Being a talented writer himself, Ratner might be interested to know that English professor and psychoanalyst Peter Rudnytsky (2002) described Groddeck's *The Book of the It* as "arguably the greatest masterpiece of psychoanalytic literature" (p. 163). Furthermore, Rudnytsky wrote, "It is not an overstatement to say that *The Ego and the Id* has become a book of the past, whereas *The Book of the It*—like Ferenczi's *Clinical Diary*—remains a book for the future" (p. 143).

Groddeck and Ferenczi's works are still being researched by the *Groddeck Gesellschaft* and the *International Ferenczi*

Society, respectively. Each has international conferences and numerous valuable publications. Freud's works also stimulate ongoing discussion and debate, albeit marginalized from medicine and saddled with the baggage related to the political power structure that Freud created, just as Bleuler predicted. That's where I agree with Ratner that a scientific basis for testing and pruning would be useful. But beyond the historical political barriers, the objective study of an intersubjective process remains a daunting task. When Freud ventured into the realm of psychology, he understood that his efforts would, at best, build a scaffolding for others later to build upon. Ratner's call is consistent with Freud's wish.

Mark F. Poster, MD
1600 Washington Street, Apt. 121
West Newton, MA 02465

mfpmd@comcast.net

References

Alexander, F.G., and Selesnick, S.T. (1966). *The history of psychiatry: an evaluation of psychiatric thought and practice from prehistoric times to the present*, Harper and Row: New York.

Breger, L. (2009). *A dream of undying fame: How Freud betrayed his mentor and invented psychoanalysis*, New York: Basic books.

Brown, T.M. (2000). The rise and fall of American psychosomatic medicine, New York Academy of Medicine, November 29, 2000 (Rise_&_Fall_PSM.pdf).

Corpt, E. (2017). Maternal ethics and the therapeutic work of protecting open futures, *Psychoanalytic Inquiry* 37 (6): 412–418.

Eisold, K. (2007). The erosion of our profession, *Psychoanalytic Psychology* 24 (1): 1–9.

Ferenczi, S. (1933a). Freud's influence on medicine, *Psychoanalytic Movement* 5 (3): 217–229.

__(1933b). Language confusion between the adults and the child: The language of tenderness and passion, *International Journal of Psychoanalysis* 19 (1–2): 5–15.

Freud, S. (1910a). Five Lectures on Psycho-analysis, *Standard Edition*, Vol. XI, London: Hogarth Press, 1953, 1–56.

__(1910b). Wild Psycho-Analysis, *Standard Edition*, Vol. XI, London: Hogarth Press, 1953, 226–227.

Gilligan, C. (1982). *In a Different Voice: Psychological Theory and Women's Development*, Cambridge, MA: Harvard University Press.

Groddeck, G. (1923). *The Book of the It*, 1950, London: Vision Press.

Horney, K. (1926). The flight from womanhood: The masculinity-complex in women, as viewed by men and women, *The International Journal of Psychoanalysis* 7: 324–339.

Hristeva, Galina (2008). *Georg Groddeck. Präsentationsformen psychoanalytischen Wissens*, Würzburg: Königshausen & Neumann.

Hristeva, G. and Poster, M. (2013). Georg Groddeck's maternal turn: Its evolution and influence on early psychoanalysts, *American Journal of Psychoanalysis* 73 (3): 228–253.

Lipsitt, D.R. (2000). Consultation-liaison psychiatry and psychosomatic medicine: The company they keep, *American Psychosomatic Society* 63: 896–909.

Poster, M.F., (2009). Ferenczi and Groddeck: Simpatico. Roots of a paradigm shift in psychoanalysis, *The American Journal of Psychoanalysis*, 69, 195–206.

Poster, M.F., Hristeva, G., and Giefer, M. (2016). Georg Groddeck: "The Pinch of Pepper" of Psychoanalysis, *American Journal of Psychoanalysis* 76 (2):161–182.

Ratner, A. (2019). *The Psychoanalyst's Aversion to Proof*, New York: IPBooks.

Rudnytsky, P. (2002). *Reading Psychoanalysis*, Ithaca, NY: Cornell University Press.

Stepansky, P.E. (2009). *Psychoanalysis at the Margins,* New York: Other Press.

Whitehead, A.N. (1916). Presidential address to the British Association for the Advancement of Science, Newcastle-on-Tyne.

Discussion of the Article by Austin Ratner "George Groddeck and the Interelation Of Art and Science in Psychoanalyis"

Marco Conci

I thank Austin Ratner for his thoughtful and stimulating paper, and also Daniel Benveniste and Arnold Richards for having invited me to join this discussion.

Reading the paper by Austin Ratner also stimulated me to read his recent book, *The psychoanalyst's aversion to proof*, and thus better understand both his critical approach to Freud and to psychoanalysis, and the nature of his preoccupation for the future of our field. Freud and his followers' allergy to the empirical confirmation of psychoanalysis as a theoretical body makes it hard for Austin Ratner to see any future for psychoanalysis.

But let me now come to the paper under discussion. Reading it not only reminded me of Saul Rosenzweig's attempts to empirically confirm psychoanalysis in the 1930s and of Freud's lack of interest for such a work, which Austin Ratner does deal with in his book. It also reminded me of a similar preoccupation which Harry Stack Sullivan (1892–1949) had expressed already in the 1930s, in terms of the necessity to find empirical and even statistical confirmation of our clinical work. As far as Georg Groddeck (1866–1934) is concerned, it is true that he founded psychosomatic medicine not in terms of controlled clinical trials, as Franz Alexander and Florence Dunbar would start doing in the 1930s, but in terms of using his creative imagination to explore the pathogenesis of a whole series of organic and physical symptoms and illnesses. From this point of view, it is true that he was as one-sided as many other pioneers have been. But we do have to be still thankful to him for such a pioneering contribution as *The book of the It,* that is, for having tried to describe the ways in which our psychological life and conflicts influence our bodily functions.

As to the question "Art versus Science," we of course have to do with a false dichotomy. As a medical doctor and a psychoanalyst, I see myself as working with my patients as an "artist," committed to working in a very individual way with every one of them, and, at the same time, as a "scientist," applying to the work a whole series of theoretical principles and scientific laws discovered and formulated by Freud and by the following generations of psychoanalysts. For example: working with a hysteric patient, I can see how the general law of psychic repression (formulated by Freud and Breuer in 1895) plays a role in the genesis of her particular and unique symptoms. The scientific law according to which a symptom is the result of a failure in our memory system is still valid!

From this point of view, we can even say that Freud was very much inclined to offer to his patients, in every single session, more than one proof of the way of functioning of their unconscious mind.

In other words, from this point of view I would more clearly distinguish —as Austin Ratner does not seem to me to do in his book—between what I would call "clinical proof," on the one hand, and "empirical" or "experimental confirmation," on the other hand. From this point of view, I do not believe that we can talk of an "aversion to proof" on Freud's side, but only of his aversion vis-a-vis the second meaning which I am giving to the word "proof."

At the same time, it is true that if we go back to Freud's presentation of his way of working in an article such as his 1912 article "The beginning of treatment," we can see that he seems to take for granted that patients will want to work with him because of his fame rather than only once he will have demonstrated to them "the power of the unconscious." On the other hand, not having the chance of inducing in their patients the kind of transference that Freud seems to have been able to produce in his patients from the very beginning, post-Freudian authors ranging from Sullivan to Bion are very preoccupied to show to their patients "the unconscious in action" from the very first session. In other words, from this point of view, we can say that most post-Freudian authors did not share Freud's apparently minor interest in showing to his patients the way of working of psychoanalysis from the very beginning of the treatment. This is why he could use the first session talking about time and money, that is, something which we can not allow ourselves to do any more. At variance with him, we have to prove that psychoanalysis works from the very first contact with our patients—otherwise, why should they come back?

Last but not least, we cannot allow ourselves to forget the fact that the pressure toward empirical and experimental confirmation of psychoanalysis is much bigger in our time than in Freud's time, because of the different *Zeitgeist*. Not to talk about the fact that many of the patients who avail themselves of our experience and competence are still—at least in my country—people psychologically predisposed to the kind of work we do, as opposed to them being people who come to us only after having read a piece of empirical research confirming the quality of our work. The relative scarcity of such studies might influence social media and the opinion-makers, but this is mostly a problem in the sociology of knowledge and influence. In my experience, any patient who sees the connection between words, emotions and relationships is a potential patient of ours—under the condition that we know how to do our work.

Reply to Poster's and Conci's Discussions of My Paper

Austin Ratner

Many thanks to Dr. Poster and Dr. Conci for their erudite discussions of my paper and my book, *The Psychoanalyst's Aversion to Proof.* I would like to correct a few misimpressions which their discussions may have inadvertently created. Dr. Poster amends my account of the marginalization of psychoanalysis by noting that "the reasons for this [marginalization] are much more complex than Freud's personality defects." I could not agree more. While my book focuses on resistances within the field, it also acknowledges the significance of external obstacles to the public validation of psychoanalysis, including critics' resistances, anti-Semitism, and the influence of the drug and insurance industries. More than half my book looks beyond Freud to the widespread phenomenon of aversion to proof in the field of psychoanalysis at large. Proof aversion is not a "defect" belonging to any one individual but a general species of defense mechanism triggered by the task of public demonstration of psychoanalytic ideas.

Dr. Conci suggests that I am pessimistic about the future of psychoanalysis. I would put it more narrowly, but more strongly: those quarters of psychoanalysis that continue to shrink so resolutely from the task of public validation have invited their own extinction. As I state in my book, however, "The 21st century could be a good one for psychoanalysis." I devote considerable space to the many past and current thinkers—from Jacob Arlow to Mark Solms and many, many others—who have assisted in the public validation of psychoanalysis. Despite Freud's bouts of proof aversion, no one did more to explain and validate psychoanalysis, of course, than the founder himself. A diagnosis of proof aversion is in other words not a death sentence. I also devote one of four major sections of my book to the future of psychoanalysis, and include detailed, practical ideas for overcoming proof aversion in the psychoanalytic community.

On the other hand, I won't dispute Poster and Conci's observation that I fail to distinguish between various forms of proof—clinical research versus experiment, as Conci puts it, or as Poster delineates it, "idiographic" versus "nomothetic" research. Without a doubt, individual case studies are critically important to the validation of psychoanalytic ideas and remain relevant to many other disciplines, even in an age that's infatuated with statistics to a fault. I sympathize with psychoanalysts' objections to rote methods when it comes to studying a phenomenon so complex and elusive as the psyche. I would question, however, how much is really gained by making categorical distinctions between research methods. The premise behind such compartmentalized methodology is that the psyche cannot be studied from all angles like other phenomena. The end result of such compartmentalized methodology has generally been to rule out and avoid new approaches to validation and to justify and preserve old ones, or to insist that validation is a private affair among psychoanalysts, not a public goal. Why not instead treat case studies and experiments as mutually compatible strategies for psychoanalytic fact-finding and public validation? In other words, why not think in terms of "both/and" instead of "either/or"?

Psychoanalysis: Art or Science?

Arlene Kramer Richards

There used to be a name for this kind of problem: chicken or the egg? But dinosaurs laid eggs. So that one is solved. Now I asked the eminent psychoanalyst Sheldon Bach the art or science question. He said, "When I was young, I was a scientist, now I think I am more of an artist." This was a little like the chicken saying, "When I was young, I was an egg, now I am a chicken." One way of understanding this is that science is the activity of exploring the unknown while art is the communication of feelings that the artist did not know she had until she created the work of art. Without this connection to the previously unknown, the work becomes polemics decorated with beauty. The mysterious process of finding something new by communicating it is what we call art.

In other words, at the beginning of a career as a psychoanalyst, there is a great deal to be learned and learning it makes a person able to use the knowledge to communicate with patients. This learning something new is the method of science. So, the young analyst is thinking like a scientist. And the key new things for the young analyst to learn are what the patient is feeling and what the patient is thinking. Knowing how to think like a patient enables an analyst to create a dialogue that can be felt as an empathic interchange. Feeling becomes thought when the analyst inquires about it, prompting the patient to think about her own feelings and to try to put the feelings into words. The patient becomes the scientist in searching for new knowledge about her own feelings. Finding out about feelings is science; communicating them is art. In psychoanalysis, art and science are indissoluble, discovery is made in the act of communicating. Lest this sound too abstract, here is a clinical example.

A patient in the later stages of analysis said to me recently: "When you gave me that interpretation about why I gamble, I knew you were against it. So, I stopped telling you about it." I recalled the interpretation as my having made a connection between his adolescent superman fantasies and the wish to hit the jackpot. I had said both were ways to succeed without doing hard work. I thought I was being empathic. He heard my comment as disapproval. I thought I was speaking to how hard he has had to work to get to where he is in life and how uncertain he had been as an adolescent about whether he had what it took to become as successful as he wanted to be and has been.

I connected this to his experience by saying: "Now I have an even worse interpretation to give you. I think the gambling has a connection to your parents' religious faith. They believe they will have everything and be totally happy after they die. They will hit the jackpot."

I believed that the second interpretation was the result of my knowing that the first one had caused him pain and that by acknowledging that, by calling the second interpretation "even worse," I was shielding him from the worst of the injury caused by the first one. That was an artistic use of scientific knowledge. I had long ago discovered that prefacing an interpretation with an acknowledgment of how wrong, limited, and/or inaccurate it probably was gave the patient room to experience rejecting what was too soon or too painful. The immediate rejection could be spoken aloud after I had already welcomed it into the discourse. And welcoming it into the discourse gave the patient the power to think further about it without having to accept my "superior wisdom."

So, what I did know helped me to explore what I did not yet know. Specifically, I did not know whether the fantasy of winning the lottery was derived from his parents' religious beliefs. I did not understand what fed his compulsion. I had a hypothesis and his response to that hypothesis would lead us further into understanding it. The hope was that understanding it would free him from the compulsion to act it out.

From previous analyses I understood that gambling is an attempt to ward off death. Because death has no odds, all living things are destined to die from the moment of conception, there are no odds. Yet figuring out the odds for other events, like which horse will win the race, gives the gambler a sense of control over the future that cannot be attained over death. Another patient who had been orphaned at an early age taught me that. And one whose parents had been in a death camp confirmed it. His parents rejected the religion that had failed their families in the camp, but became people who played cards with their friends every weekend evening. Although they gambled for tiny stakes, they became passionate about it, surrounded it with special foods they served during the games, left their children home alone or with a teenage baby-sitter evening after evening, and even went to gamble when they were ill or exhausted. While his parents were out the little boy had the fantasy that they would die in a car crash and never come home. He stayed up until they returned, unable to sleep until he was sure they would return.

All of this experience fed my feelings about my then current patient's gambling and about how he could understand its relation to his own childhood fears. I felt scared of going too fast and getting it wrong. As the analyst, what I was feeling I called the counter-transference. I understood my fear as a clue to his feeling. I hypothesized that he was feeling fear. Giving up belief in a protective god entailed an existential fear. If there was no god to protect him, only fortune or Lady Luck could do it. And what motivated me to treat him was a wish to protect him from losing both his money and the time he could otherwise be spending with family and/or friends.

Counter-transference was a tool I had learned to use from reading Racker (2018)* when I wondered what I could do with erotic feelings towards one of my patients early in my practice. Racker helped me to understand that I could be feeling what my patient was feeling. Or I could be feeling the complement of what my patient was feeling or I could be feeling an alternation between the two. Maybe Racker's neatly bifurcated theory might more clinically be seen as an alternation of the two. If we take Racker's work as an example of a psychoanalytic clinical theory, the use I put it to was an example of the artful use of theory by an experienced clinician. This was, I think, an example of Bach's comment. I think, as well, that scientific theory is useful to the beginning clinician and helps support the work as the clinician develops her art and that it becomes less necessary as she gains experience and confidence.

References

Racker, H. (2018) *Transference and Countertransference,* New York: Routledge.

---

*Originally published in 1968, it was something I read early in my analytic training.

Discussion of Arlene Richards's Paper Psychoanalysis: Science or Art?

Adriana S. Prengler

Much has been written about psychoanalysis as both a science and as an art. While psychoanalysis as a science has roused much controversy, its artistic aspect seems less controversial.

Freudian thought began within the context of science—the environment in which Freud was immersed. He developed his "science" at the center of the Austro-Hungarian empire and as a direct disciple of many notable scientists of his time. His work as a neurologist and his years conducting histological research confirmed his scientific credentials. He started his project for a scientific psychology on a purely scientific basis to create the postulates that gave rise to psychoanalysis, explaining psychic functioning in terms of energy and dynamic forces. That is how Freud argued that psychoanalysis began within the natural sciences. But when the subject of investigation shifted to the invisible unconscious, and the instrument used became interpretation, psychoanalysis moved away, for some people, from the basic postulates of the measurable scientific method. By making this move psychoanalysis approached, at the same time, the pole of artistic creation. The fact that every unconscious is unique, and that there is the unconscious of the patient and of the analyst that are involved, gives rise to a very particular and unique space in each analytical relationship. But it is also true that we often need a measure of artistic ability to create something new.

If in psychoanalysis we were guided only by the scientific aspect, we would be understanding all patients in the same way,

191

and following the theory and technique in a uniform fashion. But the ability to make use of the theory to understand each patient in a unique and particular way adds an artistic component to our practice. Any understanding of the patient taken in a "scientific" way would lead the analyst away from the connection with his/her patient. Part of our art consists in awakening, in our patients, the desire to learn about themselves—the art of inquiring into their unique unconscious. Thus, we turn to art to immerse ourselves in the work.

It is interesting to think that in Freud's work, art has been a privileged aspect to explain some of his concepts, making science and art coexist in his work, using painting, sculpture, poetry, classical and ancient writings to explain some of his central concepts.

Art is the bearer of non-scientific knowledge, it is not the power of reason, but it gives rise to knowledge. And in our practice, a science-art hybrid is consolidated, both being insufficient by themselves, but very powerful when they come together.

Learning and mastery of the psychoanalytic theory and technique with which we identify ourselves, is not enough for a successful analysis. We need to create an environment of trust and empathy, which allows the patient to connect with the analyst with a freedom to express themselves without fear. To this we need to add the ability to find the right words so that the patient understands our interpretations and can respond affectively. These right words may reveal some of the unconscious, leading to a new discovery, and transfer to the here and now what happened there and then. It is not just about what we study, learn, understand and practice, but about a much more complex dynamism that has to do with a creative act. So, the question remains, is psychoanalysis a science or an art?

According to Wikipedia, Science is "an orderly system of structured knowledge that studies, investigates and interprets natural, social and artificial phenomena. Scientific knowledge is obtained through observation and experimentation in specific fields. Such knowledge is organized and classified on the basis of explanatory principles, whether theoretical or practical. From these questions and reasoning are generated, hypotheses are formulated, scientific principles and laws are deduced and scientific models, scientific theories and knowledge systems are constructed." Could we define psychoanalysis within this framework?

Wikipedia's definition of Art is "any activity or product carried out with an aesthetic and also communicative purpose, through which ideas, emotions and, in general, a vision of the world are expressed, through various resources, such as plastics, sound, body and mixed ... reflects the transmission of ideas and values inherent in any human culture throughout space and time ...Art is synonymous with ability, skill, talent, experience. However, art is most commonly considered as a creative activity of the human being ... as a means of human expression of a creative nature".

As Arlene Richards put it, *"One way of understanding this is that science is the activity of exploring the unknown while art is the communication of feelings that the artist did not know she had until she created the work of art. Without this connection to the previously unknown, the work becomes polemics decorated with beauty. The mysterious process of finding something new by communicating it is what we call art."* Arlene states that, art and science in psychoanalysis are indissoluble. We can say that both science and art need to be linked to have their full meaning.

Within the context of theory and technique we employ the art of metaphor: words, images, voices, that offer meaning to our patient's associations.

In the clinical case of the gambler, presented by Arlene, she offered the patient an interpretation about his gambling and when he rejected it he just avoided talking about his gambling any further. When Arlene heard of this she replied, "Now I have an even worse interpretation to give you." This prelude brought humor and empathy, as well as a freedom for the patient to disagree. That kind of intervention would also give freedom to the patient to avoid the pain of poor timing or an incorrect interpretation influenced more by the counter-transference of the analyst, than the internal reality of the patient. But more than that, it helps the patient to trust himself and his own criteria instead of just accepting the voice of the analyst as the only truth. The patient knows about himself and the analyst is there to help the patient discover his own deeper truths.

When Arlene tells us about her patient and her countertransference feelings, she shows us that using the countertransference as a tool to understand our patients is also an art. We cannot escape our countertransferential feelings, but we can use them to the benefit of the patient, if we can perceive ourselves and use our creativity to metabolize them and return them to the patient.

We could say that the emotional connection between a patient and his/her analyst also has an artistic component as it needs to be created in each interaction. Arlene not only took hold of the theory to understand her patient but also added a particular space, taking into account the uniqueness of her patient.

The analytic listening of the analyst, opens interventions with the objective of discovering new readings of the patient's history, tied to the present with repeated feelings and dynamics in the here and now, in the transference. This listening means listening far beyond science, theory, and technique. It involves an artful way of listening, that creates meaning, that may or may not be admitted and elaborated by the patient. In turn, the patient will also need to listen so that it opens the doors to creativity—the ability to transform what he/she hears from what we say and to create something new. This intervention, like Arlene's, will give the possibility that where there was more of the same (where the patient repeated the gambling behavior), new behaviors, new thoughts and feelings, new scenes, will allow him to rewrite his history through the art of modifying the role the patient plays within it. This art helps strip the analyst of the role that the patient thought the analyst should "play," as in a theater scene. It is an artistic task to be able to find a way out for what was "the usual," the repeated, the expected in the patient's life. But that interpretation, as Arlene points out, when she confesses her countertransferential feelings, tells us not only about the patient, but also about the one who formulates it, that is, about the creator of that interpretation. It will depend on the connection between the one who formulates the interpretation and the one who receives it, and on the ability of both to create and maintain a bond between them.

In psychoanalysis, we seek to connect the patient with his/her historical predeterminants, so that the past stops functioning as though it is still present through repetition. When the past finally becomes past, the repetition ceases, giving space for a future.

Each feeling, act, word, symptom, dream, can have more than one dimension, understanding or interpretation, consequently there is no absolute truth. After learning our science, this is where our art comes into action. Obviously, we do not know or prepare the interpretation in advance, but we build it in each session, from the patient's speech, using what is created in each session, which emerges and surprises the analysand-and ourselves, opening the possibility to a new understanding.

The process of finding something new by communicating it, is what Arlene calls art. When we put feelings in words, they become thoughts and the patient becomes the scientist investigating about him/herself. Arlene Richards states: *"Finding out about feelings is science, communicating them is art... In psychoanalysis, science and art are indissoluble."*

The example she gives shows that the way she communicates her interpretation to her patient is itself an art. She could have interpreted the same thing differently, but it might have created more resistance in the patient. Communicating it was an art, a new creation, something that has a meaning that is not necessarily received in the same way it was sent. It is something that is neither good nor bad, nor verifiable. It is a creation, something that did not exist before in that place. This is what we do in psychoanalysis. We create a new sense, neither good, nor bad, but always unique. Art is the ability to discover something new, and that is precisely what we strive to achieve in psychoanalysis, to discover something we did not know.

Arlene Richards cites Sheldon Bach who said that when he was young he was scientific and now he is more artistic. Perhaps beginners need to rely more on science for not being so sure of their own recently acquired abilities and sources of wisdom. That is when there is the need to rely on something verifiable, but when we grow in our practice, we can give ourselves the luxury of being more artistic, more creative, trusting that we don't need scientific proof at every step along the way. However, to get to there, it feels necessary to have been a scientist, to have been able to test our hypotheses about mental health, and then later be able to trust our art.

Arlene, echoing Bach, says that when we are more experienced, we rely more on art because our science, our knowledge, and experience have already been internalized. We know that nobody has the ultimate truth, but that everyone has their own truth. Helping others find their truth is indeed an art.

———

Science Needs Criticism: Debating the Clinical Aspects of Diverging Theoretical Schools

Joseph Schachter
Judith S. Schachter
Horst Kächele

Freud considered psychoanalysis to be a scientific discipline and psychoanalysis today continues to embrace a scientific identity. Stimulated by a recently published paper by T. Lubbe about an eight-year analysis and its termination, we have accepted Bernardi's advice to encourage discussions of clinical issues across those diverse psychoanalyses newly recognized by the IPA. However, our original paper criticizing the evidence Lubbe provided was rejected by his publisher, Psychoanalytic Review, on the basis of an "editorial policy" of not publishing critiques of previously published papers in that journal. Criticism is essential in assessing the scientific value of theoretical hypotheses. While Lubbe asserts as an empirical, clinical fact that "There is a reworking of the Oedipus complex in every termination" (p. 852), we question whether his clinical material supports this position, because we found a lack of descriptions of expressions of his patient's anger at either the therapist, his wife or other figures throughout the eight-year treatment, including termination itself. Without taking on the task of bridging the Klein/Freud chasm, we direct ourselves to his theoretically anchored but in our eyes clinically evident failure to address and deal with fundamental unresolved aspects of the patient-analyst relationship.

These are issues of science as we co-exist and seek a common ground. Moreover, even if formidable, we believe that evidence from a single analytic treatment is grossly inadequate to support a generalization of scientific value in psychoanalysis.

Introduction

The theoretical and clinical diversity inside and outside the IPA has been acknowledged. Differences of opinion are no longer solved by exclusion, formerly the stimulus for the formation of many independent associations outside the IPA. The struggle of the founder and his closest pupils towards "unity" belongs to the past. This recognition of diversity forces our professional community to clarify the areas of agreement as well as the areas of difference. We are, however, still confronted with the old problem of theory influencing therapeutic thought and deed (Fonagy 2006).

It is now officially acceptable to talk about **the** psychoanalyses, thus bringing the issue of co-existence and the *common ground* to the fore (Wallerstein 1988). Today's trend is towards a pluralistic approach, both theoretical and technical, which Tuckett (1998, p. 446) believes requires formulating criteria for competent treatment to be drawn up; "first, do no harm," being the very least (Tuckett 2005). This expansion has made it even harder to differentiate between various directions than it was during the spread of psychodynamic psychotherapy in the fifties.

It is our belief that the scale of pluralism, which in its entirety can be said to give psychoanalysis a chaotic image, is largely under-estimated. Earlier, Wallerstein (2005), for example, sought and found binding similarities in clinical observations by stating that both general elucidative theories and those specific to certain schools have a metaphorical character which only questionably matches the phenomena that are to be observed. While these metaphors function to make sense of clinical data, they are an impediment to dialogue as well as empirical research since it is not possible, at present, to check these data in comparative studies. In this context we offer a critical conception implementing Bernardi's (2002) suggestion that "research should centre on particular instances though it should at the same time arrive at conclusions that could be generally valid "(p. 852).

The Issue: The Oedipus Complex in Termination

This paper is a response to a recent published case history by T. Lubbe, a Tavistock trained analyst, entitled "The Preoedipal and Oedipal Structure of Termination: An In-depth Case Study" published in Psychoanalytic Review (2016). In it he summarizes an eight-year psychoanalytic treatment conducted at four sessions per week, while focusing on the termination phase. He posits that the Oedipus Complex is the central organizing force in all psychoanalytic terminations during which it is recapitulated. This demonstration is of a "universal": "There is a re-working of the Oedipus complex in every termination" (p. 852).

Although PEP lists 223 papers about termination, Lubbe limits his bibliography to nine Kleinian analysts and three papers by J. Novick. He fails to note the large number of criticisms of the concept of termination. His publication preceded our recent proposal (Schachter et al., 2018) to formulate a new concept of termination which we have named, "Progression."

Psychoanalytic Review, the journal which published this paper, rejected our limited initial responsive paper on the basis of its "editorial policy" not to publish critiques of papers it had published. This struck us as a blow to the future of psychoanalysis as a science and so we reoriented our focus from a clinical critique to a critique in defense of the scientific nature of psychoanalysis. Consider, for a moment, if *all* psychoanalytic journals adopted the "editorial policy" of the Psychoanalytic Review and refused to publish manuscripts that were critical of papers previously published by their own journal, making it necessary to seek other outlets and further splintering dialogue. That might make it *impossible to publish any critique of a previously published psychoanalytic paper.* The absence of criticism of theoretical, clinical and empirical psychoanalytic papers would undermine any scientific aspirations or credentials of psychoanalysis, separating our field from other sciences.

Parenthetically, the author, T. Lubbe, failed to respond to our inquiry about the outcome of the post-termination contact which the analyst – to our real surprise—had proposed and to which the patient had agreed. If evaluation of the effects upon the patient of this post-analytic contact could be assessed, it could add to the growing psychoanalytic interest in and controversy about post-analytic patient-analyst contact (Schachter, J. & Johan, M., 1989; Novick, J. & Novick, K.K., 1991; Novick, J., 1997; Schachter, J., Martin, G., Gundle, M., & O'neil, M.K., 1997; Schachter, J. & Brauer, l., 2001; Roose, S. P., Yang, S., Caligor, E., Cabaniss, D.L., Luber, B., Donovan, J., Rosen, P., & Forand, N.R., 2004; Geller, J.D., & Freedman, N., 2011; Kantrowitz, J.L., 2015).

Progression (Termination)

An alternative conception of termination, named "progression," has been derived from a "Family Model" of psychoanalytic treatment (Schachter, J., Kächele, H. & Schachter, J., 2017). "A patient who has completed treatment may have become independent, self-aware, and engaged in a more satisfying life, while also valuing subsequent periodic contacts with the former analyst" (p. 160).

The complexity of the concept of "progression" (termination) is illustrated by the 223 published clinical papers in the psychoanalytic literature. A book about progression (termination), "Good Enough Endings," edited by the relational oriented author J. Salberg (2010) presented 16 papers while another book by the ego-psychological author J.L. Kantrowitz (2015), "The Myths of Termination," provided further important contributions.

In addition to hundreds of *clinical* papers, there are numerous *empirical* studies that investigate the phenomenon of progression, without specifically including Oedipal formulations (Kantrowitz, Katz & Paolitto, 1990; Schachter, 1990; Schachter, 1992; Schachter & Brauer, 2001; Craige, 2002; Tessman, 2003; Craig, 2006; and Geller & Friedman, 2011).

Lubbe's proposed original, but otherwise unsubstantiated hypothesis, that "oedipal structures take hold of the termination process so that the final working through and the resolution of the transference/countertransference can be maximized" (p. 819) is, we believe, an example of the analyst finding in his patient's analysis what he expected to find, just what Fonagy had warned of.

The psychoanalytic literature is studded with examples of analysts presenting corroborating clinical evidence for theoretical assumptions, only to discover later that the theoretical assumptions themselves were faulty. Most recently, e.g., homosexuality was regarded as intrinsically psychopathological, but both extensive empirical and psychological studies decimated that belief. We strongly propose that clinical findings, therefore, should be viewed cautiously until empirically substantiated. The conclusion that "There is a reworking of the Oedipus complex in every termination" (p. 852) falls within this parameter, particularly since its base is the Oedipus complex, which itself still lacks empirical validation.

The Role of Anger in Lubbe's Psychoanalytic Treatment

We were attracted to this paper in part because we felt the rich descriptions provided an opportunity for interactional psychoanalytic discussion. Once the patient set a date to terminate treatment, Lubbe writes, "a pall of superficiality fell over the work" (p.835). This, we believe, may reflect the patient's failure to express anger about the analyst's decision to end treatment. We note, however, that five months prior to the end of treatment the patient forgot to pay his bill and also dreamed that his nipples seemed to be in the wrong place; he cut them off with a scissors, but put them in the wrong place, so he cut them off again and placed them where they belonged. We see this ample material as replete with significant enactments and messages; the analyst himself declares shock at the dream. He recognized that it reflected the patient's concern about ending the psychoanalytic treatment: *"My patient seemed to fear expressing anger or any sense of outrage about ending"* (p. 839, our italics added). But he fails to describe exploring or discussing this significant possible insight with the patient.

Three sessions before the end of the analysis the patient reported a dream in which he killed a man. The patient said "he had never had it out with his father ..." (p. 846). While Lubbe reflected that it was "his intention to stir up doubt in my mind as to whether I had done the right thing in going along with his ending" (p. 849), he also commented that "he seemed unaware of how similarly he sometimes behaved like her (his mother), especially when he was dealing with his therapist" (p. 849). No further transference interpretations are presented.

The Role of Anger in Psychoanalytic Theory and Practice

Before we return to the issue of the need for an open dialogue about theoretical disagreement, we want to explore further one of the clinical characteristics of this analytic treatment. We accept that the evidence of Lubbe's patient's hostility toward his father and identification with his mother is clearly consistent with theoretical oedipal factors in the patient's development and in treatment, as we know them. However, we find that the more significant *clinical data* described in this treatment was the patient's inability, during the eight years of analytic therapy, to express anger directly toward his therapist, his wife, or others, which we believe reflects a fundamental undiscussed and unresolved aspect of the patient-analyst relationship not expressed other than in the noted bill default. The occurrence of a psychoanalytic patient's expression of angry feelings are distinctly different from a patient's *acts of aggression*, i.e., acts interpreted as hostility, such as a patient's failure to pay a bill. For example, while Lubbe admits to being "shocked" about the patient's dream about cutting off his nipples, he does not mention the possibility that it expresses anger toward the analyst redirected towards the self.

We considered that our reading of the clinical material might be idiosyncratic, so in order to gain a perspective on the patient's apparent failure to express anger during treatment, we started by reviewing the frequency with which various concepts, including anger and aggression, were listed in each of the indexes of twenty-one volumes of Freud's collected works

Table 1

Number of Freud Volumes with Listing Number of Papers in PEP		
Sexuality	21	526
Anxiety	20	590
Aggression	18	364
Depression	12	486
Anger	2	46

(two volumes contained no index) to evaluate Freud's interest in these concepts. The frequency of listing of these concepts in the indexes is presented in the first column in table 1. The second column provides the number of psychoanalytic papers catalogued by PEP for each of these same concepts. This table enables us, for example, to see that sexuality is listed in the indexes of all twenty-one volumes, whereas anger is listed in the indexes of only two volumes of the collected works. The number of PEP papers in each category is listed in column 2.

Absent a statistical test, clearly the number of papers published in PEP for each concept parallels the distribution of the frequency of these concepts in the indexes of Freud's collected works. Freud's interests have had a pervasive effect upon the formation of psychoanalysis and the conduct of psychoanalytic treatment. The rare listings of feelings of 'anger' suggest it was not considered as significant a psychoanalytic concept as 'aggression,' which is an *action*, not a *feeling*. PEP lists 364 papers about aggression compared to the noted 46 in the table about anger.

How do we regard this disparity? We agree with Liekierman (1987) that "Anger, being a familiar everyday feeling of an obvious kind, has received minimal attention in analytic thinking, which has preferred instead to concentrate on the concept of aggression" (p. 143). Leverenz (1975), among others, highlights the developmental significance of anger: "Yet also anger provides the first sense of self as a separate being who needs and fears" (p. 423). In this context, Fonagy, Moran and Target (1993) suggest that aggression is not an instinct in Freud's terms but a defense against threats to the psychological self (p. 482) as well as a sign that separation is recognized. Pizer (2014) provides a rare example in the literature of the therapeutic benefits of a patient's expression of anger against her analyst. The patient said: "I came to you in the first place because I could not work...And you kept telling me I'd start soon as a result of our work. That didn't happen. But after I expressed my anger about your paper something changed. I just realized I was on my own, as always, and I better get on with it" and then the patient lets Pizer know that even before receiving the analyst's revision, "I intended to email and tell you that I started working again" (p. 27).

In practice, we believe that Lubbe may have failed to address and deal with fundamental unresolved aspects of the patient's anger in transference and counter-transference, because of his focus on those theoretical oedipal factors he deemed critical in ending analysis.

Conclusion

Freud was concerned that a focus on the therapeutic demands of analytic treatment might distract from the creation of psychoanalytic theory: "I only want to feel assured that the therapy will not destroy the science" [theory] (1926, p. 254). As noted, Lubbe appears more concerned about analytic theory than about the clinical aspects of this analytic treatment, leading him to neglect the need to address the patient's failure to express anger at the analyst while defensively allowing his patient to recapitulate a recognized childhood role to satisfy his parents.

As Bernardi (2002) elegantly has noted, major difficulties for psychoanalytic science occur whenever "defensive states aimed at keeping each theory safe from the opposing party's arguments" (p.851) prevent the selection of the most useful conceptions of psychoanalytic treatment. Consideration of such alternate clinical and theoretical conceptions must be debated, discussed, and critically evaluated by empirical research for psychoanalysis to be considered a science. Our hope for our science is to use such explorations to enable the selection of the most useful psychoanalytic conceptions. Criticism is the lifeblood of science. To eschew it, is to condemn psychoanalysis to mediocrity.

References

Bernardi, R. E. (2002). The need for true controversies in psycho-analysis. The debates on Melanie Klein and Jacques Lacan in the Rio de la Plata. *International Journal of Psycho-Analysis, 83*: 851–873.

Craige, H. (2002). Mourning analysis: The post-termination phase. *Journal of the American Psychoanalytic Association, 50*:507–550.

__(2006). Termination, terminable and interminable: Commentary on a paper by Jody Messler Davies. *Psychoanalytic Dialogue* *16*:585–590.

Fonagy, P. (2006). The failure of practice to inform theory and the role of implicit theory in bridging the transmission gap. In J. Canestri (Ed.), *Psychoanalysis: From practice to theory* (pp. 69–86). Chichester: Wiley.

Fonagy, P., Moran, G. S., & Target, M. (1993). Aggression and the psychological self. *International Journal of Psycho-Analysis, 74*: 471–485.

Freud, S. (1926). The question of lay analysis. *The Standard Edition of the Complete Psychological Works of Freud,* London: Hogarth Press, *20*:179–258.

Geller, J.D. & Freedman, N. (2011). Representations of the therapeutic dialogue and the post-termination phase of psychotherapy. In N. Freedman, M. Hurvich, R. Ward, J. Geller & J.D. Hoffenberg (Eds.), *Another kind of evidence: Studies on internalization, annihilation anxiety, and progressive symbolization in psychoanalytic process* (pp. 55–66). London: Karnac.

Kantrowitz, J. L. (1993). Outcome research in psychoanalysis: Review and reconsideration. *Journal of the American Psychoanalytic Association, 41S:* 313–329.

Kantrowitz, J. L. (2015). *Myths of termination* New York: Routledge.

Kantrowitz, J.L., Katz, A.L., & Paolitto, F. (1990). Follow-up of psychoanalysis five to ten years after termination: Stability of change. *Journal of the American Psychoanalytic Association, 38*: 471–496.

Leverez, D. (1975) Anger and individualism. *Psychoanalytic Review, 62*:407–428.

Likierman, M (1987) The function of anger in human conflict. *International Journal of Psycho-Analysis, 14*:143–161.

Lubbe, T. (2016). The preoedipal and oedipal structure of termination. An in-depth case study. *Psychoanalytic Review, 103*:819–854.

Pizer, B (2014) A clinical exploration of moving anger forward: Intimacy, anger and creative freedom. *Psychoanalytic Dialogue, 24*:14–28.

Salberg, J., ed. (2010). *Good enough endings: Breaks, interruptions, and and terminations from contemporary relational perspectives.* New York: Routledge.

Schachter, J. (1990). Post-termination patient-analyst contact: Analysts' attitudes and experience; II. Impact on patients. *International Journal of Psycho-Analysis, 71:* 475–485.

Schachter, J. (1992). Concepts of termination and post-termination patient-analyst contact. *International Journal of Psycho-Analysis, 73:137–154.*

Schachter, J. & Brauer, L. (2001). The effect of the analyst's gender and other factors on post-termination patient-analyst contact: Confirmation by a questionnaire study. *International Journal of Psycho-Analysis, 82:*1123–1132.

Schachter, J. & Kächele, H. (2013). An alternative conception of termination and follow-up. *Psychoanalytic Revue, 100:*423– 452.

Schachter J, Kächele H, Schachter J (2018). "Progression": An alternative conception to "termination" to denote the ending of successful analytic treatment, *Psychoanalytic Psychology, 31:* 60–167

Tessman, L.H. (2003). *The analyst's analyst within.* Hillsdale, N.J.: The Analytic Press.

Tuckett, D. (1998). Evaluating psychoanalytic papers: Towards the development of common editorial standards. *International Journal of Psycho-Analysis, 79*: 431–448.

Tuckett, D. (2005). Does anything go? Towards a framework for the more transparent assessment of psychoanalytic competence. *International Journal of Psycho-Analysis, 86*: 31–49.

Wallerstein, R. S. (1988). One psychoanalysis or many? *International Journal of Psycho-Analysis, 69*: 5–21.

Wallerstein, R. S. (2005). Will psychoanalytic pluralism be an enduring state of our discipline? *International Journal of Psycho-Analysis, 86*(3), 623–626.

Critique on the Article: Science Needs Criticism: Debating the Clinical Aspects of Diverging Theoretical Schools

Zerrin Emel Kayatekin and Mehmet Sagman Kayatekin

No Critique Allowed—Politics of Exclusion

Perhaps it is not surprising that the editors of Psycho-analytic Review adopt a policy of not publishing critiques of previous papers. It may be symbolically concretizing the widespread criticism about psychoanalysis, that it's a closed system of thought; monastic in the way it is protected in its enclosed figurative walls; and dogmatic in the way in which it is interpreted within these walls.

This encapsulating, cocooning stance might not be limited to the aforementioned journal but it may be an example of an endemic trend in the circles of our guild; it might be a reflection of the current status of organizational psychoanalysis as a system of thinking, or as some of us may prefer to refer to it, our "science." Even further, this may not be an attitude of theorizing but of guarding of the organizational hierarchy, shrouded under the guise of protecting the scientific purity of theoretical narrative.

Here, we are reminded of the excommunication of Bowlby and his fertile ideas, and still widespread, ongoing hostility towards the attachment theory, possibly the most empirically tested school in the multiplicity of psychoanalyses, as a symbol to such practices of exclusion. In our history, this attitude can easily be applied to many fertile theoreticians/schools, like Kleinians, Kohutians, Jungians and some others. Or we can be reminded of the struggles of the non-MDs for their inclusion into the psychoanalytic profession.

It is probably fair to say that we have a rich tradition of exclusion, banning.

Is Psychoanalysis a Science? Does It Have to Be?

We would like to broaden the context of the discussion; is psychoanalysis a science? Or is it a hermeneutic, linguistic discipline? Or does it straddle both?

This was a major struggle in the times of its founder, Sigmund Freud. He came from a solid scientific background and did want to pursue a career along the lines of physiology and neuroanatomy, as the wonderfully detailed, intimate biography of Ernest Jones suggests. And he made quite significant contributions as a young scholar. As he was betrothed to Martha Bernays, Freud was faced with the harsh reality that he had to make a living for his new family, and thus followed the realistic recommendation of his revered teacher Brucke, and agonizingly abandoned his dreams and opened his private practice, with the significant anxieties and uncertainties of such a work.

To use the incisive insights Freud brought to the understanding of human mind and soul, we may use his theories to analyze him. We may easily postulate, with supporting evidence from the multiple biographies about him, that he was deeply ambivalent all around about this new context of the private practice he found himself in, and might have considered it as second class to basic science. This was clearly demonstrated in his attempts to define psychoanalysis as a science, sometimes overtly and more often covertly in his prolific writings.

Thus, at the root of this century-old "science-or-not" debate might be the mourning of and strivings for the reparation of Sigmund Freud's unfulfilled ambitions and narcissistic injuries. Many analysts and critiques of analysis joined this debate as it flourished on the fertile intellectual politics of the times; a time when science was seen as the pinnacle of human knowledge, and was revered as monotheistic religions were of the previous millennia.

Perhaps the wish to create a science was symbolized in the translating transition of "Das Ich" to "the Ego" and "Das Es" to the "Id" and "Trieb" to "Instinct." In the linguistic transformation, these ideas changed character—from experience-near, vague constructs to experience-distant structures with theoretical clarity, that had almost autonomous lives and relatedness—as it was masterfully detailed and crystallized in the works of Hartmann/Kris/Lowenstein and Rapaport. In sum, one may hypothesize that the translation of Strachey created a new narrative of psychoanalysis, which even impacted Freud's thinking. These were the times we were talking about "our science."

So, within this broader context, let us narrow down our critique to the paper.

The Paper

The authors of the article rightfully state that criticism is essential in assessing the scientific value of theoretical hypotheses. Intolerance of critique, encapsulated presentations, turn psychoanalytic thinking and writing into semi-religious texts, or maybe interpretations of the "Text" which is the massive Oeuvre of Freud, that needs a Talmudic reading. Talmudic readings naturally create an endless permutation of interpretations as most monotheistic religious texts display.

On the other hand, the authors seem to be content with a very narrow definition of science. The authors' critique on the termination around the revival of Oedipal constellations and the counter debate is an evocative one, but not an evidence for science. An "n" of 1 (one), i.e., a case study, is barely sufficient to prove anything beyond speculative, though helpful, ideas. And the authors' critique is equally insufficient to meet the criteria of being "scientific."

Basic criteria of the definition of science would include: developing a question about a phenomenon, reviewing the research done on this issue, constructing a hypothesis, testing the hypothesis by doing an experiment, analyzing the data, drawing a conclusion and sharing the findings and hoping for replication of the results.

This is probably a restrictive description, but it applies to most definitions of that mystical concept of "science."

But then, is recognition of black holes, or some supernova or a new galaxy unscientific? Can we do a double-blind study on the already found new galaxy? Probably not, though we can for sure find some other astrophysicists that can replicate the finding.

It could also be argued how much "evidence-based treatments" in psychiatry are "scientific." What makes most psychopharmacological, double-blind, placebo-controlled research fail is not that the active medication does not work, but placebo works equally well. If active medication's effect differentiates from placebo, and especially if it is duplicated, then it may become an "evidence-based treatment.

So, the issue of how to think about scientific aspects of psychoanalysis is a complicated one.

Is medicine a science?

We would like to consider our training in medicine as a paradigm to think about psychoanalysis.

Medical training and practice is not just a "science"; it has scientific elements as a solid foundation, from biochemistry to biology, but then it has many "non-scientific" elements. Would any MD consider anatomy as scientific? Would any MD consider physical examination as "scientific"? We doubt they would. And further, would a surgical intern consider repairing an inguinal hernia or performing appendectomy as "scientific" and just "scientific"? We doubt that too. It is a combination of scientific and nonscientific knowledge that we practice on a daily basis.

Our basic assertion is that "science" is not necessarily the ultimate and most powerful source of information; tradition is another source, improvisation is another one, etc. At the best "scientific" base of medicine can be annotated as "primus inter pares".

So, if we apply this millennia-old healing profession to a hundred plus year-old healing profession, does psychoanalysis have to be a "science" or just a "science?"

Response to Kayatekin Discussion

Joseph Schachter, Judith Schachter and Horst Kächele

The Kayatakins have written a thoughtful review of the thesis of our article "Science Needs Criticisms: Debating the Clinical Aspects of Diverging Theoretical Schools," which was in turn stimulated by Psychoanalytic Review's policy of refusing to publish critiques of its published papers. This position registered as "unscientific" and antithetical to those of major medical journals. And it was interpreted by the Kayatkins as a metaphor for the closed theoretical systems of psychoanalysis, not only in its publications but in its organization.

They elegantly segue from the history of exclusion (of Bowlby, the Kleinians, Kohutians and Jungians) to an analysis of the proposed origin in Freud's pragmatic need to abandon scientific research and a career as a professor for marriage and clinical practice, a second-class career. The pressure to define psychoanalysis as a science is therefore reparative of the loss.

The authors then transform the criticism of the original paper's plea for the freedom to evaluate disparate theoretical postures into a discussion of "science or not" in psychoanalysis based on Freud and his followers need to create a science—not quite our point. While appearing to accept the need for such critiques in a science, they criticize Schachter, Schachter and Kaechele for their narrow definition, although the latter had never claimed that their speculation was more "scientific" than the author they were criticizing. They only claimed that science demands that well-formulated criticism is essential to any science and that their critique should be published within the usual rules of propriety.

Indeed, they join the Kayatekins in their criticism of single case studies as well as their further afield examples of "evidence-based treatments in psychiatry." A straw man is constructed however, when they say "that 'science' is not the ultimate and most powerful source of information." All information must be reviewable and on examination must satisfy standards of validity and replicability to be considered "scientific." Criticism is the path to elucidating that result.

The Facts About the Neubauer Twin Study: An Interview About Controversy or a Controversial Interview?

Lois Oppenheim

The interview that follows was conducted for the purpose of revealing the facts about the so-called Neubauer Twin Study, for much has been grossly distorted in the media and in recent films. Dr. Peter Neubauer, Director of the Child Development Center in New York City from 1951 to 1984, undertook with colleagues a prospective study of twins reared apart, a study funded in part by the National Institute of Mental Health. The study has stimulated a number of highly complex questions ranging from the psychological impact of separating multiples put up for adoption to the ethics of research involving adoptive families who knew virtually nothing of the study in which they were participating. At issue as well is how one views today the practices of a bygone era: Do we consider them in accordance with the standards maintained at the time or with the standards developed many years later (the study was conducted in the 1950s and '60s; the Institutional Review Board was established in 1974, the Belmont Report in 1978)?[1]

None of these controversial questions prompted this interview, however, as significant as they are. Rather, I wished to set the record straight and bring to light the truth about the study as well as about Dr. Neubauer, a highly respected child, adolescent, and adult psychiatrist and psychoanalyst, the John Turner Lecturer at Columbia University, Clinical Professor at the Downstate Medical Center, the President and Founding Member of the Association of Child Psychoanalysis, long-time co-editor of *The Psychoanalytic Study of the Child*, and the author of numerous publications. Dr. Neubauer had been unjustly vilified in the film *Three Identical Strangers*, a film that achieved its considerable dramatic and commercial success by ignoring facts, employing 2019 practices and conventions to denounce good faith actions taken over a half-century ago, and falsely maligning a widely admired leader of the profession. The thesis of the film is that, in 1961, Dr. Neubauer inhumanely separated identical triplets who had been given up for adoption in order to enable him to conduct a study of their separate development. Additional villainy attributed to him is that he did not tell the adoptive parents that the babies were triplets. Whether the film's falsification was willful or attributable to ignorance, the accusations are without factual basis, for the triplets were separated for adoption for reasons having nothing to do with Dr. Neubauer's study. Years before Dr. Neubauer's involvement, the Louise Wise adoption agency, under the guidance of its chief psychiatric consultant, Dr. Viola Bernard, was separating identical twins for adoption in the belief that this was in the best interest of the twins. The film's proposition that the study was a heartless scheme undertaken at the expense of the children's well-being to enable a scientific study is but a fabrication. And it is shocking that the film either willfully conceals, or is shamefully ignorant of, Dr. Bernard's role. Moreover, the laws and practices of adoption have changed dramatically in the last half-century. In the 1960s, it was conventional, if not also required by law, that adopting families not be told the facts of the children's biological families. This also was believed at the time to benefit the children.

Adopting parents signed consent forms which explicitly acknowledged and agreed that they would not be told the facts of the birth family. But, again, it is the study itself that is the primary subject of the interview.

I had access to material that was virtually unknown to exist by anyone other than the source of that access, the Project Director of the study. She was willing to grant but a single interview, an interview with me. What she recounted in response to my questions was illuminating. But then there was this: Placing the interview—though it contained much significant information both new and corrective—proved in itself unexpectedly complicated necessitating, as a result, consideration of a question I had not anticipated when the desire to make known the truth about the study took form: What, if anything, is to be done when one or more answers by an interviewee are deemed by potential publishers to be ethically unacceptable?

Surely, asking an individual to modify a response in order to render it more palatable to a journal editor, and perhaps even to some portion of the public at large, is nothing short of censorship. Yet the replies of two editors were immediate and unambiguous: The seeming lack of regret expressed by the researcher—though she, like the others on the team, had not been in any way responsible for the separation of the siblings— made publication in those journals impossible. The next response was more stunning still: The interview failed not only to speak sufficiently to the "trauma," but to the "evil of these circumstances." But here's the rub: The interviewee was of the opinion that no evil had been wrought, certainly not by the research team that came on board with their study only after the separation of the twins/triplets took place. In fact, she believed then and continues to believe today that such separation is better for multiples for reasons touched upon in the interview. One can certainly cite evidence for both sides and this has been done. As to the trauma, she was extremely sensitive to the pain that some study subjects endured later in life when they learned of the existence of their sibling(s) and of the study. Yet, once again, neither that nor the separation was intended to be the primary issue at hand. The focus of the interview was to be the study itself, not the policy that was put in place by others before it was begun, not the anguish suffered decades later with the reuniting of some siblings. The question that rapidly presented itself as editors were approached was whether readers should or should not be informed of the truth about such a study—how it was conducted, for what purpose, and what happened with regard to the results—when beliefs of the interviewee are incongruent with those of the editor or other reviewers.

Child development subsequent to the no-longer practiced policy of twin separation, its benefit or harm to such siblings, produces profoundly emotional responses in many a clinical theorist. And, though only a small part of the interview, it was enough to cause more than one editor to shy from publication. An interviewee who believes in the value of such separation was clearly not to be heard from. But it cannot be over-stated: the policy on such separation had nothing to do with the research team, a fact hardly of negligible significance and one that needs to be made known. Censorship, moreover, in itself is unethical. Is it justifiable to withhold publication based on what an editor determines an acceptable belief on the part of an interviewee? When might that be legitimate? When not? What became apparent was that the interview — never conceived as one about controversy—became the subject of controversy itself.

Above all, however, is the notion that this interview focuses in large part on the existence of an unknown manuscript. Is it unethical to make the existence of that draft known when it is not available to the study subjects or researchers? So say some. The subjects would feel much better if they knew such a manuscript existed, that the study did have real results. So say others. One could make the argument that it would depend upon the individual, that it is not a case of one size fitting all. One could also make the argument that there may be both responses in a single study subject. Only with the publication of the interview by a courageous journal publisher/editor will we come to know.

* * *

"It's true, every word of it." So we are told near the start of the 2018 documentary Three Identical Twins, directed by Tim Wardle. But is it? (Natasha Josephowitz's credit in the film as Peter Neubauer's "research assistant" though she has said she knew nothing about the study and learned about it only by "hearsay," by virtue of being "in the office,"[2] already throws into question the film's status as a documentary. And a so-called "documentary" in which the principals are paid for their "life rights" raises additional questions.[3]) "There's no study, no anything." So we hear in The Twinning Reaction, another documentary, this one directed in 2017 by Lori Shinseki. Just how accurate is that? The films themselves and the media coverage of what is commonly referred to as the Neubauer Twin Study have displayed the pain—the deep sense of loss and regret, the anguish—suffered by those separated from their sibling(s), from other offspring produced by the same pregnancy. But there is another dimension to this pain as well: "What they feel is most egregious is not just the separation, but that no good has come of it," Wardle told a television interviewer referring to subjects of the study. And, he further commented, "It would make it much easier for them if there were answers or definite information that had been found as a result of tearing these lives apart."[4] The truth? There is.

In 1986, Samuel Abrams, M.D. published a paper entitled "Disposition and the Environment."[5] In 1990, Peter Neubauer, M.D. published a book called *Nature's Thumbprint: The New Genetics of Personality.*[6] In 1994 Abrams and Neubauer together published "Hartmann's Vision: Identical Twins and Developmental Organizations."[7] And in 1996, Neubauer and Christa Balzert, Ph.D. published "Genetik und Psychotherapie."[8] All four publications were drawn from results of the study. In addition, several presentations devoted to the study outcomes have taken place. To cite but two, "Genetic Findings and Their Impact on the Psychoanalytic Theory of Development" was written by Dr. Balzert and presented at the Institute for Child, Adolescent and Family Studies in New York and Neubauer and Balzert co-presented "Genetics and Psychotherapy" in a meeting of The American Academy of Psychoanalysis. And then there is this: An approximately 200-page manuscript bearing the title *Becoming Mind: Identical Twins Reared Apart.* Written by Neubauer, Abrams, and Balzert,[9] it remains an unpublished, incomplete draft.

Dr. Balzert agreed to be interviewed for the purpose of correcting flagrant misrepresentations and errors that have been floated by the media since the 1980s and particularly since the release of the two highly spectacularized films. As mentioned above, she made it eminently clear that this was to be the *only* interview on the Twin Study she would give and that the manuscript draft would *not* be made available for reasons that become evident in what follows. The interview took place (following two preliminary discussions) in New York City on April 25th, 2019.

Lois Oppenheim: At the center of the media coverage of the Twin Study is the Louise Wise Services, the adoption agency in New York that primarily placed Jewish babies from early in the 20th century to 2004 (when it closed and turned over all of its voluntary adoption records to the Spence-Chapin agency). Also at the center is Dr. Peter Neubauer who saw in these adoptions what he considered an extraordinary opportunity. What was the purpose of the study undertaken by Neubauer, the Director of the Child Development Center, a division of the Jewish Board of Family and Children's Services?[10]

Christa Balzert: In the late '50s and early '60s it was the adoption agency's policy to place twins separately. This created the unique opportunity for the *prospective* comparison of the development of genetically identical children growing up in different environments, in contrast to the existing *retrospective* twin studies. We expected to learn how the unique dynamics of each of the otherwise comparable middle-class adoptive families affect the developmental progression of children with identical genetic blueprints.

L.O.: There is much disagreement over the actual number of subjects in the study. How many were there?

C.B.: Originally, there were four sets of twins and one set of triplets. One set of twins dropped out early, and so did one of the triplets.

L.O.: Before we get to the manuscript itself, how would you describe the role of Dr. Neubauer in the separation of the twins? Contrary to what is distinctly claimed in one of the films, in much of the media hype, and elsewhere as well, it is my understanding that he did not separate the children and that Dr. Viola Bernard, the psychiatric consultant to the agency, did. In other words, Neubauer developed his study *after* that policy was in place. Is that correct?

C.B.: That is correct. It is my understanding that Viola Bernard, based on the assumption that it would be advantageous to the development of the individual, recommended separating twins at adoption.

L.O.: Do you feel that Dr. Bernard had any undue influence on Dr. Neubauer?

C.B.: As colleagues they did exchange ideas, but there was no "undue" influence.

L.O.: The focus of the study was nature vs. nurture. What specific aspects of that long-standing conundrum were you, the team, most interested in? Can you summarize that?

C.B.: We never thought of nature vs. nurture, but rather of their interplay. Many areas of interest emerged in the course of the study but, as child psychoanalysts and psychologists, our main focus became how disposition, as determined by genetic and epigenetic givens (nature), interacts with external stimuli (nurture) to create experiences that ultimately form the mind of the individual.

L.O.: The manuscript (or draft, such as it is) outlines four primary goals of the study: Refining aspects of the relationship between nature and nurture; exploring issues relevant to adoption for the purpose of distinguishing what in the environment promotes and what inhibits development; increasing understanding of the etiology and progression of psychopathology and examining the notions of abnormality and normality (i.e., the usefulness of considering psychopathology in terms of adjustment vs. deviation from developmental standards); and establishing ways of studying the emergence and growth of what we call 'mind'. Do you feel there was achievement in all four areas?

C.B.: Yes, I believe so.

L.O.: What is your thinking on the notion of the so-called "twinning reaction," the idea that a particular kind of bonding takes place between such siblings? Many years ago, Susan Farber described "twinning" as an "exceedingly complex and idiosyncratic interaction" in which there is "close identification with and exaggerated independence of the other."[11] Not long after, Muriel Chaves Winestine wrote of the "mutual interidentification," the "part fusion of the self representation and the object representation of the other member of the pair."[2] Do you believe, given the more recent research in this area, that there is such a phenomenon? It has been said that that "mutual interidentification" can occur in non-twin siblings and even non-siblings.[13] If this is true, what does that say about the validity of the "twinning reaction"?

C.B.: The term "twinning" does not exclusively refer to the special relationship between twins. It is used to describe a number of different situations, ranging from a specific form of transference in the analytic relationship to interidentification or "psychic twinning," as Ronald Britton called it,[14] whether with imaginary companions, non-twin siblings, admired figures or best friend. Of course, one has to assume that this reaction is more pronounced and powerful between twins, who normally find themselves from birth on in constant presence of an other who is at the same developmental stage. Seeing one's every reaction reflected may create a sense of comfort and security, but also make it difficult to recognize oneself as a separate individual and to develop a distinct sense of self.[15] I suspect that the children in the Neubauer study showed "twinning reactions" while together, but that no specific attachment to the cotwin had been formed at the time of their adoption around six months of age. In their review of the literature and their own study of twin relationships from an attachment-theoretical perspective, Caroline Tancredy and R. Chris Fraley conclude that twins "during the first couple of years of life ...appear to be relatively uninterested in the presence of the cotwin."[16]

L.O.: Identical siblings separated at birth not uncommonly refer to the feeling that, for as long as they can remember, they had the sense that something was not quite right, that something was missing. Parents of some of the separated twins in the study have commented that they "knew" their child was lacking something, but they didn't know what it was. Do you believe there is a possibility of such "knowing," that such a sensation (for lack of a better word) is plausible, either with regard to children or parents, or does that thinking seem too magical to you?

C.B.: I think this is one of the things one never will know for sure. There are strong opinions and feelings about the separation of multiples. The pain and sense of being deprived of an essential experience and the resulting anger which some of the reunited twins expressed affected us deeply and led to discussions about the adoption agency's policy. Still, I don't believe that "knowing" of and suffering from the early separation is plausible, since it is not likely that a strong attachment was present at that point. The feeling that something was not quite right, which some of the parents and adult twins describe, may have been retroactively attributed to the separation while actually being the result of problems in the children's development or even of feelings about adopted versus biological offspring.

L.O.: One word that is thrown around a lot is "experimentation." The analogy to Nazi-like experimenting, particularly with regard to Neubauer (an Austrian refugee who came to the U.S. to escape the war), is particularly disturbing. We have heard or read it in various interviews and the analogy is even made in at least one of the films. Director Tim Wardle refers to journalist Lawrence Wright's having "discovered that there was a science experiment going on and that these boys had been separated on purpose for this experiment."[17] And, again, the first of the two films I referred to earlier was billed as a "feature-length documentary film about a tragically failed human research experiment from the 1960s." The Washington Post published a piece on CNN's airing of the film in which the reporter wrote of the Twin Study as "just one of many unethical studies in the 1950s and 1960s that used subjects as means to an end" and of "the unethical experiment" that was so damaging.[18] Was there any sort of experimentation—any kind of experimentation whatsoever—involved in this study, either on the children or on the families?

C.B.: This is one of the most glaring misconceptions about the study. Our *research* did not involve any *experimentation*. Our method was *natural observation*. The data were collected during home visits (more frequent in the first year of life; later on, twice a year) where standard tests, child observation, parent interviews, and filming of play situations were conducted.

L.O.: So it was pure observation.

C.B.: Yes, this was an observational study. No manipulation of elements was involved, as would be the case in an experimental study.

L.O.: The essential disparities between psychoanalytic thinking and attachment theory have long been recognized. More recently, however, some have noted what Peter Fonagy and Mary Target describe as "a move toward greater interest in attachment theory by psychoanalysis," a move they refer to as "striking." Would it be correct to say, given the purely observational nature of the study, that if that move—said to result from greater recognition of embodied cognition in the development of mind, from the view of the brain as "more continuous with the mind, which is seen as ever reflecting its bodily origin"[19]—had occurred earlier, historically speaking, the study would have not been different in any way?

C.B.: Attachment theory was not at all a focus of the study. And it therefore doesn't appear in the manuscript. Had the shift you refer to taken place prior to the study, I don't think it would have significantly altered it. I might have thought somewhat differently about our work had the more recent thinking on attachment been known at that time, but I don't think it would have altered anything for Neubauer or Abrams.

L.O.: Do you think the observing of the siblings, the testing and filming of them at various stages of development, might have had an impact on them, hypothetically speaking?

C.B.: Any experience has an impact. I imagine that for some families the visit may have been a welcome event, with the children receiving special attention and the mothers having an opportunity to discuss some of their concerns. For others it may have felt more like an intrusion. I don't recall that any of that was ever articulated to us.

L.O.: It has also been claimed that the selection of the families was related to the design of the study in one way or another. Is there any truth to this?

C.B.: The selection of the families had nothing to do with the design of the study. As I understood it, it was the agency's policy to place the children in families of similar middle-class background with no known unusual circumstances, like chronic illness, unemployment, and so on, and one older (preferably adopted) sibling present. So, again, the placement of the children had nothing to do with the study.

L.O.: Did you, Neubauer, and Abrams discuss among yourselves your own reactions to some of the siblings having discovered each other? How did you all feel after some of the study participants learned they had identical siblings?

C.B.: We had strong and mixed reactions and had many discussions about it. The anger at having been deprived of the experience growing up with their twin and being misled by the adoption agency and the researchers was difficult for us to contemplate and deal with. We had to reevaluate our original approach in the light of the changed rules about informed consent. Yet there was also curiosity and excitement to find out about the young adults whom we had known so well as children twelve years earlier. How did their later development confirm or disprove our observations and predictions? How did they feel about having been part of the research project? Beyond these considerations we were concerned how the sensationalized reports and misrepresentations of the role of the agency and the study could affect other adoptees.

L.O.: Did any of the three of you feel any regret at that point?

C.B.: Although there was a good deal of media coverage critical of the study and negative feelings expressed by the reunited siblings, none of us felt regret.

L.O.: In your paper, "Genetic Findings and Their Impact on the Psychoanalytic Theory of Development," one reads that the team was more impressed with the likenesses than the dissimilarities between particular siblings, "with the fundamental similarities ... found in spite of significant differences in environmental offerings." You state, "These similarities may be related to three dispositional leanings which the research team catalogued ... within the first three months: inner-directness, problems in effectively engaging persons or things, and a limitation in integrative capacity." Can you say more about those three areas in terms of the study?

C.B.: We were impressed with striking *intra-twin* (children of the same set) similarities, in spite of differences in the parents' attitudes and child-rearing practices. At the same time, we noticed from early on *inter-twin* (children of different sets) similarities. In each set one twin tended to have more difficulty integrating experiences, to be more inner-directed and thing-oriented, the other more outer-directed and person-oriented. We came to speculate that this, along with other possible factors, correlates with higher birth weight, birth order, and laterality (right-left brain dominance) as evidenced, with one exception, by the fact that in each set one child was right-handed, the other left-handed.

L.O.: That's fascinating! In the same paper, you also say that "Focusing primarily on the developmental dimension, [the research team] found a high concordance of the emergence of phase sequences as well as phase dominance" and you then go on to discuss the persistence of certain phase expressions and, in certain subjects, "evidence of reorganization into new hierarchies and of appropriate self and object differentiation." That goes back to what you were just referring to, but do you think that if you were observing the same children today, you would be looking through the same developmental lens? Might any subsequent theorizing on developmental organization (or its vicissitudes) alter your view of the subjects or your approach to the study if you were undertaking it today?

C.B.: I suppose that, as analysts, we would look for the same developmental landmarks today, but perhaps include other aspects; more specifically, for instance, separation/individuation and attachment type and history.

L.O.: And do you think Neubauer and Abrams would be on the same page with you about that?

C.B.: I can't be sure, but I think so. I know that, as the study progressed, we were impressed with new observations and formulated new hypotheses. At the same time, however, I don't think there would be any real substantive difference in the study, certainly not in its overall purpose or our approach.

L.O: Had the manuscript been published, it would likely have forestalled the accusations of secrecy, the embellishment of the idea of secret experimentation, and the extraordinary villainizing of Peter Neubauer. But it wasn't. Wright is of the opinion,[0] and his expression of this has subsequently snowballed to an astonishing degree, that the draft was never published because of the findings, because of the determination that genes play a far greater role in development and pathology than expected. To clarify once and for all: Why was the manuscript not ever published?

C.B.: We intended to publish our findings all along, but felt constrained by clinical considerations and reasons of confidentiality. At that time most of the families were not aware that their children were multiples. It was to be expected that the publication of any kind of study would easily become sensationalized, as present events show, and come to the attention of the adoptive families without clinical assistance. We also struggled with how best to present our findings. Data based on natural observation do not easily lend themselves to traditional statistical methods. In the first draft, we presented the findings in the form of hypotheses with different levels of certainty.

L.O. The existence of the draft was not even known to the Jewish Board of Guardians, with which the Child Development Center had merged, presumably because it was written not only well after the study ended, but after all materials related to the work had been donated to Yale University where they remain sealed until 2065. Is that accurate?

C.B.: Yes.

L.O.: What do you feel are the most important parts of the draft?

C.B.: We were interested in nature/nurture and adoptive issues, the study of possible psychopathology, and the growth of the mind. The growth of the mind, however, became our main focus, which accounts for the working title of the unpublished manuscript: "Becoming Mind." Observing the development of separated twins created the opportunity to understand better the environmental role in the formation of psychological meaning, the minds of children with identical genetic make-up.

L.O.: Certainly one of the most interesting findings of the study is that, unlike in other studies, there was a clear indication that, as it was written, "a more accommodating or attuned environment does not necessarily lead to a more coherent internalization of self and object representation nor to a greater adaptedness beyond the contained family setting." In other words, the assumption that an "attuned environment inevitably yields a greater degree of structuralization and adaptedness" is not upheld by the study outcomes.[21] That has been floated as a primary reason for there not being the kind of comprehensive publication one would expect from such a study; in other words, that genes play a stronger role not only than one might anticipate, but than one—namely, psychoanalysts—would have wanted to discover. In fact, however, what you are really saying, as I understand it, is that constitution and environment are integrated in more complex ways than had previously been acknowledged; that it's neither this nor that, but the way that an individual's developmental disposition is facilitated by or interfered with by all that makes up the environment. How did that lead to the choice of the title "Becoming Mind" as opposed to, say, "Becoming Oneself"?

C.B.: Far from ignoring its importance as a facilitating or interfering factor, the unique nature of the study allowed for a better understanding of the interplay between environment and inherent equipment (for example, the pull forward, disharmonies in emerging faculties, and engagement in the overall progression) in the process of "becoming mind." We could see how a child's constitutional givens will, to a certain extent, determine what can be extracted from the environment to become formative mental experience.

L.O.: Very generally speaking, were you aware of some of the children in the study being symptomatic at a very early age?

C.B.: It depends what you mean by "symptomatic." We certainly saw variations of different kinds and severity in the children's developmental progression, but nothing that would count as a "symptom" requiring intervention.

L.O.: Were you concerned about the mental health of the children at the time?

C.B.: During our home visits we looked for signs of potential pathology and discussed this during our regular team meetings. It was understood that the parents would be notified should there ever be reason for concern and intervention.

L.O.: So if you had found something very serious in one twin you would have gone to the family of the other twin, but you didn't ever have to do that?

C.B.: We would have notified the parents of the other twin if a problem appeared to have a genetic basis.

L.O.: Did any of you ever relate any area of potential concern to the separation itself from an identical other? My emphasis here is on separation as opposed to rearing apart.

C.B.: We did not attribute any emerging problems to the early separation, but rather to unevenness in development. For instance, we understood the prolonged and intense clinginess of one pair of twins to their mothers to be the result of their lack of developmental pull forward, not as the result of separation.

L.O.: To the broad categories in which clinicians are trained—ego function, object relations, trauma, and the like—you, Abrams, and Neubauer uncovered an invaluable category to add: disposition. How therapy can remediate disturbances in the undeniable interaction between nature and nurture, modify interference by disposition in the pull toward maturation, might well have been significantly altered by the discovery of the very strong role played by disposition had it not been determined, despite the write-up of the study and the desire to publish it, that confidentiality of the subjects had to override all else. In other words, the findings of the study might well have served all those who influence—be they educators, therapists, or parents—the maturational process. But the struggle with how to put the manuscript in print without breaching the most pressing ethical issue of confidentially prevented its publication. Do you have any regrets about that? Any thoughts about what might have helped scores of children had you published the draft? It is clear that so much learning took place on the part of the team. So much could have been done with that had the issue of confidentiality not played a part, which of course it rightly did. Confidentiality is the most important consideration and you could only do as you did, refrain from publishing the manuscript however much you wanted to. But does that remain problematic for you?

C.B.: It was not a new idea that environment in interaction with "disposition" affects a child's development. What our study showed more clearly was the extent to which dispositional factors determine the developmental process, especially in specific areas. Taking these findings into consideration could inform the approach of professionals working with children, help parents to understand and accept their child's dispositional limits, and alert therapists to how a child's disposition contributes to the presenting problem. For those reasons, I regret that we felt we could not publish our findings.

L.O.: While there is much science related to twinship that we don't yet understand—the role of the sharing of amniotic fluid in attachment, the significance of non-shared intrauterine experiences, the potential implications of differences in the size of the placenta or umbilical cords, the placement of the fetuses in the womb—more is known now of the pre- and post-natal epigenetic variables, of differences in gene activity and their expression.[22] And adoption today in the State of New York is not what it was in the 1950s and 1960s when those adoptions took place. Given the scientific and legal changes, would you do the study today?

C.B.: If started today, the study would not exist in its present form as the policy regarding the separation of twins no longer exists. However, a practical consideration regarding separation remains, given the difficulty of finding adoptive homes for multiples and the strain on the caregiver. Personally, I might have more questions about the design of the study than I had then, having learned of the negative feelings expressed by some of the twins. But I still do believe that engaging the world as a singleton is advantageous to the development of a clear sense of self.

L.O.: You speak of the benefit to autonomy and individuation that a child reared alone has over one reared as a singleton. But you also mention the change in policy, the fact that "the separation of twins no longer exists." Why do you think the policy changed? Aren't there certain implications inherent in that change of policy that would contradict your belief?

C.B.: I cannot speak to the reasons why the adoption agency changed its policy in the early sixties. It may have been the result of re-evaluating the clinical reasons behind it, new rules about informed consent, or even negative reactions from the public. All these reasons deserve consideration, but I still feel that growing up with a twin creates a challenge for the separation/individuation process and self representation (see, for example, Farber and E. D. Dibble and D.J. Cohn[2]),[24] which has to be weighed against the positive effects of growing up with an identical other.

L.O.: In view of all the misrepresentation and misinformation that has come from the media hype, is there anything you would like to emphasize as in particular need of clarification?

C.B.: I want to emphasize again that separation of the twins was part of the adoption agency's placement policy and independent of the study. There was no "experimentation" or manipulation for the sake of data collection involved. The method of the study was *natural observation*, which included standard developmental tests, child observation, brief videos of child play, and parent interviews, all in the children's familiar environment. The families were not aware of the existence of a twin. At the time of the study, no rules regarding informed consent existed and it was assumed that such knowledge could interfere with the bonding process. It was understood, however, that disregarding the design of the study, the families would be told of the twinship and intervention offered should a genetically linked problem become evident.

L.O.: There was not a way to publish the manuscript draft without the risks inherent in the breach of confidentiality, as you have made clear, but I do think the study exceedingly important, especially for the primary conclusion it reached:

> The environment's competence can only be comprehended in terms of the specific inherent capacities and limitations of children; this attends to the reciprocal interaction between the components of the equation rather than either in isolation. This also shifts the focus of attention away from 'nature vs nurture' to the process of becoming mind and to the necessary experiential products.

> This recognition of the mutual interdependence of disposition and the environment seems to provide a more felicitous framework for understanding the process of becoming mind than does any approach that isolates

the one from the other or sees one as more 'causative' than the other.[2]

References

[1]See Hoffman, L. and Oppenheim, L. (2019). "Three Identical Strangers and The Twinning Reaction: Clarifying History and Lessons for Today From Peter Neubauer's Twins Study." JAMA, Vol. 322, No. 1, pp. 10–12.

[2]Joseph, J. "'Three Identical Strangers' and the Nature-Nurture Debate," https://www.madinamerica.com/2019/06/three-identical-strangers-nature-nurture-debate/

[3]Jacobs, M. "In 'Three Identical Strangers,' A Saga About Triplets Grows More Twisted By The Minute," https://www.huffpost.com/entry/three-identicalstrangers-documentary_n_5b2d165ee4b-00295f15c1b18

[4]pbs.org Metrofocus 01/11/2019.

[5]Abrams, S. (1986). "Disposition and the Environment." *The Psychoanalytic Study of the Child* 41: 41– 60. Yale University Press.

[6]Neubauer, P. (1990). *Nature's Thumbprint: The New Genetics of Personality* (co-authored with Alexander Neubauer), N.Y.: Columbia University Press.

[7]Abrams, S. and Neubauer, P. (1994). "Hartmann's Vision: Identical Twins and Developmental Organizations." *The Psychoanalytic Study of the Child* 49: 49–59. Yale University Press.

[8]Neubauer, P. and Balzert, C. (1996). In *Der psychoanalytische Prozeß* (1996), Sylvia Zwettler-Otte and Albrecht Komarek, eds. Wien: Turia + Kant.

[9]Dr. Neubauer died in 2008, Dr. Abrams in 2016.

[10]At the time, the organization was known as The Jewish Board of Guardians.

[11]Farber, Susan L. (1981). *Identical Twins Reared Apart: A Reanalysis.* New York: Basic Books, Inc. p. 5.

[12]Winestine, Muriel Chaves (1969), *Journal of the American Academy of Child Psychiatry,* vol. 8, issue 3, p. 437.

[13]See, for example, Joseph, E. D. and Tabor, J. H. (1961). Simultaneous Analysis of an Identical Twin Pair and the Twinning Reaction. *Psychoanalytic Q.,* 30:319–320

[14]Britton, R. (2013), Commentary on Three Papers by Wilfred R. Bion. *Psychoanal. Q.* 82 (2), p. 315.

[15]See Winestine, *op. cit.*

[16]Caroline M. Tancredy and R. Chris Fraley (2006). The Nature of Adult Twin Relationships: An Attachment-Theoretical Perspective. *J Pers Soc Psychol* 90 (1), p. 80.

[17]pbs.org Metrofocus 01/11/2019.

[18]Lerner, B.H. "'Three Identical Strangers': The high cost of experimentation without ethics," washingtonpost.com.

[19]Fonagy, Peter and Target, Mary (2007). "The Rooting of the Mind in the Body: New Links Between Attachment Theory and Psychoanalytic Thought," JAPA 55 (2), pp. 415 & 445.

[20]See, for example, Whittaker, R. "Twins, Genes, and Destiny: Lawrence Wright Meets *Three Identical Strangers,*" The Austin Chronicle, July 23, 2018, austinchronicle.com.

[21]Neubauer, P. B., Abrams, S., Balzert, C., "Becoming Mind: Identical Twins Reared Apart," unpublished draft, p. 30.

[22]See Jeffrey Craig's remarks in Hayasaki, Erika. "Identical Twins Hint at How Environments Change Gene Expression." *The Atlantic.* May 15, 2018. Theatlantic.com

[23]Farber, *op. cit.* and Dibble, E. D., & Cohen, D. J. (1981). Personality development in identical twins: The first decade of life. The Psychoanalytic Study of the Child, 36, 45–70.

[24]However paradoxical, separated twins are often more alike than twins growing up together, which indicates that the genetic disposition shows more clearly when the twinning reaction is avoided.

[25]"Becoming Mind: Identical Twins Reared Apart," p. 183.

Ethical Questions Remain in Controversial Twins Study: Further Information and Sources are Required to Find Resolve

Adam M. Kelmenson and Ilene Wilets

In Response:

Dr. Oppenheim writes a commentary with an accompanying interview segment in order to "set the record straight" about the Neubauer Twins study.[1] Oppenheim's piece offers an unwavering defense of Neubauer as a pioneer in psychological research while failing to answer the legitimate ethical question raised by critiques. Her commentary also presents obscure and antithetical information that we believe perpetuates misunderstanding about the problematic research. This misunderstanding, in turn, yields a missed opportunity for learning from historic ethical missteps and from seeking reparation of such errors of judgment and conscience.

Oppenheim opens with a caustic review of Tim Wardle's documentary "Three Identical Strangers." Her primary criticism rests on Wardle's artistic license in which several key aspects of the study are not mentioned. Oppenheim's intention, we believe, was to bring truth to the flaws she sees in the film that create misconceptions of Neubauer's research conducted from the 1960's to the 1980's. It was during that time that several biological mothers relinquished their newborn identical twins for adoption with the Louise Wise Services Adoption Agency (LWS), who enrolled the identical siblings

---

[1]Oppenheim L., "The Facts about the Neubauer Twin Study: An Interview about a Controversy or a Controversial Interview?" *International Journal of Controversial Discussions* 2020 1(1): 171–188.

in longitudinal psychological research and then secretly placed them into different homes. According to first-hand accounts from adoptive parents, the agency described the already ongoing research as important to understanding key aspects of child development but did not mention the existence of identical siblings or the true purpose of the study.[2] Parents also describe an implicit pressure to agree to continued research participation as a condition of adoption.[3]

Decades after the study's onset, several sets of separated siblings discovered the separation and research. Many of the study participants experienced personal crises of identity and anger towards those that organized the study. After attempts to access study materials in order to learn more about the circumstances of adoption, participants faced restrictions put in place by deeds of gift from several key study organizers.[4] At present, materials from the project are held without access at Columbia University and Yale University until the years 2021 and 2065 respectively.[5,6] Adoption records, in which descriptors of placement decisions exist, are likely housed at Spence-Chapin adoption agency, who absorbed the defuncted LWS in 2005, with access determined by the organization's executives.[7,8]

The author's view of the study is shaped by an exclusive

---

[2]*Three Identical Strangers*. Directed by Tim Wardle. United States: CNN Films, 2018.

[3]Paparella A., Strauss EM., Effron L., Valiente A., "Twins Make Astonishing Discovery that They Were Separated Shortly After Birth and Then Part of a Secret Study." ABC News. March 9, 2018.

[4]*The Twinning Reaction*. Directed by Lori Shinseki. United States: Fire Horse Pictures; 2017.

[5]Finding Aid. Viola Wertheim Bernard Papers, Archives & Special Collections, Columbia University Health Sciences Library. New York, NY; 2003.

interview with Christa Balzert, a project director and, according to Oppenheim, a co-author, alongside Neubauer and Samuel Abrams[9] (Clinical Professor of Psychiatry at NYU Psychoanalytic Institute and colleague of Neubauer), of an unpublished and inaccessible manuscript reporting the study's findings. The author's opinions of the study are similarly shaped by the manuscript's contents, though, it is unclear if she has reviewed it.

One cannot help but question Oppenheim's access to such revealing sources given that participants themselves have tried unsuccessfully to review study materials. Though Oppenheim never claims to have read the manuscript, in her article, and other academic installments, Oppenheim reveals previously unknown details about its contents. For example, even the name of the manuscript, though included in Oppenheim's commentary, is not listed on the Columbia University or Yale University finding aids.[10, 11] What is more, in a 2019 article published in JAMA, Oppenheim describes the manuscript in detail without citation, leaving the reader to assume she has

---

[6]Guide to the Adoption Study Records of the Child Development Center. Yale University Manuscripts and Archives. New Haven, CT; 2004.

[7]Interview with Bernard, V. Conducted by Wright L. for "Double mystery" The New Yorker; July 31, 1995.

[8]Dickter A. "Home Found For Louise Wise Records." *New York Jewish Week;* December 10, 2005.

[9]Abrams S. "Disposition and the environment." *Psychoanalitic Study of the Child,* 1986; 41:41–60.

[10]Finding Aid. Viola Wertheim Bernard Papers, Archives & Special Collections, Columbia University Health Sciences Library. New York, NY; 2003.

[11]Guide to the Adopotion Study Records of the Child Development Center. Yale University Manuscripts and Archives. New Haven, CT; 2004

reviewed the document herself.[12] If she has not read the manuscript, but is aware of its details based on descriptions from Balzert who allegedly contributed to the manuscript some 40 years ago, then Oppenheim's commentary on this topic must be viewed in light of her limited, secondhand knowledge.

We also question the identification of Balzert as an expert on Neubauer's study. Oppenheim states that her interview is a "one-time exclusive." Balzert, however, gave at least one other interview on her involvement in the study. Lawrence Perelman, research assistant working on the Neubauer project in 1968, summarizes his own interview with Balzert in a 2005 article published in the Journal of Twin Research and Human Genetics.[13] There, it is revealed that Balzert joined the project in 1969, well after its onset in 1961, and left the project in the mid-1970's, prior to its conclusion. During her tenure, she "worked peripherally on the study," mostly in data analysis.[14] Balzert further discloses to Perlman that she neither conducted any of the home visits nor met any of the subjects. This account conflicts with Oppenheim's portrayal of Balzert as an authority on the topic.

Oppenheim admonishes other journals for rejecting her commentary and interview, an action she equates to academic censorship. She claims that her work was rejected because various editors disagreed with Balzert's viewpoint that the research was in fact ethical. It is not inconceivable, however, that legitimate academic forums rejected the work on the basis of its concealed sources—both the manuscript and the exclusive interview with Balzert. Without access to the sources

---

[12]Hoffman L., Oppenheim L., "Three Identical Strangers and The Twinning Reaction—clarifying history and lessons for today from Peter Neubauer's Twins Study." JAMA 2019; 322(1): 10–12.

[13]Perlman LM, Segal NL. "Memories of the Child Development Center of monozygotic twins reared apart: An unfulfilled promise." *Twin Research and Human Genetics* 2005; 8(3): 271–281.

[14]Ibid.

in her article, it is impossible for academic peers to respond to Oppenheim's viewpoints or answer the valid ethical questions raised by critiques in response Neubauer's study.

Nevertheless, Oppenheim presents her work as unbiased interpretation of the interviewee's response. The author poses interview questions that direct the reader to regard the continued secrecy of the study design, the manuscript and the research records as a means to protect subjects' privacy. However, the reader will notice that Balzert herself never speaks to the concealment of study data or manuscripts as a helpful means to secure subject privacy. In contrast to Oppenheim, Balzert notes, "At that time most of the [adoptive] families were not aware that their children were multiples. It was to be expected that the publication of any kind of study would easily become sensationalized, as present events show, and come to the attention of the adoptive families without clinical assistance."[15]

Balzert seems to suggest that study orchestrators came to recognize that the study caused harms that would require clinical care, leading researchers to hide their work out of fear of being demonized for their actions. All the while, Balzert fails to acknowledge the researchers' ethical obligation to provide ancillary care for ailments discovered during, or harms caused by the study. We might further question the motive of keeping the manuscript and research data hidden from participants after Oppenheim's claim in 2019 that all those involved in the study are now aware of their participation.[16] At this point, we believe that participants should be afforded

---

[15]Oppenheim L., "The Facts about the Neubauer Twin Study: An Interview about a Controversy or a Controversial Interview?" International Journal of Controversial Discussions 2020 1(1): 171–188.

[16]Hoffman L., Oppenheim L. "Three Identical Strangers and The Twinning Reaction—clarifying history and lessons for today from Peter Neubauer's Twins Study." JAMA 2019; 322(1): 10–12.

wider access beyond the limited documents already given, including the information from the unpublished manuscript.

In addition to concerns about Oppenheim's motives and sources, her tendentious defense of Neubauer includes a number of inaccuracies and contradictions about 20th century scientific practices, adoption procedures, and application of bioethics in research. One of the most egregious errors in the author's writing is the assertion that the adoptive parents provided consent to research participation and withheld disclosure of the existence of siblings. Oppenheim writes, "Adopting parents signed consent forms which explicitly acknowledged and agreed that they would not be told the facts of the birth family." Yet, adoptive parents had no reason to assume a sibling existed as LWS was the only agency that routinely separated siblings, and did so in secret.[17]

Though Oppenheim minimizes consent, this issue is tantamount to ethical concerns in Neubauer's work. Notes from an LWS adoption committee meeting held on October 11, 1960, available to the public at Columbia University Special Archives Library in the Bernard Estate, include Gertrude Sandgrund, head case worker for LWS, describing the context, actions and adoption procedures leveraged by the agency during the time of the study. Sandgrund says:

> The children referred to us by the JCCA [Jewish Child Care Association] are usually not surrendered children; and we have to take responsibility for this. In the simpler situations where the natural parents have indicated to the JCA some readiness to sing surrender, the only thing we need to do is ask the Department of Welfare to accept surrender from the parents. These simpler situations are rare; most of the JCCA situations are those where the mothers have absconded, or mothers are in mental hospitals;

---

[17]Kelmenson AM., Wilets I., Historical practice of separating twins at birth. *JAMA* 2019 322(18):1827.

or there are two parents, one of whom is not available to sign surrender. In these cases JCCA refers the situation to us and we have to grapple with the problems and have our lawyers work on them. In the last few years we have become quite skillful in the 384 procedure which is to remove custody from the parents and transfer custody to us thus enabling us to place the children without participation of the parents. Of the 15 children on referral, seven have been freed for adoption thru[ough] our efforts which have gone on for a year or two. The other seven children are not yet available for adoption and we are at various stages of working on these legal proceedings.[18]

The above is damaging not only in its reveal of LWS's indifference for the wellbeing of biological mothers, but also in its militant use of legal loopholes used to acquire twins for adoption. The 384-procedure referenced by Sangrund served as the functional basis for twin separation and subsequent enrollment in Neubauer's study. The spirit of this procedure created a protection for children with deceased or unfit parents, and with no appointed guardian. To enact the 384-procedure for a child with a living birth mother, the parent was required to willingly surrender the child to the agency or be "declared insane or mentally defective."[19] After securing a surrender or mental illness diagnosis, the law allowed certified agencies to assume legal custody of children before finding an adoptive family.

Oppenheim contends that voluntary informed consent was not a concern during the time of Neubauer's study. It is true that informed consent, in the absence of the codified

---

[18]Sandgrund G., "Louise Wise Services Adoption Committee Meeting Minutes 10/11/60." Viola Wertheim Bernard Papers, Archives & Special Collections, Columbia University Health Sciences Library, Box 154, Series 7.4.

[19]McKinney's 1960 Session Laws of New York; Chapter 717, page 1202, §384 S 4.

federal regulation, was not as well developed and documented in the 1960's as it is now. However, the Nuremberg Code, developed in 1947 and formalized into research policy soon after, notes that "the voluntary consent of the human subject is absolutely essential."[20] For minors, permission is provided by the parent or legal guardian. After enactment of the 384-procedure, the guardian in this case was LWS. Records indicate that psychological study began during foster care while infants waited for adoption placement, at which time research participation consent and separation permission was given by LWS.[21] Based on this clear conflict of interest, it is more accurate to say that consent was not absent but immoral.

Oppenheim might dismiss the above as irrelevant given her claim that LWS held no interest in the research. She asserts that LWS separated siblings into homes solely based on the advice of Columbia Professor and LWS Chief Psychiatrist Viola Bernard. However, our own research suggests LWS concerned itself with the success of Neubauer's study. A 1965 letter to Bernard from Florence G. Brown, executive director of LWS, contains the following quote: "I was very happy to learn that you did succeed in getting renewal of funds for the CDC-LWS [Child Development Center–Louise Wise Services] study. I do hope that the other agencies will participate so that the sample can be large enough."[22] If

---

[20]The Nuremberg Code. Trials of War Criminals before the Nuremberg Military Tribunals under Control Council Law. Washington, D.C.: U.S. Government Printing Office, 1949;2 (10):181–182.

[21]Perlman LM, Segal NL., "Memories of the Child Development Center of monozygotic twins reared apart: An unfulfilled promise." *Twin Research and Human Genetics* 2005; 8(3): 271–28.

[22]Brown FG. Letter to Viola Bernard from Florence G. Brown. New York, NY; 1965. Viola Wertheim Bernard Papers, Archives & Special Collections, Columbia University Health Sciences Librarary, Series 5.4.

Oppenheim is correct that that LWS did not concern itself with the research, then why should the agency's executive director discuss the study's sample size? Further, why should Brown refer to the "CDC-LWS study," an implication of joint participation?

Given the agency's involvement in the Twins Study, especially in regard to sample size, it is not unreasonable to suggest that LWS's practice of twin separation was at least perpetuated by Neubauer's study—the agency's vested interest in the research reveals conflicts of interest that render its actions unethical.

We argue that Oppenheim's writing is lacking in its review of sources and ethical analysis of Neubauer's work. Further, we believe that the Twins Study perpetuated the separation of siblings, coerced families into participation in research, and willfully withheld family information. The author, unwittingly, does a further disservice to biological mothers and adoptive parents by insinuating that they, rather than Neubauer or LWS, allowed for twin separation.

Our review of Oppenheim's commentary demonstrates the need for redress on the part of study organizers but further access to study documents is required to achieve this goal. As a start, access to study materials must be offered to participants before the year 2065. Many questions remain about the method of study design that passed through institutions undetected for decades, as well as the full extent of harm imposed upon participants, families, and even non-identical siblings placed by LWS. Until the full scope of Neubauer's work is understood, bioethicists and policy makers alike cannot ensure corrective action on behalf of participants or the prevention of further research harms. To avert future missteps, academics and policy makers alike should join our call for continued introspection, access and analysis of Neubauer's research.

Rebuttal of Response by Kelmenson and Wilets

Lois Oppenheim

It is most unfortunate that Kelmenson and Wilets' vitriolic response to my piece on the so-called Neubauer Twins Study not only goes in so many directions that it would require another very long paper (if not an entire volume!) to address the issues raised, but contains a truly astounding number of blatant errors and misrepresentations. As the purpose of my paper was to put truth in high relief, I will focus here on rectifying their many mistakes and inaccuracies.

To begin, I am faulted for defending Neubauer while failing to answer the (as if there were but one) "legitimate ethical question…" As I make clear from the start, my objective was neither to voice an opinion on any of the highly complex ethical matters nor to correct what they term "errors of judgment and conscience." Rather, my objective was simply to set straight the facts. I am faulted for my critique of "Wardle's artistic license." There is a world of difference between "artistic license" and misrepresentation of facts. A documentary is meant to provide an accurate record of what took place. *Three Identical Strangers* does not. The separation of the twins, whatever one's judgment of it, was neither a practice instituted by Neubauer nor initiated for the purpose of the study. To say otherwise is grossly inaccurate and constitutes an inaccuracy extending well beyond any notion of "artistic license." Crediting Natasha Josephowitz as Peter Neubauer's "research assistant" despite her having said she knew nothing of the study and learned about it only by "hearsay" [see reference in my paper] is, of course, far less significant. Nonetheless, it too is a misrepresentation that can hardly be considered "artistic license" in a documentary film. The identification of Samuel Abrams as "professor of Psychology at Yale"—as it appeared in the version of Kelmenson and Wilets' commentary to which I was invited to respond and which was later, unbeknownst to me, corrected—is also, in a word, simply wrong. As they appear to have realized late in the game, Abrams was Clinical Professor of Psychiatry at NYU-Langone School of Medicine. Though he held several other positions as well, he was never affiliated with Yale. The unpublished manuscript to which I refer is cited by Kelmenson and Wilets as "Abrams, 'Disposition and the Environment,'" which makes no sense whatsoever. That paper by Abrams *was* published and was cited by me as one among several places where information on the study was presented in print or as a lecture. Even more astonishing is the claim that my "opinions of the study are similarly shaped by the manuscript's contents, though, it is unclear if [I have] reviewed it." How can one be unclear as to whether I have "reviewed" the unpublished study given that I not only discuss its contents, but quote from it, indeed rather extensively at the end, and even go so far as to say from the start "I had access" to it? How remarkable that my access to this unpublished manuscript is questioned because, as Kelmenson and Wilets write, "the participants themselves have tried unsuccessfully to review study materials." How remarkable that my access to this unpublished draft is questioned because its name "is not listed on the Columbia University or Yale University finding aids related to the concealed documents from the study." It really is not rocket science! How could it not occur to Kelmenson and Wilets that the unpublished manuscript might have been produced *after* the materials in question were deposited in those locations?

Also thrown into question is the "identification of Balzert as an expert on Neubauer's Study." Balzert was a member of the three-person study team at the time the manuscript was written, a team that consisted precisely of Neubauer, Abrams, and Balzert, a team that met weekly to produce the 183-page unpublished manuscript. "Balzert further states," claim

Kelmenson and Wilets with a nod to a paper by Perlman, "that she neither conducted any of the home visits nor met any of the subjects." How much more wrong could this be? While she did work initially more on data analysis, she most certainly also made home visits. Indeed, Christa Balzert was Project Director of the study. As for what I termed my "exclusive interview" with her, this is refuted by the responders to my paper on the basis of a telephone conversation between Balzert and Perlman. Recently asked if she had ever been interviewed by him, Balzert replied, "Perlman called me once and wanted to interview me, as two filmmakers had already wanted and I had refused. With Perlman, I had a chat about our respective times at CDC and the twin study" (personal communication). More to the point, however, is that my referring to the interview as "exclusive" was simply a means of saying that Balzert had made very clear to me that she would grant one interview, the interview I have now published in this journal, and not give any interviews to anyone going forward.

The going gets really good, however, when the authors discuss my claim that my piece was rejected by other journals "because various editors disagreed with Balzert's viewpoint that the research was ethical in nature." "It is not inconceivable," they write, "that legitimate academic forums rejected the work on the basis of its concealed sources, both the manuscript and the exclusive interview with Balzert." This is careless in the extreme: How is the exclusive interview with Balzert "concealed"? *It appears right there, in the article itself; indeed, it constitutes the article almost in its entirety!* As for the study remaining concealed, that hardly kept JAMA (the *Journal of the American Medical Association*) from publishing in 2019 a piece I co-authored with Leon Hoffman, M.D. in which reference is made to the then anonymous as well as concealed study. Moreover, the rejections to which I refer came only from editors whose personal exchanges with me offered very precisely (and respectfully) their reasons, which were just as I stated them.

"The reader will notice that Balzert herself never speaks to the concealment of study data or manuscripts as a means to secure subject privacy." Did Kelmenson and Wilets actually read the article they are critiquing? Christa Balzert was very clearly quoted as saying: "We intended to publish our findings all along, but felt constrained by clinical considerations and reasons of confidentiality." Similarly, they say, "Balzert fails to acknowledge the researchers' ethical obligation to provide ancillary care for harms discovered during, or caused by, the study." Once again, I must ask: Did Kelmenson and Wilets actually read the article they are critiquing? Balzert explicitly says in the interview: "During our home visits we looked for signs of potential pathology and discussed this during our regular team meetings. It was understood that the parents would be notified should there ever be reason for concern and intervention."

Kelmenson and Wilets argue that my work "is lacking in its review of ethical sources and ethical analysis of Neubauer's work." Had the purpose of my paper been to discuss the ethics of the study, how right they would be. I am an academic, a scholar who takes very seriously the review of sources and the scope of my areas of expertise as well. Ethics is not one of these areas. I would not engage in an ethical analysis of this kind without the appropriate qualifications to do so. I did not aim in this paper to discuss from a personal perspective any of the ethical issues related to the study. Once again, that was made clear from the outset. Thus to argue that my noting, for instance, that "Adopting parents signed consent forms which explicitly acknowledged and agreed that they would not be told the facts of the birth family" rendered "counterintuitive" my noting that informed consent, such as it exists today, was not endemic to scientific research before the 1972 implementation of the Belmont Report is nonsensical. Both are true, despite their claim that I made a significant error in my statement about the consent forms. But to state that I made much of the "alleged informed consent in the adoption process as a defense of the study's actions" is to misunderstand

and misrepresent my intentions. For, once again, my purpose was not to defend either the study or the researchers on any sort of ethical basis, but rather to expose falsifications.

I wish now to address the two most stunning articulations of Kelmenson and Wilets' response to my paper, the "Louise Wise Services Adoption Committee Meeting Minutes" containing notes by Gertrude Sandgrund and the 1965 letter to Viola Bernard from Florence G. Brown that refers to sample size of a study. With regard to the first, the JCCA, the organization referred to in the Sandgrund notes, is not to be confused with any other organization. It is an establishment separate from any other mentioned in my paper and had then, and continues to have today, its own programs. There is no evidence whatsoever in what is quoted in the critique that any dealings they may have had with the Louise Wise Services were in any way related to Peter Neubauer and the Twins Study. Concerning the second, there too there is no evidence that the study in question is the Twins Study. Sample size may well refer to any study either undertaken or merely proposed for funding. Supposition is not fact.

Space prevents me from extending this corrective further. But I cannot close without making two additional points. The first concerns Kelmenson and Wilets' complete failure to recognize that this study, as clearly articulated by Balzert, involved *no form of experimentation*. It was purely observational. I wish to reiterate that here as vociferously as I can and add to it that the implication that the study was in any way like the Nazi or Tuskegee experiments is as outrageous as it is false. Moreover, the comparison in *Three Identical Strangers* of Neubauer to Nazi experimenters is not only defamatory but potentially libelous. My saying so in no way constitutes an approval or disapproval of the study or of his work. The second point concerns my dismay at the carelessness with which the authors reviewed my paper. I looked forward to an engaging "controversial discussion." Instead, I met with an ensemble of contentious and egregious errors. I hope nothing more than to have set the record straight.

Book Review: *The Emergence of Analytic Oneness: Into the Heart of Psychoanalysis,* by Ofra Eshel (Routledge, 2019).

Reviewed by Nathan Szajnberg

King Solomon, Eshel reminds us, that wise king, that son of Batsheva and David, that man who was permitted to build the Temple (denied to his father, King David, who had too much blood on his hands), Solomon prayed to God for a Hearing Heart (Lev Shomeah). His prayer is unfulfilled, Eshel suggests, because a hearing heart must be earned, not given, by, per Eshel, opening one's heart to another human being.

Eshel shifts easily from ancient Hebrews to Dante's Medieval genius, the *Inferno*. She recounts the scene in the lowest circle of Hell, the Circle of betrayal, a sea of frozen tears. We see Ugolino gnawing at the skull of Archbishop Ruggieri (for eternity, we recall). This Archbishop imprisoned Ugolino and his four sons and starved them. His sons died at their father's feet and after four days, Ugolino's "hunger had more force than grief." The father ate his sons (Canto 33, 186–188).

But, after this recounting by Ugolino to Dante, Ugolino resumes his eternal gnawing of Ruggieri's skull. Eshel suggests that Dante, unable to bear witness further, needing to forward his own redemption, resumes his journey with Virgil's guidance, and in Ugolino's eyes, abandon's this man. For Eshel, it is Dante's absenting himself that denies what Ugolino needs: someone to be with him in this most painful moment.

Yet, this book should be read for its compelling case histories of deeply disturbed, wounded people and the psychoanalytic techniques Eshel uses to redeem them of their suffering. The case histories read like other classics, such as Milner's *Hands of the Living God,* or Winnicott's *The Piggle (1980), (Szajnberg, 2017)* which bring alive the moments in the session when transformations occur. She cautions us that there are long, overly long periods when little appears to improve, when misery may increase, but remaining close to the patient's material, a state of mind, is the analytic frame that benefits these wounded souls (Giovacchini, 2000).

And she is frank that it is not easy to bear the life experiences of such pain and misery.

For the case histories alone, this book should be read, especially by those who choose to work intensively with the deeply troubled soul.

Eshel presents us with two aspects of technique: first the more experience-near concepts such as "with-nessing" (as opposed to witnessing), "two-getherness," "two-in-oneness," analytic "presencing." Later, she reviews the more experience-distant (particularly later) ideas of Bion (such as his mathematical attempts to codify analysis in his later works or use abstract letters to signify deeply felt experiences) and Winnicott (1974). Eshel even tries to convince us that there is a new paradigm shift[1] in psychoanalysis that she calls "quantum" (psycho)analysis. But, the philosopher of science, Stephen Toulmin (trained as a physicist, student of Wittgenstein) wrote in 1978 and 1984 that psychoanalysis often falls back on physics to explain itself, from the earliest hydrodynamic metaphors of Freud, through quantum mechanics and possibly even the most recent "field theory" (borrowing from a nineteenth century fields of electromagnetism discovered by Maxwell and colleagues at Cambridge). Toulmin's well-argued point is that these are all metaphors or analogies: reifying them into concrete statements that psychoanalysis is "hydrodynamic," or "field theory" or "quantum theory," misleads us. In fact, Eshel hints to us that she began developing her clinical techniques with primitive more disturbed patients as early as three decades back, well-before she armed herself with quantum mechanics or paradigm shifts. Let these arguments rest and not interfere with the fine clinical work Eshel articulates. I draw analogies to other attempts to compare psychoanalysis to physics, as Toulmin articulated in his classical monograph.

Eshel's moving, compelling clinical accounts sound familiar to this reader. This may be because I was first introduced to Winnicott by Bruno Bettelheim in the late 1960s through the mid-70s, who suggested I re-read the Transitional Object/ Phenomenon paper. Perhaps because this was Chicago, new ideas were investigated with critical care: Kohut taught Klein in the 1950s; in the 1970s, I studied Winnicott with Alfred Flarsheim (one of Winnicott's analysands) and Peter Giovacchinni and Gene Borowitz. We took up the challenge of working with primitive mental states (I use this phrase rather than more specific diagnoses for now) and learned that Winnicott's techniques, Klein's ideas, and Giovacchini's

---

[1]While paradigm shift has become notorious from Kuhn, his last book, The Essential Tension, was intended as a course correction on its misuse. Kuhn argues there that most science is "normal' science (not paradigmatic). This is not bad science, just the very pedestrian, patient slogging-through repetitive work, while remaining aware of mismatches between data and theory. That is not a model for clinical work: an "essential tension" between the normative daily details, while remaining aware of the surprising moments (Winnicott) that occur to shift our "paradigm" of the patient's inner life.

tactics could meet the regressed or regressing analysand at his or her level of need.

However, Bettelheim cautioned us (in our work with children at the Orthogenic School): while we may never fully grasp the child's descent into Hell, we can reach down, extend a ladder or arm and help the child clamber out. This is a variation, I think, from Eshel's technique. In other terms, Flarsheim taught (and here he was talking from Winnicott's couch, so to speak) the analyst suspended in evenly hovering attention can mesh his or her primary processes with the analysand's. Then, the analyst periodically sits back and, now with secondary process, asks: "What just happened? What's that about?" referring to what occurred when the two primary processes were enmeshed. In the state of secondary process, the analyst can winnow out what part of the primary process came from his (neurotic) countertransference contributions from what was evoked by the analysand (a different version of countertransference, perhaps we can call this counteridentification or response to projective identifications).

But, this, to quote Rabbi Hillel, is commentary. The nucleus of this review is "Read the book, be moved by the case histories, listen to the inner work of the analyst."

Eshel spends at least two chapters on tough technique issues that should also be a warning to us. First, she describes her inner (non-neurotic) vicissitudes that she sorted out *in order* to help the patient. Giovachinni described this as a form of the analyst internalizing the pathology, metabolizing it (that is reforming it) and then presenting something back to the patient. (That "something" could be as simple as not attacking after being attacked.) David Rosenfeld (1992), in his last book on psychosis, emphasized that he could not have done this work without ongoing therapy or supervision. (He travelled to London and Paris for the supervision.) While Eshel doesn't mention what supported her heroic efforts, she does express gratitude to supervisors in the past. Second, Eshel gives some vignettes about her falling asleep during session *as a consequence* of something going on with the patient. She reflects on this and uses it.

Two cautions to those of us who choose to work with primitive mental states (and this is a choice, not an obligation): we must know ourselves well, and when not well-enough, do the internal work in order to be more available to the analysand. First, Eshel nor this reviewer would countenance falling asleep (for one's personal reasons), then foisting this on the patent. Second, Eshel, like Winnicott, did not shy away from regressions. Yet, we need to distinguish regression in service of the ego (Kris) (or self), versus regression due to errors in our technique. Neither Eshel (nor WInnicott) would countenance an adverse regression due to errors in technique; no reason to attack the patient twice! Anecdotally, colleagues in Britain have reported that some therapists believe that unless one digs to the deepest depths of regression, an analysis is neither complete nor satisfactory. This runs contrary to Ticho's (1972) classical paper distinguishing analytic from life goals.

For an internal autobiographical account of what it is like to undergo such dedicated analysis, one can read *The Last Asylum*, by Barbara Taylor (2015). It is reminiscent of Cardinal's *The Words To Say It*. Their compelling accounts of their own deep miseries, alcoholism, drug use and recovery (which included for Taylor, stays at one of the last asylums in the U.K.) is a powerful counterpart to Eshel's elegant and touching account.

References:

Cardinal, M. 2013 *The Words to Say It.* Van Vector and Goodheart.

Giovacchini 2000. *Impact of Narcissism: The Errant Therapist on a Chaotic Quest*, Jason Aronson.

Rosenfeld, D. (1992) *The Psychotic.* Karnac.

Szajnberg, N. (2005). Impact of Narcissism: The Errant Therapist on a Chaotic Quest, by Peter Giovaccini, Jason Aronson, 2000. J. Amer. Acad. Psychoanal., 33(4):761–763.

Szajnberg, N.M. (2017). The Piggle: Decoding an Enigma. Brit. J. Psychother., 33(4):470–491.

Taylor Barbara *The Last Asylum*, 2015 U of C Press.

Ticho, E.A. (1972). Termination of Psychoanalysis: Treatment Goals, Life Goals. Psychoanal Q., 41:315–333.

Winnicott, D.W. (1980). The Piggle: An Account of the Psychoanalytic Treatment of a Little Girl. Edited by Ishak Ramzy. The International Psycho–Analytical Library, 107:1–201. London: The Hogarth Press and the Institute of Psycho-Analysis.

Toulmin, S. 1978 "Psychoanalysis, Physics, and the Mind-Body Problem." Annual of Psychoanalysis 6 (1978): 315–336

Toulmin, S. 1984 The Inner Life: the Outer Mind Heinz Werner Lectures, Clark University

Winnicott, D. W. (1975). Through Paediatrics to Psycho-Analysis—Basic.

Response to Nathan Szajnberg's Review of My Book

Ofra Eshel

I am very grateful to Dr Nathan Szajnberg for his rich and thoughtful review of my book, and his close reading of my clinical cases. Over the years of my analytic work, and particularly through my work with more disturbed patients, the lived experiences with my patients and enriching psychoanalytic theoretical and clinical influences have crystallized and developed into my own way of psychoanalytic clinical thinking. I tried to describe them in my writing as close to my own analytic experiences and thoughts as I could, even when going through obfuscating darkness in difficult treatments of severely disturbed patients, and beyond more established psychoanalytic terms. Thus, it is especially important to me that Szajnberg—with his helping inner influences of Winnicott, Bettelheim, Flarsheim, and primarily Giovacchini—could go along with me into and through these challenging and difficult clinical cases.

Yet, in this response I would allow myself, with the deepest respect, to add to, emphasize, refine, or even challenge and disagree with some of his points.

The book describes the evolution of my theoretical-clinical psychoanalytic approach over the years. This approach is grounded in the essential role of the analyst/therapist's "presencing" (being there) within the patient's experiential world and the grip of the analytic process, and the ensuing deep patient-analyst interconnectedness or "withnessing" that goes beyond the confines of their separate subjectivities and the simple summation of the two. Two-in-oneness, with its challenges, struggles, and mysteries.

Over the last decade, I have further expanded this dimension of patient-analyst interconnected being and experiencing, beyond recent analytic notions of intersubjectivity and witnessing, to more radical patient-analyst deep-level interconnectedness or "withnessing" that may grow into at-one-ment or being-in-oneness with the patient's innermost experiences. I have come to believe that this dimension of analytic functioning, with its profound ontological implications, engenders markedly new possibilities for extending the reach of psychoanalytic treatment to more severely disturbed patients and to the most difficult treatment situations. It has become an essential and integral part of the way I practice, think of, and envision psychoanalytic work—I went-with my patients thorough "black holes," dissociation, deadness, sleepiness, petrifaction, silence, longings, the depths of perversion, and the enigmas of telepathic dream; we "weave other-than-me objects [and experiences] into the personal pattern" as Winnicott writes in his "Transitional object" paper (1971, p. 3; Ogden, 2019)—the paper, Szajnberg tells us, through which Bruno Bettelheim introduced him to Winnicott.

But, Szajnberg writes that Bettelheim cautioned us that while we may never fully grasp the child's descent into Hell, we can reach down, extend a ladder or an arm and help the child clamber out. This, he thinks, is a variation from my technique. And, indeed, it is. For in an abyss and the depths of deadness and death, extending a ladder or an arm to help would not be enough to reach the patient. I came to learn from within my clinical experience that only the analyst's being thoroughly there with the patient, will enable the crucial possibility of going through and living through the patient's psychic reality of profound deadness, breakdown, and despair—this time t(w)ogether with the analyst—and eventually coming through it differently. No easy challenge, but a sustaining, life-giving struggle.

Supported by Winnicott's posthumous writings on early

breakdown and madness (1974,1965) and Bion's late work (1967,1970), I regard the profound interconnected being of patient-analyst within deeper levels of traumatic or core experiences as the only state of analytic being that can stand in opposition to destruction, dying, and non-being; the state that can cut the lethal cycle of abuse and annihilation, and experientially transform the patient's most extremely dissociated, unknown, unrepresented states—mainly of unthinkable breakdown and mental catastrophe. Unlike Szajnberg, for me, Bion's late writing is not "experience-distant." But it requires the suspension of memory, desire, and even understanding (Bion, 1967) for the analyst to become "at-one" with the patient's unknown and unknowable emotional reality-O by being in-tu-it ("intuit"), and thus to experience the "dark night" of the soul (1965, p. 159).

The critical question here is to what extent the analyst is willing and able to open his or her psyche and heart to the patient, especially in difficult, unbearable and devastated-devastating states.

And finally, some comments on Szajnberg's reservation that relies on the philosopher of science Stephen Toulmin, regarding the borrowing of terms from physics for psychoanalytic phenomena.

I love the use of interdisciplinary terms and ideas—from physics and astrophysics, as well as from biology, literature, theater, poetry, the Bible, mythology, and films. I feel that this interdisciplinary correspondence enables us to capture in a particularly vivid way something fundamental to the very nature of psychoanalytic experience and the psychoanalytic process. I encountered the issue of using terms from physics in an exciting occurrence 21 years ago, when my first paper in English "'Black Holes', Deadness and Existing Analytically" (1998) was published in the International Journal of Psychoanalysis. In this paper I made metaphorical use of the astrophysical term 'black hole' to describe a difficult analytic encounter with massive, devouring deadness. The term "black hole" had previously been used in psychoanalysis by Bion, Tustin, and Grotstein to describe the internal space in primitive mental disorders. But I expanded the metaphorical analytic application of the astrophysical black hole and the "event horizon" to an interpersonal phenomenon with regard to less disturbed individuals, whose interpersonal/intersubjective psychic space is dominated by a central object that is experienced as a black hole—the psychically 'dead' mother (Green, 1986) because of the intense grip and compelling pull of her world of inner deadness.

A few months later, I received an amazing letter from James Grotstein in Los Angeles (a letter with an envelope and stamps). I still treasure it today.

He wrote:

> Dear Dr. Eshel,
>
> I just read your paper, "Black Holes…" in volume seventy of the International Journal of Psycho-Analysis. I read it with great delight and admiration—even before I saw that you had graciously cited my own work on the black hole. I very much appreciate the perspective you took on the phenomenon and congratulate you for not shying away from using the metaphor of astrophysics. I, myself, received a lot of criticism for invoking astrophysical metaphors.
>
> I am in a process of rewriting my papers in preparation for a book and would very much like to cite your work. […]
>
> Congratulations.
>
> Sincerely yours,
> Jim

Not only was I astonished to receive such an appreciative letter from James Grotstein; but I was even more amazed to hear that he had received a lot of criticism for invoking these astrophysical metaphors. I used and developed the astrophysical terms "black hole" and "event horizons," and added "wormhole" in my article following physicists Hawking (1988) and Gribbin (1992). But I used them when I saw that James Grotstein had introduced astrophysical terms into psychoanalysis. And this was what I wrote back to him.

In the years that followed, I wrote an article about "My use of concepts from modern physics in psychoanalysis" (2002). "Black hole" (including my "Black hole" metaphorical analytic application) became an entry in Akhtar's Comprehensive Dictionary of Psychoanalysis (2009). And perhaps most importantly, when I grappled with the mysterious transfer of thoughts, impressions and information in patients' telepathic dreams as the embodiment of an enigmatic "impossible" extreme of patient-analyst deep interconnectedness, this was facilitated by the far-reaching changes within science, technology and psychoanalysis in the 20th century, and particularly the quantum mechanics revolution in physics. The prevailing scientific world view has become one of entanglement and connectedness. I think that reflecting upon the enigma of telepathic information-transfer is more feasible from within the post-Einsteinian world view, which is underlain by the enigmatic basic interconnectedness of particles in quantum physics, or the "mythic implosion" of electric age telecommunication (McLuhan, 1994). For today, this mysterious "sort of 'other world' lying beyond the bright world governed by relentless laws which has been constructed for us by science" (Freud, 1933, p. 31), lies at the very basis of modern science and technology.

I thank Dr Szajnberg for the opportunity to reconsider and to feel once again that the correspondence with interdisciplinary metaphors and analogies in general, and from physics, in particular, has become over the years part and parcel of the way I revere psychoanalysis and the analytic endeavor. And if so, why not say it?

Author Bios

Daniel S. Benveniste, PhD, is a clinical psychologist in Sammamish, Washington. He is an Honorary Member of the American Psychoanalytic Association and is author of *The interwoven Lives of Sigmund, Anna, and W. Ernest Freud: Three Generations of Psychoanalysis* and the forthcoming *Libido, Culture and Consciousness: Revisiting Freud's Totem and Taboo.* He served as guest editor of the first edition of the *International Journal of Controversial Discussions* in February 2020.

Robert Bergman, MD graduated from college, medical school and psychiatric residency at the University of Chicago. He has served as chief of the mental health program of the Navajo Area of the Indian Health Service, chief of mental health programs of the IHS nationally and director of psychiatric residency programs at the University of New Mexico. He is a graduate of the Seattle Psychoanalytic Society and Institute and is a training analyst. He is a clinical professor of psychiatry at the University of Washington.

Lucy Biven MAEd, BA, trained in child & adolescent psychotherapy at the Anna Freud Center in London England. I have been in private practice and have worked as head of child & adolescent psychotherapy in the Leicester NHS. I have studied neuroscience for the past 25 years and in 2012 co-authors *The Archaeology of the Mind* with Jaak Panksepp.

Marco Conci, MD is an Italian psychiatrist and psychoanalyst, working in Munich (Germany) and Trento (Italy). He is a full member of the German and of the Italian Psychoanalytic Society and of the IPA. Since 2007, he is the Coeditor-in-chief of the *International Forum of Psychoanalysis,* and is the European Co-chair of the Int. Council of Editors of Psychoanalytic Journals (ICEPJ). His latest book publication: *Freud, Sullivan, Mitchell, Bion, and the multiple voices of international psychoanalysis* (New York, IPBooks, 2019).

Margaret Crastnopol (Peggy), PhD is on the faculty of the Seattle Psychoanalytic Society and Institute, and a supervisor of psychotherapy and faculty, William Alanson White Institute in New York City. She is a training and supervisory analyst at the Institute for Contemporary Psychoanalysis and Psychotherapy, Los Angeles. She is also an associate editor, *Psychoanalytic Dialogues,* and on the editorial board of *Contemporary Psychoanalysis.* Dr. Crastnopol is on the executive committee and the board of directors of the International Association for Relational Psychoanalysis and Psychotherapy. She is the author of *Micro-trauma: A Psychoanalytic Understanding of Cumulative Psychic Injury,* Routledge, 2015, and other works. Dr. Crastnopol is in private practice for the treatment of individuals and couples in Seattle, WA.

Ofra Eshel, PsyD is a faculty member, and training and supervising analyst at the Israel Psychoanalytic Society, and a member of the International Psychoanalytical Association (IPA); co-founder, former coordinator and faculty member of the Program of Psychoanalytic Psychotherapy for Advanced Psychotherapists at the

Israel Psychoanalytic Society, and of the Israel Winnicott Center, and she is on the advisory board of the International Winnicott Association (IWA); founder and head of the post-graduate track "Independent Psychoanalysis: Radical Breakthroughs" (2016) at the advanced studies of the Program of Psychotherapy, Sackler Faculty of Medicine, Tel-Aviv University. She is book review editor of *Sihot-Dialogue, Israel Journal of Psychotherapy.* Her papers were published in psychoanalytic journals and presented at national and international conferences.

Gerald J. Gargiulo, PhD maintains a practice in NYC and Stamford CT. He is the author of four text the latest of which *Quantum Psychoanalysis* won the Gravida Award for best book of 2016. He has published numerous articles and is a published poet. He is a graduate of the NPAP psychoanalytic institute, of which he was both President and chair of faculty. He is also on the editorial boards of *The Psychoanalytic Review* and *Psychoanalytic Psychology.* He had the fortunate opportunity to study with Theodor Reik.

Jeffrey H. Golland, PhD is Clinical Professor, Department of Psychiatry, Mount Sinai School of Medicine, and practices near Union Square in New York City.

Horst Kächele, Dr.med. Dr.phil. is a psychoanalyst and psychotherapy researcher. From 1990 to 2009 he held the chair for psychotherapy and from 1997 also medical director of the *Clinic for Psychosomatic Medicine and*

Psychotherapy at the University of Ulm. From 1988 to 2004 he headed the Center for Psychotherapy Research S tuttgart. He is considered an advocate of empirically based psychoanalytic research, sometimes also as *Ulm School of Psychoanalysis* designated doctrine. Since the International Psychoanalytic University Berlin was founded in 2009, Horst Kächele has held a professorship there for research methods.

Susan Kavaler-Adler, PhD, ABPP, NCPsyA, DLitt. is Fellow, American Board and Academy of Psychoanalysis, Founder and Executive Director, Object Relations Institute for Psychotherapy and Psychoanalysis (www.orinyc.org), Psychologist/Psychoanalyst/Group Therapist/Psychoanalytic Training Analyst and Senior Supervisor/ Psychotrauma, Developmental Mourning, Grief, Self-sabotage/Writing & Creative Blocks. Psychoanalytic Author & Theorist; 16 Awards for Psychoanalytic Writing, including 2004 Gradiva® Award from NAAP.

Mehmet Sagman Kayatekin, MD earned an MD from Hacettepe University Medical School, Ankara, Turkey. Residency training in Adult Psychiatry, Department of Psychiatry and Behavioral Sciences, Medical College of Wisconsin, Milwaukee, Wisconsin, USA. Post-Doctoral Fellowship. Sleep Disorders and Research Center, Department of Psychiatry, Baylor College of Medicine, Houston, Texas, USA. Fellowship in Hospital based Psychoanalytic Therapies The Austen Riggs Center, Stockbridge, Massachusetts, USA. Candidate in Adult Psychoanalysis, Wisconsin Psychoanalytic Institute, Milwaukee, Wisconsin, USA. Candidate in Adult Psychoanalysis, Boston Psychoanalytic Society and Institute, Boston, Massachusetts, USA. Currently Chinese American Continual Training Program, For Senior Psychodynamic

Psychotherapists, Wuhan, Peoples Republic of China. Faculty, Center for Psychoanalytic Studies, Houston, Texas, USA. Medical Director, Professionals Program, The Menninger Clinic, Associate Professor of Psychiatry, Menninger Department of Psychiatry, Baylor College of Medicine, Houston/Texas/USA. Visiting Professor of Psychiatry, Wuhan Mental Health Center, Tongji Medical College. Huazhong University of Science and Technology; Hubei, Peoples Republic of China. Dr Kayatekin has published/presented and taught locally/nationally and internationally.

Zerrin Emel Kayatekin, MD is Associate Professor of Psychiatry, The Menninger Clinic, Baylor College of Medicine. She received her medical degrees from Hacettepe University Medical School, Ankara, Turkey and other advanced degrees from Mass Medical School, Worcester, MA, and Berkshire Medical Center, MA She has been in practice for 42 years and is board certified in Psychiatry. Her recent publication include with co-writer Kayatekin, MS, a chapter on "The Team and the Milieu in the Psychotherapeutic Hospital" in "Psychoanalytic Conversations: From the Psychotherapeutic Hospital to the Couch." August, 2016 and was a presenter at Wuhan Mental Health Center, Tongji Medical College, Huazhong University of Science and Technology, Wuhan, Hubei, Peoples Republic of China 2015, 2016, 2017, 2018 and 2019.

Adam M. Kelmenson, MS, is an assistant lecturer of Bioethics at The Chinese University of Hong Kong, Faculty of Medicine. He also serves as coordinator of the Columbia University—Chinese University of Hong Kong bioethics academic partnership. Adam is active in bioethics curriculum development in the Asia-Pacific region focusing on local

adaptations for traditional western bioethics teaching modalities. Adam holds a Master's of Science in Bioethics from Columbia University and a Bachelor of Arts in Biological Basis of Behavior from the University of Pennsylvania.

Kimberly Kleinman, LCSW is a Life Cycle Training and Supervising Analyst. She has co-edited "from Cradle to Couch, Essays in Honor Sylvia Brody" and "The Plumsock Papers, Giving New Analysts a Voice." She has taught developmental approaches to understanding therapy in various institutes including the Contemporary Freudian Society and the Harlem Family Institute as well as in China.

Rómulo Lander, MD is a Psychoanalyst doctor dedicated to the practice of Psychoanalysis. He is a member of the Caracas Psychoanalytic Society (SPC) and a training analyst at the SPC's Institute of Psychoanalysis. He is an active member of the International Association of Psychoanalysis (IPA) and of the Latin American Psychoanalytic Federation (FEPAL). He was a Psychiatrist graduated from UCV (1967) and Child Psychiatrist graduated from Harvard University (1970). A student of the teachings of Jacques Lacan since 1979. He exercises teaching and clinical supervision functions in various postgraduate degrees in Caracas. He has exercised administrative functions in psychoanalytic institutions at the national, Latin American and global levels. He has published more than 150 psychoanalytic articles in national and international magazines and several books.

Arthur Leonoff, PhD is a Supervising & Training Analyst with the Canadian Psychoanalytic Society (CPS). He is a past-president of the CPS and a recipient of the Society's Citation of Merit. He is also an Honorary Member of APsaA as well as a co-recipient of the Association's presidential citation. Dr. Leonoff is a former Board member of the IPA and remains very active in supporting this international organization. He is a committed teacher, supervisor and author.

Henry Zvi Lothane, MD, Clinical Professor of Psychiatry, Icahn School of Medicine at Mount Sinai. Author, 85 publications listed in PubMed on the practice and history of psychiatry and psychotherapy, including the book *In Defense of Schreber: Soul Murder and Psychiatry* and the published papers in journals about C.G. Jung & Sabina Spielrein, the Schreber Case, and the concept and method of dramatology.

Merle Molofsky, NCPSYA, LP is a psychoanalyst, fiction writer and poet, a produced playwright, and the recipient of the 2012 NAAP Gradiva Award for Poetry. She serves on the faculty of the Training Institute of NPAP, on the faculty and the Advisory Board of the Harlem Family Institute, and as a member of the Editorial Board of *The Psychoanalytic Review*. She has published numerous psychoanalytic articles in various journals, and chapters in psychoanalytic books, including Pedro *Almodóvar: A Cinema of Desire, Passion and Compulsion* (IPBooks, 2019). Her two works of fiction, *Streets 1970* (2015) and *Necessary Voices* (2019), were published by IPBooks.

Lois Oppenheim, PhD, is University Distinguished Scholar, Professor of French, and Chair of the Department of Modern Languages and Literatures at Montclair State University. She has authored or edited fifteen books, the most recent being *For Want of Ambiguity: Order and Chaos in Art, Psychoanalysis, and Neuroscience* (co-authored with Dr. Ludovica Lumer) and *Imagination from Fantasy to Delusion* (awarded the Courage to Dream Prize from the American Psychoanalytic Association). Other titles include *The Painted Word: Samuel Beckett's Dialogue With Art*; *Psychoanalysis and the Artistic Endeavor: Conversations with Literary and Visual Artists*; and *A Curious Intimacy: Art and Neuropsychoanalysis*. In addition, Dr. Oppenheim has published over 100 articles and is the co-creator of two documentary films.

Mark F. Poster, MD, Staff Psychiatrist, Veterans Administration Boston Healthcare System (VABHS); Assistant Professor of Psychiatry, Part-time, Harvard Medical School; Psychoanalytic Institute of New England Center; Private practice, West Newton, MA.

Adriana Prengler, LMHC, FIPA. is a native Spanish speaking Licensed Mental Health Counselor in Sammamish, Washington. She provides psychotherapy and psychoanalysis to adults, couples, adolescents and children. She has taught and supervised advanced psychotherapists for many years in graduate school programs as well as in advanced institutes training. She also lectures and writes on clinical topics. She did her training in clinical psychology and psychoanalysis in Caracas, Venezuela, where she worked for 30 years. She

emigrated to the U.S. in 2010 and is bilingual in Spanish and English. She is currently Vice-President of the IPA.

Austin Ratner, MD, is author of 4 books, 2 novels and 2 works of non-fiction, most recently *The Psychoanalyst's Aversion to Proof,* published in 2019 by Arnie Richards's press IPBooks. Before becoming a full-time writer, Austin received his M.D. from Johns Hopkins Medical School and studied psychoanalysis through an APsaA mentorship with a training analyst at the New York Psychoanalytic Institute. His essays have appeared in the *New York Times Magazine, The Wall Street Journal, USA Today,* and other publications and he has published journal articles in *The Psychoanalytic Review* and *The Journal of the American Psychoanalytic Association.* His first novel *The Jump Artist* won the 2011 Sami Rohr Prize for Jewish Literature.

Arlene Kramer Richards, EdD, is a psychoanalyst and a poet. She is a Training and Supervising Analyst with the Contemporary Freudian Society and the International Psychoanalytic Association and Fellow of IPTAR. She is currently faculty at the CFS and Tongji Medical College of Huazhong University of Science and Technology at Wuhan, China. Her psychoanalytic writings have helped clarify and bring to life issues of female development, perversion, loneliness, and the internal world of artists and poets.

Arnold Richards, MD, was Editor of *JAPA* from 1994 to 2003 and before that was an Editor of *TAP.* He is a member of the Contemporary Freudian Society, and an honorary member of the Karen Horney Clinic. He is currently on the faculty at Tongji Medical College of Huazhong

University of Science and Technology at Wuhan, China. He has written two volumes of selected papers: *Psychoanalysis: Critical Conversations* and *Psychoanalysis: Perspectives on Thought Collectives* and co-edited four books. He is the publisher of <u>internationalpsychoanalysis.net</u> and <u>ipbooks.net</u>. He is in private practice.

Joseph Schachter, MD, PhD received a PhD. from Harvard University, an M.D. from N.Y.U. Bellevue and psychoanalytic training from the Columbia University Psychoanalytic Center. He was a Training Analyst at the Pittsburgh Psychoanalytic Center, and is an Honorary Member of the William Alanson White Society.

Judith S. Schachter, MD is a graduate in adult psychoanalysis at the Columbia Center and subsequently from the Pittsburgh Psychoanalytic Center in child and adolescent psychoanalysis. She is a member of the American Psychoanalytic Association and has held psychoanalytic administrative posts both locally and nationally.

Leonie Sullivan, BSW, Psychoanalyst, Visiting Professor and Balint Group Leader & Supervisor, Wuhan Psychotherapy Hospital and Balint Group Leader and Educator, Peking Union Hospital & Peking Union Oncology Hospital, Beijing, China. Bachelor's degree in Social Work, University of New South Wales.

Nathan Szajnberg, MD, attended the University of Chicago BA '74, MD '74. He was Freud Professor, the Hebrew University (2007–10) and Wallerstein Research Professor (2005–2016). He has written several books (*Reluctant Warriors, Sheba and Solomon's Return, Jacob and Joseph, Judaism's Architects; Lives Across Time* (with H Massie); and edited *Bruno Bettelheim and Psychoanalytic Development.* He has written two novellas: *JerusaLand* and *Breathless.*

Ilene Wilets, PhD, serve as Chair for the Institutional Review Board within the Program for the Protection of Human Subjects at the Icahn School of Medicine at Mount Sinai. She is an Associate Professor within the Department of Environmental Medicine and Public Health. Dr. Wilets is active within the field of bioethics, and is on faculty with the Clarkson University-Mount Sinai Bioethics Program and a lecturer for the Columbia University Masters Program in Bioethics. She also serves on the Advisory Board for the Global Bioethics Initiative, an international non-profit organization dedicated towards fostering public awareness and understanding of bioethical issues.

Author Emails

Daniel S. Benveniste	daniel.benveniste@gmail.com
Robert Bergman	daghazhin@hotmail.com
Lucy Biven	lucybiven@gmail.com
Marco Conci	concimarco@gmail.com
Margaret Crastnopol	crastnopol@gmail.com
Ofra Eshel	eshel211@bezeqint.net
Gerald Gargiulo	jerrygargiulo@gmail.com
Jeff Golland	jeffgolland@gmail.com
Horst Kaechele	horst.kaechele@uni-ulm.de
Susan Kavaler-Adler	drkavaleradler@gmail.com
Mehmet Sagman Kayatekin	hakamesk@gmail.com
Zerrin Emel Kayatekin	ekayatekin@menninger.edu
Adam M. Kelmenson	amk2310@columbia.edu
Kim Kleinman	kim@kskleinman.com
Rómulo Lander	rlander39@gmail.com
Arthur Leonoff	leonoff@rogers.com
Zvi Lothane	Zvi.Lothane@mssm.edu
Merle Molofsky	mmpsya@gmail.com
Lois Oppenheim	oppenheiml@mail.montclair.edu
Mark Poster	mfpmd@comcast.net

Adriana Prengler	lalipren@gmail.com
Austin Ratner	austinratner@gmail.com
Arlene Kramer Richards	arlenerichards89@gmail.com
Arnold D. Richards	arniedr15@gmail.com
Joseph Schachter	jschachter22@gmail.com
Judith Schachter	judithsschachter@gmail.com
Leonie Sullivan	lesull1984@gmail.com
Nathan Szajnberg	nmoshe@Gmail.com
Ilene Wilets	Ilene.wilets@mssm.edu

www.ingramcontent.com/pod-product-compliance
Lightning Source LLC
Chambersburg PA
CBHW062119020426
42335CB00013B/1029